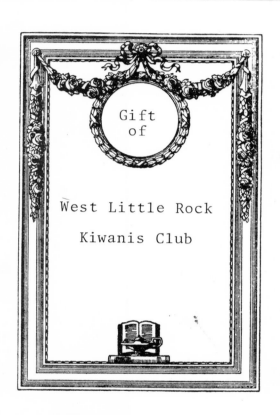

MISSION TO TEHRAN

General Robert E. Huyser

MISSION TO TEHRAN

INTRODUCTION BY
General Alexander M. Haig

A Cornelia & Michael Bessie Book

1817

HARPER & ROW, PUBLISHERS, New York
Cambridge, Philadelphia, San Francisco, Washington
London, Mexico City, São Paulo, Singapore, Sydney

FIRST U.S. EDITION

Library of Congress Cataloging-in-Publication Data

Huyser, Robert E., 1924-
    Mission to Tehran.

    "A Cornelia & Michael Bessie book."
    Includes index.
    1. Iran—History—Revolution, 1979—Personal narratives. 2. Huyser, Robert E., 1924- —Journeys—Iran. 3. United States—Foreign relations—Iran. 4. Iran—Foreign relations—United States.
I. Title.
DS318.825.H89   1987   955′ .054   85-45641
ISBN 0-06-039053-0

---

87 88 89 90 91 RRD 10 9 8 7 6 5 4 3 2 1

CONTENTS

ACKNOWLEDGEMENTS

My deepest gratitude to my wife Wanda, my two daughters, Christine Harris and Tracy Murphy, my son-in-law Mike Murphy and many other great people for their prayers and dedicated support.

My constant companion while in Tehran, Lieutenant General Philip C. Gast, was, through his loyalty and brilliant mind, an invaluable asset to me – many thanks Phil. Thanks also to Colonel Ray Burnette and the entire MAAG staff for their unwavering support.

My most heartfelt gratitude goes to Frank Johns and his team for their concern for my well-being and the superior protection which they provided. Without them it is questionable whether I would even be here today to relate these events.

My sincere appreciation also to Ambassador and Mrs Sullivan for being such gracious hosts and accepting me as a boarder during my stay in Tehran.

Last, but not least, a very special word of thanks to Thomas C. Reed, whose support and encouragement were instrumental in my decision to document this important piece of history.

INTRODUCTION

In early January 1979, while Supreme Allied Commander in Europe, I was called by an official of the Office of the Secretary of Defence about the deteriorating situation in Iran. The President wished to send General Robert E. 'Dutch' Huyser, my deputy as Commander of US forces in Europe, to Tehran. His mission was murky. Subsequent conversations with officials in the White House suggested that his purpose was to make a military coup. This impression, however, was contradicted by other officials at State. The dominant impression was of confusion in the face of growing danger to American interests.

Experience teaches that confusion at the centre usually dooms efforts at the periphery. I opposed what became known as the Huyser Mission because its objective was ambiguous and because it was preeminently a political and not a military task. President Carter, as then Secretary of Defence Harold Brown told me, did not agree. General Huyser went and the rest, as they say, is history.

The reader of this book will find Dutch Huyser's own chronicle of that history. As the story of one man's odyssey in the face of tragic events, and as a cautionary tale of how uncertainty in Washington breeds disaster, it must rank among the most valuable accounts to be found anywhere. No one can emerge from this experience without the most profound respect for Dutch Huyser's character and talent. Equally certain is the astonishment and dismay, even five years after these events, that one must feel about the last days of an Iran friendly to the West.

The outcome of the Iranian crisis sealed more than the fate of the Shah. It provoked another oil price escalation, and a further cycle of inflation, debt and international economic recession from which we are still recovering. It created the image of a triumphant fundamentalist anti-Western Islam and led to the Iran-Iraq war still bloodying the Persian Gulf. It diminished American prestige and humiliated the United States in the course of the hostage crisis, an early act of open state-sponsored terrorism. Finally, it led to an American commitment to defend the Gulf against Soviet aggression, a far-reaching and expensive proposition of uncertain duration.

Yet in all the controversy over Iran, we should guard against the recrimination of a particular incident. As Dutch Huyser suggests in his final chapter, a larger issue is at stake: how the United States deals with historic change in developing countries caught in the throes of modernization. Their governments and political traditions are rarely democratic and usually authoritarian. Our interests are engaged often on behalf of governments that cannot meet the test of democratic purity. Iran was a classic case, but there are others today and there will surely be others tomorrow.

The time is long past due when the United States should have adopted some general principles for dealing with such situations:

First, an effective US policy towards change abroad requires a balanced approach at home. A public aroused over the human rights violations of a foreign government will not respond well to the sudden discovery by the White House that American interests may be seriously damaged if that government falls. The reverse is also true. No American policy that ignores oppression by US allies in the name of *realpolitik* is likely to endure. So a President must educate the American people to a balanced policy that advances American values but in the context of a realistic strategic setting. The Carter Administration manifestly lacked such a balance.

Second, our policy must recognize the limits of intervention yet the necessity to defend our interests. We cannot remake the world in our own image. We cannot resolve the crisis of identity that may beset a nation caught between its traditions and modernization. Yet, at the same time, we have interests to defend and values to advocate without fear or shame. To fail to defend these interests and values suggests to our adversaries a lack of confidence and belief that can only lead to escalating violence. In many instances, there may be no substitute for an American presence, even an American military presence.

In the case of Iran, the original and fundamental error was to put upon this developing country the burden of the 'policeman of the Gulf', largely because neither we nor our allies were prepared to assume that historic stabilizing role when the British gave it up in 1971. Iran, under the Shah, began to remake itself in the American and European image of an advanced society, a forced modernization that called forth a reaction whose first victim was the foremost advocate of a changing Iran – the Shah himself.

Third, our policy must understand the impact of local change in regional and even global relationships. The Iranian crisis affected the international economy, the balance of power in the Middle East and Soviet appreciation of American resolve. We face similar circumstances in Central America today. Will necessary historic change take place peacefully under the guidance of law or will it be determined by violence, often abetted by the Soviet Union and its local allies? Our response cannot ignore the roots of local destinies but our actions must reflect a comprehension of the broader consequences.

Fourth, we must coordinate our diplomatic, economic and military actions. The differences between Dutch Huyser and Ambassador Sullivan reflected an infirmity of purpose in Washington. Even where unity of purpose exists, however, an Administration must have the organizational discipline to coordinate its actions. This problem persists and unless it can be overcome, even the best knit schemes will fail of execution.

Ultimately, a nation's foreign policy is a test of its character. Dutch Huyser's portrayal is not only of Iran but of America as well. His Americans are courageous, the most important quality, as Churchill observed, because it guarantees the rest. But character alone cannot carry the day. Leadership and wisdom are its necessary escorts. Let us hope that America, educated in part by the Iranian experience, has emerged with a wiser resolve to deal with the crises of the future.

Alexander M. Haig, Jr

PRELUDE

39 Richard Wagner Strasse, Stuttgart, Germany. 4 January 1979, 2 am. The sharp ring of my secure telephone jolted me from a sound sleep. I lifted the receiver and the crisp voice of General Alexander Haig delivered the fateful message: 'Dutch, we lost. You are going to Iran.'

This was the beginning of a story that has never been accurately told, one that started with desperation and disunity and ended in disaster, the story of the Huyser mission to Tehran in January of 1979. Although much has been written on the subject in books and periodicals around the world, most of the coverage has been disappointingly ill-informed. Yet this is an area where reliable facts are specially important. As all the world knows, the crisis in Iran was perhaps the most explosive international problem of its time – so much so that it became one of the decisive issues in the US Presidential election of 1980. This makes the story of President Carter's final initiative one of prime importance not only to historians but also to future Western policymakers.

It is a plot of Shakespearean fascination. The decisive factors in the final showdown were the characters of a dozen or more personalities, their behaviour under appalling stress, their ambitions, enmities and vacillations, their reaction to events, and their response to each other's reactions. Who could be relied on? What were his real motives? Could he be trusted to think the same thing tomorrow, or next week? Nor did these questions refer only to the Iranian protagonists. There were moments when I was asking them about some of my own side.

In the following pages I have tried to disentangle these threads by telling the story as it happened to me. In doing so, I hope to eliminate some of the misconceptions and misrepresentations which have grown up around the story.

For example:

Associated Press, Paris, 8 December 1979: 'Shah Claims He Was Thrown Out Like A Dead Mouse.'

Answer to History, by Shah Mohammed Reza Pahlavi: the Shah quoted Air Force General Rabii as having said just before he was executed by a firing squad: 'General Huyser threw the emperor out of the country like a dead mouse.'

The *New York Post*, 26 November 1979: 'Did Carter Send A General To Hasten The Shah's Fall?'

The *New York Times*, 17 January 1980, 'The Huyser Mission' by William Safire: 'A generation ago, as most students of Iranian history know, the American who helped place the Shah on his throne was CIA operative Kermit Roosevelt. In 1979, as most students do not know, the American who may have carried out Presidential orders to discourage a military coup aimed at blocking the power grab of Ayatollah Khomeini was U.S. Air Force General Robert E. (Dutch) Huyser.'

Pravda, Moscow, 29 January 1979: 'The United States sent Robert E. Huyser to Iran to function as Vice-Regent, and as such he is guiding a creeping *coup d'etat* by the pro-monarch military leaders who are still receiving orders from Shah Mohammed Reza Pahlavi. This really means that General Huyser bears the responsibility, together with the government, with the top military leadership, for the daily bloodshed in the streets of Tehran and other towns.'

Pravda, Moscow, 30 January 1979: 'General Huyser is carrying out the role of "Governor-General" in Iran. In Washington it was said the General has "successfully replaced the Shah".'

Pravda, Moscow, 31 January 1979: 'General Huyser's successful leadership is the main reason why the people's will for
an independent and democratic path of development for Iran
is not being implemented . . . he is conducting a creeping
military coup . . . he is creating obstacles to the return to Iran
of political and religious leader Khomeini.'

The above should be enough to confuse anyone; but there is
much more. I now possess eighteen books and over five hundred
articles about the 'mysterious Huyser mission', and the most
striking thing about them is that a minimum of eighty per cent of
their content is speculation, and no more than twenty per cent fact.
Because I believe there are many cautionary lessons to be learned
from this story, I have decided to set the record straight.

1

To help others to form a judgement of my account, I think they
should know a little of my career and life-style, and some of the
events which formed my character. I had a long, interesting career
in the military – 38 years, 85 days. When it ended, on 1 July 1981 in
a moving retreat ceremony, I received expressions of personal
gratitude from the governors of twenty-two American states.

I was born in Colorado on Flag Day, 14 June 1924, to an
immigrant father and devout Christian mother who taught me
early in life about the greatness of the American nation. Both my
parents helped to create in my heart a deep appreciation and love
for God and the United States of America. It was because of this
upbringing, which gave me a deep sense of dedication and
responsibility, that I eventually chose a military career. But the
actual decision to build a life in the military did not come quickly.

In April 1943, following high school graduation, I was drafted as
a buck private in the US Army. As a red-headed, freckle-faced
farm boy, I received three important pieces of paper almost
simultaneously: a high school diploma, a draft notice, and a
marriage licence – the latter two becoming lasting commitments.

While I was a draftee progressing up through the ranks, and then
as a young officer, I had no thought of serving for more than the
duration of World War Two plus six months, as specified in the

draft notice. I greatly enjoyed service as a bomber pilot, but when the war ended, I was told by regular officers that anyone without a military academy background or a regular commission would stand little chance of advancement in the service.

Yet things did not work out that way. The government had left many bombers in the Pacific Islands, and wanted them returned to the United States. When the call for assistance came, it was a combination of my strong feelings for my country and my experience as a bomber pilot that persuaded me to stay on for a few more months. I decided to help complete the project as a reservist, and then return to civilian life.

Again, not so. By early 1946, when I had finished ferrying aircraft home, the Soviets were beginning to build an atomic weapon. They were also clearly determined to expand, as indicated by the pressures they were exerting on Turkey and Greece. To counter Russia's aggressive behaviour, the US government decided to establish a new command, the Strategic Air Command. It put out a call for highly experienced military personnel, and the urgent need was for instructor pilots. Once again I put my country first by volunteering to help set up SAC's new Bomb Wings.

Just as this project approached maturity, the Korean war broke out. There was no way I would shirk my duty to my country during a conflict, so I fulfilled my obligations by direct involvement. My principal duty was Chief of Combat Operations for the Far East Bomber Command. In this capacity I planned the missions for our strategic bombers and published their daily operations orders. I also flew many of the missions myself: as an active crew member I was able to ensure that missions were properly planned and executed. I had never been shot up in World War Two, but I was in this one.

Following the Korean truce, I returned to the United States and was once again faced with a career decision. The Air Force was converting from propeller bombers to jets – from B-29s, B-50s and B-36s to B-47 aircraft. My extensive experience in bombers would make me useful in this process, and when I was asked to remain in uniform for the next few years I elected to do so.

Finally, in 1957, after nearly fourteen years of active service in the Air Force, the government informed me that I had served long enough as a reserve, and should make a decision as to whether or not I wanted to make a career of the military. If I chose to remain,

I was to apply for a regular commission; if not, I was to apply for discharge. This was at the time when Khruschev was making threatening speeches, Sputnik had just been launched, and the missile gap debate was beginning. It appeared to me that there was one thing which could keep the balance between the two great powers: our own strategic nuclear capability. Consequently, I elected to apply for a regular commission, and was accepted as a regular officer in the United States Air Force.

By this time I was a Lieutenant Colonel, having made that grade in 1956. To have reached that rank at the age of thirty-two was something I could hardly have predicted. When I was drafted in 1943, the rank of Technical Sergeant had been the summit of my ambitions. So my professional background was unusual among my colleagues, and it seemed to give me a certain independence of outlook. There are people who do their job, not as they believe it should be done, but rather in ways by which they themselves may benefit. I have always been highly critical of such people. I have never been a rebel or a maverick, but I most certainly consider myself to be a man of principle.

When I was granted a regular commission in 1957, I decided to complete at least twenty years of service, since this would make me eligible for retirement. In 1966 I was approached by certain heads of industry to enter the business world. I was in the process of leaving Strategic Air Command headquarters to enter a unit as a Vice-Wing Commander when I received several lucrative offers. The businesses which contacted me realized that I had already served sufficient time in the service to retire; and they also knew that my daughter Tracy was in college, working towards a doctorate. Their offer of additional pay was thus very enticing.

Yet I decided to stay in the Air Force. My decision was prompted by many reasons. The most important was that I knew the formidable problems my country was facing. The Vietnam war was raging at the time; and the Soviets had not changed their doctrines, quite the reverse. I also had a personal motive. If I could prove myself as a Vice-Commander, I would have the opportunity to become a Wing Commander, one of the most sought-after posts in the Air Force.

Being a Wing Commander was indeed one of the most gratifying jobs I ever had in the Air Force. I commanded my own unit, enjoyed great independence, and was able to perform at peak efficiency, relying completely on my own ingenuity and initiative to guide the men and women and provide the leadership to cause their wing to be a success. After nearly two years as a Wing Commander, I returned to Strategic Air Command headquarters, where I received my first star, and began progressing through the general officer ranks. Advancement proved more rapid than I anticipated, and in 1972 I was promoted to Major General and assigned to the Pentagon.

During my three years there, I served first as Director of Plans, and later was appointed Deputy Chief of Staff for Plans and Operations, which brought my third star. I had the responsibility of monitoring worldwide foreign military sales for the Air Force, and ensuring that the programmes we established with other countries ran effectively. It was in this capacity that I received my first introduction to the officers and people of Iran.

In 1975 I was appointed by the President as a Four-Star General, and on 1 September I travelled to Stuttgart, Germany, to assume the duties of Deputy Commander-in-Chief of the US European Command under General Alexander Haig. It has sometimes been reported that I was part of the NATO command structure. This is not so; my job was purely American, and one that was unique in the US military. The US European Command is the only one in our military structure which has two four-star Generals assigned. It is structured in this way to accommodate the Commander-in-Chief in his duel-hatted position, since he is also NATO's Supreme Allied Commander in Europe.

The Commander-in-Chief's headquarters is in Mons, Belgium, and he operates there solely with a NATO staff. As Deputy Commander-in-Chief, my headquarters and the entire US staff were in Stuttgart. My duties were to administer command of all US forces on a day-to-day basis and keep the Commander-in-Chief advised. In the event of a crisis I would then assign the US forces to NATO units. At the same time, I re-entered the field of foreign military sales. For in addition to overseeing the 320,000-plus United States personnel in the theatre, I was responsible for all the foreign military sales and military assistance programmes to forty-four countries. During my stay, about eighty-five per cent of US foreign military sales were in the European theatre, and we were doing an average of $12 billion business a year with the countries in my area of responsibility. This work had a considerable political and diplomatic dimension. I got to know many heads of state, including Chancellor Schmidt of West Germany and King Hussein of Jordan, King Juan Carlos of Spain, King Olaf of Norway and President Antonio dos Santos Eanes of Portugal and worked with all the US ambassadors in those countries – a considerable number, since the majority were switched with the change of administration in January 1977.

One of our largest customers at this time was Iran which, from a military standpoint, was a key strategic area for the United States. If Iran could establish a significant defence capability, as it was in the process of doing, we would save our country millions of dollars. I am certain that had we not lost the close ties we established with Iran, and had that country continued to increase its military capability, we would not have had to lay out huge sums on setting up a Rapid Deployment Force for the Persian Gulf area. Iranian forces would have guaranteed the area's stability and guarded America's vital interests.* By the mid-1970s, following the Yom Kippur war of 1973, it was clear that the West needed better protection for its interests in the Middle East (otherwise known as South-West Asia). The price of the Shah's downfall was a heavy one for the American people.

From 1975 to 1979 I made numerous visits to all the friendly Middle East and North African countries. I worked directly with government and military leaders at the highest level to develop defence programmes throughout the area. A sizeable US-Iran programme was now being established, and this required me to travel to Tehran frequently to deal with Iran's military leaders. I had many audiences with the Shah, at which a mutual respect and trust were established.

Early in 1978 the Shah asked the United States to help him to set up a command control system, and to develop doctrine and operational concepts for the reorganization of his armed forces. Up till that time he had managed the armed forces single-handed, carrying all his doctrines in his head, and never putting them on paper. He preferred to operate in this way, as insurance against a

*Of course, a capability for rapid deployment has long existed in the United States. It was originally developed when the US wanted to cut its forces in Europe without weakening its commitments to NATO. Men and equipment were kept in the US, ready to deploy forward when needed. The same principle was later applied in Korea.

military coup, although the Iranian military had no history of subversive behaviour. He requested that I be sent to accomplish this task, and in mid-April 1978 the Department of Defence sent me to Iran to work with His Majesty. I was accompanied by experts on Iranian affairs, and reviewed with the Shah his hopes and requirements. With the growth of his armed forces, he wanted a command control system as modern and automated as possible. Work had already been done in this area, but the system had been set up piecemeal, with no formal integration between the old and new procedures.

An effective command control capability requires a 'systems' approach. In other words, *all* elements of the armed forces must be included. When I had the US European Command, the elements I found necessary to make the American forces effective were intelligence, logistics, the command line, and operation. Each of the four elements had to provide about the same amount of information at the various command levels, so they were integrated into one functioning system. I used much the same philosophy later when I was in charge of the Military Airlift Command, except that I obviously added the ingredient of transportation. The Shah told me he was pleased that I was to head the project, as he believed I understood his method of government, his armed forces, and the differences between the American system and his monarchy in Iran. He told me that one of his principal requirements in designing a command control system was that he should be able to maintain absolute control. He wanted a foolproof system to protect him from a coup.

During several of our meetings, he expressed concern about the threatening forces around him. He was extremely worried about Soviet intentions, and believed that Russia had long been planning to gain control of Iran's natural resources and to get a hold on a strategic location which could be the key to eventual control of the world's economy. On one occasion, he gave me a lengthy history lesson about Russia's designs on Persia. He discussed Peter the Great, who had said, in 1725: 'Whoever controls the area between Constantinople and India will rule the world. The doctrine should be to excite continual wars in Turkey and Persia, and then penetrate as far as the Persian Gulf.' In 1907 Russia had nearly succeeded in turning the north of Iran into a satellite country. In 1918, they had declared: 'If Persia is the gateway to India, we must

foment a Persian revolution.' He mentioned the 1921 Treaty of
Friendship between the Soviet Union and Iran, and cited the
clause which gave Russia 'the right to advance her troops into the
Persian interior for the purpose of carrying out military operations
for her defence' – a dangerous precedent, he suggested. He also
talked of the 1930s and 1940s, giving President Harry Truman full
credit for ousting the Russians from Persia in 1946. He said that if
it had not been for the United States, Iran would have become a
Russian satellite.

Afghanistan also worried him. (Remember that this was long
before the Russians invaded.) He viewed the Soviets' political
intervention as a step toward a Persian Gulf takeover. He hoped
the world would recognize Russia's intentions quickly, since a
victory in Afghanistan would bring the Soviet Union a long step
closer to massive oil reserves and warm-water ports. Here he
expressed concern about the Baluchis, whose homeland straddled
the Pakistan-Iran border. They were an independent-minded
community whom he could not trust. He feared that Moscow
would seduce them into allowing it access to the Indian Ocean
after it had established itself in Afghanistan. Chah Bahar, in
south-eastern Iran, was due to be developed into Iran's largest
port, and he feared it might fall prey to the Soviets.

A further threat was Iraq, a long-time enemy. The Shah had
deployed much of Iran's military warning system and equipment to
cope with an attack from that quarter.

He then discussed a new threat. It was at one of these meetings,
in April 1978, that I first heard the name of Ayatollah Khomeini.
Just four months earlier, on 7 January, Khomeini had issued a
threat to destroy the Pahlavi dynasty. (I later learned that it was
not his first such threat.) The Shah said he feared that the West
would not fully understand the meaning of this threat, and would
probably construe it as either a religious or a minor political
problem. They would be wrong to do so. For the history of the
Pahlavi-Khomeini relationship was far deeper. Ayatollah
Khomeini's father was killed early in the century by Iranian
government agents as he was embarking on a religious pilgrimage.
In late 1977 Khomeini had lost one of his sons, Mustafa, in a
mysterious death for which he held the Shah responsible. He thus
had strong personal feelings about the regime.

Earlier in his reign, the Shah had reached the conclusion that the mullahs (Iran's religious leaders) and other clerical factions had acquired too much control of the country's land and money, through their constant demands for donations. To redress this balance, he pushed through a major redistribution of assets to the people in the 1960s. This reduced the power and influence of the religious element, and did nothing to endear him to the Ayatollah. In 1963, Khomeini became very outspoken against the Pahlavi rule. The Shah took him into custody and exiled him to Turkey. From there he later went to Iraq, where he was living in early 1978.

Westerners seldom think in terms of revenge or family vendettas at this level of politics; but to the Persian way of thinking, a blood feud can be a driving political force. The Shah told me that Khomeini's threat to destroy the Pahlavi dynasty did not imply only the eviction of the Shah from the Peacock Throne: 'he wants to stretch my neck' – a phrase His Majesty graphically illustrated by a gesture as if he were pulling off his head.

Following these meetings, I returned to my headquarters in Germany to work on his projects. As the months pressed on, I heard more and more about the Ayatollah Khomeini as the tempo of his activities increased. To help me formulate the Shah's Concept of Operations and Operational Doctrine, I dispatched a team of officers to Iran to gather information. Once I had the data I needed, I sat down and personally hand-wrote a doctrine and concept that I believed was appropriate for the Iranian armed forces. This task was completed in late July.

In mid-August I went to Iran and presented my proposal to the Chief of the Supreme Commander's Staff, General Gholam Reza Azhari. The document was carefully reviewed by Azhari, and by the chiefs of the armed services and key members of the joint staff. They declared the doctrine and concept to be acceptable without change, and presented it to the Shah. His Majesty's verdict on my report still amazes me today. He accepted it in its entirety without alteration – an extremely rare occurrence for anyone dealing with the Shah. He thanked me for my personal attention, saying he was aware that I had hand-written the original.

He then said that the report would be published as a classified document to be used only by his most senior officers. I objected to this decision, as a doctrine and concept of operations should be for the use of the entire military. After prolonged debate, I was even more astonished to win a reversal of policy from the Shah. He finally agreed to publish the document in unclassified form for all his troops to read. The Concept of Operations and Operational Doctrine was to be distributed immediately.

During my visit, trouble surfaced in Isfahan, a town some 150 miles south of Tehran. Martial law was established under the command of my close friend, General Reza Naji. It was also during this time that the Rex Cinema in Abadan was bombed and gutted by fire, with hundreds of people killed or injured. Activities of the opposition forces had really moved into a new gear after 18 June when Khomeini, still in Iraq, publicly called on the people of Iran to overthrow the Shah. When His Majesty and I discussed the situation, he reminded me that he had predicted this development, but admitted that it had come more quickly than he expected. He said it was very serious, as there was now rioting in the towns of Mashad, Shiraz and Isfahan; but he did not want me to become overly alarmed. He 'might fall in high disfavour' with President Carter, but he was not going to lose control.

I assumed the 'disfavour' referred to their differences over the human rights issue. The Shah claimed he understood President Carter's views on human rights far better than the President understood his. The Shah was acutely aware that if he was to maintain control of Iran, there might be considerable bloodshed. This caused him grave concern; his own image, and that of his country, were extremely important to him, and he wondered how the rest of the world would view such carnage. I suggested that a shift towards a more parliamentary form of rule would preempt much of the criticism.

When I left to return to Stuttgart, I felt certain that the Shah had the necessary resolve to maintain control. He had shown his ability to take action in the past, and there was no question in my mind that he could do so in the future. But people can change. On 27 August, the Shah made his first concessions to the Khomeini forces. He changed Iran's calendar from the year 2537 to the Islamic calendar year 1357; and he closed the casinos and banned gambling.

On 8 September – a day to be known in history as 'Black Friday' – a number of people variously estimated at from fifty to five hundred were killed as riots filled the streets of Tehran. Martial law was decreed and severe controls were exercised. On 6 October Khomeini was deported from Iraq. He decamped to a villa at

Neauphle-le-Chateau, a suburb of Paris, and mounted a well-organized programme of pressure against the Shah. The more virulent he became with his denunciations, the more disruptive the crowds became in Iran. He was waging a war without guns, a war of nerves. His ammunition was leaflets and smuggled cassette tapes; his weapons were bullhorns, aimed from the vantage-points of Iran's mosques. He could use these mosques with impunity, since religious centres were relatively immune from prosecution.

By early October the situation had deteriorated so far that Washington felt it must reduce the number of Americans in Iran. From my headquarters in Stuttgart, I discussed evacuation plans with the government. By mid-October we began evacuating those who were ready to leave. On the 1st and 2nd of November, major demonstrations erupted in the streets of Tehran and Tabriz, despite the introduction of martial law. On 5 November, 'Red Sunday', rioting and fires spread through the capital. Neither the Army nor security forces intervened.

On 6 November, the Shah formed a military government headed by General Azhari. For some days the rioting stopped, strikers returned to their jobs, and oil production rose to 4 million barrels a day. No doubt people thought the Shah was taking control in spite of his apologetic speech when he announced the military government. But by now the opposition to the Shah, which consisted of the National Front party, Khomeini supporters, the Tudeh (Communist) party, Fedayeen, Mujahidin and various other small elements, were taking advantage of the situation and combining together to gain their objectives. In my opinion, which has not changed, the total support for the opposition never stood at more than fifteen to twenty per cent of the population. They were held together only by their opposition to the Shah; other than that, their goals conflicted. It is my opinion that the National Front, which was probably the strongest party, and the longest established in Iran, thought that they could mobilize the Khomeini supporters and still keep control in the end. I think they believed that the Ayatollah would return as a religious symbol, not as a ruler. The temporary opposition alliance soon began testing Iran's new military government. The challenge was stepped up every day, week after week. On 18 December, another really massive demonstration was held.

The Shah's position was by now acutely precarious. Much earlier both the American and British ambassadors had reached the conclusion that the bloodshed could never be stopped as long as he remained in the capital. Now he himself was coming to the same conclusion. This left him three options. He could go elsewhere in Iran, he could leave the country on vacation, or he could abdicate. His prime consideration was: which would be most conducive to the restoration of order?

In Washington, counsels were divided. President Carter was still hoping in late December that the Shah could be saved. Others were less optimistic. But the unthinkable had to be thought. The paramount factor must be the maintenance of stable US-Iranian relations, come what might; and the key to this was clearly the Iranian military leadership. As long as the Shah remained, they could be relied on. But if he left, how would they behave? Having identified themselves with the royalist cause, they would become prime targets for opposition vengeance once the Shah's protection was withdrawn. Some would most probably run for it – and their departure would open the gates to Khomeini. Others might make a fight of it by staging a military coup. Since this was bound to precipitate widespread bloodshed, could it possibly be in America's interests?

There were some in Washington who thought it might. Indeed, so black was the situation that official opinion ranged across the whole spectrum of options, from sending a naval task force to settling for the Ayatollah without delay. But as long as there was a civilian government, President Carter felt it was urgently necessary to persuade the military to throw their whole weight behind that government after the Shah had left.

How could this be done? It seemed that the President was thinking of dispatching a special emissary, and he was casting about for a senior military figure with diplomatic experience and extensive knowledge of Iran who could inspire the trust of Iran's military leaders.

2

One day late in December 1978, I received at my Stuttgart headquarters a number of telephone calls from the Military Assistant to the Chairman of the Joint Chiefs of Staff. We discussed in great detail the situation in Iran, and he asked my advice about the idea that a senior US military man should be sent there to work with the country's military leaders. When I asked what he meant by 'senior', he said they would prefer a four-star general, but would accept a three-star. The man should already know the Shah personally, and his senior military advisers, and he should have an intimate knowledge of US programmes in Iran. After much deliberation we identified only two men who met these qualifications. One was a four-star general – myself. The other was a three-star – Lieutenant General Devol 'Rocky' Brett.

Over the next several days I had lengthy conversations with the Chairman's office; but nothing was mentioned about this mission, so I figured the idea had died on the vine. But clearly things in Iran were coming to a head. The opposition had infiltrated key positions in essential industries. On 28 December, four vital sections of the economy – oil, customs, banks and civil aviation – were again paralysed by strikes, in a pattern of left-wing disruption familiar to nations in many other parts of the world. On 31 December, Azhari's military government fell. It looked as if his mantle would fall on Shahpur Bakhtiar, who commanded the Shah's support although he had been vice-president of the National Front opposition; but there cannot have been much competition for the job.

On 3 January 1979, I received a call from General David Jones, Chairman of the Joint Chiefs of Staff. He told me that I would soon be asked to go to Iran on the mission we had been discussing. He said the decision was final: President Carter had personally selected me. Since this was clearly a mission of the highest consequence, I told the Chairman that I wanted my boss, General Al Haig, to be consulted. I added that I was due to go to Saudi Arabia for high-level meetings about that country's command control system. The trip had been arranged by the Department of Defence, with my departure scheduled for Sunday, 7 January.

General Jones agreed to contact Al Haig, and then the fireworks began. Haig took violent exception to the whole idea. Both of us felt the US had failed to give proper support to the Shah, and should not have allowed the situation in Iran to deteriorate so far. General Haig never gave me a full explanation of his strong objections, but I believe that he felt that our government should be taking much stronger action. He had called our diplomatic repre-

sentative in Iran, Ambassador Sullivan, who had also expressed
objections. (I thought then that Sullivan did not want a military
man infringing on his own responsibilities.) General Haig and I
held a great many telephone conversations with Washington that
day, but by evening, both sides seemed to have quietened down.

When I called General Jones's office to ask if he thought the
situation had simmered down enough for me to leave the telephone, they thought it had, so I felt free to take time off with my
daughter, Tracy Murphy, and her husband Mike. I wanted to show
them and some other guests an example of typical German night
time culture – large beer mugs, bar snacks and um-pa-pa music – so
we went to the Königshof in Stuttgart, 'the world's largest beer
hall'. While there, I was paged to the telephone. It was rare for
such an establishment to deliver phone messages, but this one was
an urgent request for me to return to my quarters and contact
General Haig. As soon as I got home, I called him on the secure
telephone. Washington had become extremely anxious. I was to
leave immediately for Iran, although both General Haig and
William Sullivan, the US Ambassador, objected violently to the
whole plan. When Haig asked my opinions on the subject, I told
him I agreed with his views on Iran and the US government's
feebleness, but I had chosen not to express this opinion to
Washington because I was not certain that I was armed with all the
relevant facts. Haig promised he would keep me informed of any
further developments while he continued his rearguard action
against Washington. He may have believed that I was being used
as a scapegoat in the event of an American setback in Iran.

So I went to bed. But at two in the morning the sharp ring of the
secure telephone jolted me from a sound sleep. I lifted the receiver
and General Haig delivered the fateful message: 'Dutch, we lost.
You are going to Iran.' President Carter had confirmed it. Haig
instructed me to go immediately to my command post to receive
secret instructions from Washington. From that point forward, he
said, I was to deal direct with Washington. He intended to wash his
hands of the whole affair.

I dressed quickly and made the twenty-minute trip in my private
car to my command post in Patch Barracks. During the drive
through the snow-covered streets of Stuttgart, my mind raced
through a series of mental gymnastics. I had only a few minutes to
deal with one nagging question: should I accept the mission to Iran

or not? I did not see what it could achieve. We already had a capable Ambassador there. Why should the President want another emissary? Would the curse of history be on my shoulders? Would it be better to resign now rather than involve my Iranian friends in what could become a major calamity?

I had the highest respect for General Haig's overall judgement, and I agreed with him on this issue. During the years we worked together I had found his perception in political matters so good that at times it seemed to verge on clairvoyance. I also had great respect for Ambassador Sullivan. He was the President's personal representative and an extremely strong member of the diplomatic corps. Yet no matter what their views might be, I was left with two central considerations. The first was that so much was at stake: Iran's military capability in the Persian Gulf area was crucial to the Western world's interests. The second was that Washington might possess information about the situation which I did not have.

For me the whole problem raised a fundamental question of allegiance. Normally, when the Commander-in-Chief speaks, a military man must respond without question. The age-old military practice whereby 'Yes, sir', 'No, sir' and 'No excuse, sir' are the only acceptable answers still applies in most cases. However, I believe that when a man is selected to be a general officer, he is set apart from the rest of the ranks in matters of judgement and loyalty. I further believe that for the few men who reach the highest military grade of four-star rank, there is one absolute in their responsibilities, and that is loyalty to the nation. Should a four-star officer accept a directive that in his judgement is detrimental to the nation, I believe he is being disloyal to his country. In our history, there have been senior officers who have voluntarily retired or resigned because of a disagreement with a directive. In this instance, I had either to accept the mission or turn in my uniform. Above all, I could not compromise my principles.

By the time I arrived at my command post, I had completed the agony of this internal debate. My conclusion was that if there was one chance in a million of success, I should accept the mission. On that basis, I knew that if the Shah left the country, the senior military officers would want to go with him, and if they left, the entire military organization would come apart at the seams. Two, I recalled what the opposition's reaction had been to the establishment of a military government on 6 November. The military had to be key. This thought remained with me and provided the thread of hope for the days ahead.

(Had I known then what I learned some five years later, in Gary Sick's book, about Ambassador Sullivan's plan to work with the opposition; the progress he had made in that direction, unknown to any of the leadership in Washington; and about his plan to compel about one hundred senior Iranian military officers to leave the country – a plan directly opposed to my own mission, which was to keep them and assist them – then my conclusion would certainly have been different.)

I called the office of the Secretary of Defence by secure telephone. Harold Brown was away, so I spoke with Under-Secretary Charles Duncan, who was handling the situation. Mr Duncan provided me with detailed instructions, advising me to travel to Iran as covertly as possible. I was to leave immediately so as to arrive in Tehran by mid-afternoon that day. It was then getting on for three in the morning. I asked Duncan if he was aware of General Haig's intense objections to the mission. He told me that he was, and that he had never had an opinion brought to his attention more forcefully. But the President had made the decision, and it would stand.

I also learned that Washington was not intending to send me written instructions detailing my mission. This was a decision I simply could not accept. Owing to Iran's unique strategic import-ance, the low probabilities of success, and the opposition voiced by General Haig, I insisted on being sent written orders confirming the President's directive before I left for Tehran. After a lengthy attempt to convince me that I did not understand the level from which the directive came – something I certainly *did* understand – Mr Duncan finally agreed to do all he could to meet my demand. Only minutes later the clatter of the teletype told me that the secret orders were arriving. The text was headed 'Draft', which caused me some concern, but Mr Duncan assured me that I would receive final orders by the time I reached Tehran.

The orders were basic and rather indefinite. The President directed me to convey his concern and assurances to the senior military leaders at this most critical time. It was of vital importance to both the Iranian people and the US government that Iran have a strong, stable government which would remain friendly to the United States. The Iranian military was the key to the situation.

The message went on:

> The President is deeply impressed with the way the military
> have maintained their integrity during this period of trying
> circumstances. The United States believes the long-term
> interests of Iran are best served by a strong and stable
> government. The Shah's effort in establishing a civilian
> government appears to be the most likely prospect at the
> present.
>
> No civilian government in Iran can govern effectively
> without the support of the Iranian military. It is extremely
> important for the Iranian military to do all it can to remain
> strong and intact in order to help a responsible civilian
> government function effectively. The Iranian military today
> have a role of overriding importance to the future of Iran.
> They can only carry out this responsibility if they remain
> cohesive and work closely together. No Iranian military
> leaders should leave the country now.
>
> As the Iranian military move through this time of change,
> they should know that the US military and the US govern-
> ment, from the President down, remain strongly behind
> them. We are prepared to stick with them. We will maintain
> our military supply relationship, maintain our establishment
> and training consistent with their desires.

The curious feature of this message is that not only was it
ambiguous, but there was disagreement about its meaning within
the Cabinet. Brzezinski wanted it to convey to the Iranian military
a green light to stage a military coup, and considered that it did so.
President Carter intended it to convey such a meaning only as a
last resort.

The President had said he wanted me in Tehran by mid-
afternoon that day. Since I would lose three and a half hours in the
time difference between Germany and Iran, a mid-afternoon
arrival time looked pretty ambitious. Nonetheless, I was determined to do all I could to meet the deadline. I accepted the 'Draft'
instructions and asked my aide to gather all the items I needed for
the trip. These included the papers for my Saudi Arabian visit, as
at this time I still planned to be there on 7 January. There was no
time to obtain country clearances or visas, so I asked my staff to
alert our embassies. I then instructed the command centre to alert

a T-39 crew and said I wanted to be airborne within the hour. They were to get permission to overfly Switzerland, and then determine how I was to make the next leg of my trip to Iran. (The T-39 had a range of only about 1,000 miles.)

The command centre located a C-141 which would be hauling fuel from Athens to Tehran. The flight would serve our purpose well. No one would be suspicious about a passenger on such a flight. My personal driver, Sergeant Goscin, rushed me back to my residence where, in a matter of minutes, I changed into civilian clothes and packed for what I thought would be at most a three-day absence.

Within an hour I was at the controls of the T-39 Sabreliner en route to Athens. Suddenly my heart was in my throat: I realized I was missing the most important travel document – my passport. I was dressed in civilian clothes and had no country clearance and no formal orders – only my Air Force identification card. I was transiting Greece on my way to Iran, and I was planning to fly on from there to Saudi Arabia. I could picture myself being taken into custody along the way. What would the President think about that? I was stunned, but knew that I had no alternative but to press on if I was going to connect with the C-141 in Athens and meet the prescribed arrival time. The only action I could take was to warn the military in Athens of my problem. They had to handle the situation for me.

We were fortunate in getting permission from the Swiss to overfly their country. Their cooperation shortened the flight and enabled me to complete it without refuelling. When we landed in Athens, US Air Force personnel ushered me into a car and briefed me on the flight schedule to Tehran. The plan was for me to follow a group of people to one of two C-141s waiting to carry fuel to Tehran. As the group approached the aircraft, which would have its engines running, my driver and I were to proceed to the second aircraft and nonchalantly nip aboard. Since I had only one piece of baggage, I was able to do this without creating any commotion.

The flight to Tehran was not exactly routine. The Iranian air traffic controllers were on strike, and we were on our own as we entered Iranian air space. Luckily the weather was clear and the traffic light. We reached Mehrabad Airport, Tehran, by mid-afternoon.

1

The Last Days of the Shah

Thursday, 4 January 1979

Word of my arrival had been secretly passed to the Chief of the US Military Mission, Major General Philip Gast, and preparations had been made to receive me covertly. As the aircraft's doors opened, several US military personnel boarded the plane – some in uniform, others in civilian dress – to arrange for the unloading of the fuel. I stayed out of sight in the cargo compartment. When the group disembarked, I got off with them. We chatted and sauntered around, and then I casually walked to an automobile, got in, and was driven off. I was afraid the guard at the airport gate would demand my identification, but there was not even a hesitation as he waved us through. My arrival did not seem to have been detected. It was an eerie experience, because on all my previous visits the Shah's most senior military leaders had greeted me at the airport with tremendous fanfare.

   The military personnel who had met me were all convinced that the US government should, and could, help to ease the tragic situation in Iran. But they also thought Washington was on the right track in encouraging Americans to leave.*

*Out of nearly 58,000 Americans in Iran in early October 1978, there were now only about 12,000. The US had also started to move household goods out. Each officially employed family was being allowed to ship 1,000 lbs of their most valuable possessions back to the United States.

The drive through Tehran was an immense shock. This once energetic, pulsating capital was now in a state of total paralysis. The streets were empty; not a car, bus or even a motorcycle. From Shahyad Square to the far side of the city, everything appeared to be locked up tight. Shop owners had bolted their doors; newspapers had halted their presses; marketplaces were vacant, sidewalks deserted, gas stations chained shut. Every other window displayed a portrait of Ayatollah Khomeini. Opposition forces had taken control of the country's vital elements, and a frightening tension filled the air. We passed long lines of people outside gas stations, each carrying a small container. I was told they were waiting for a ration of fuel for heating and cooking. The queues did not seem to be moving.

My first stop was at the home of Brigadier General Howie Stone, Chief of the Army Section in the US Military Assistance and Advisory Group (MAAG). This was my holding and briefing point. From here, as soon as it was dark, I was to be moved to Major General Gast's home for the night. I noticed a strained atmosphere, even in Brigadier General Stone's house. He had shipped most of his important belongings back to the US and his wife had left the country. Crisis was setting in fast. The dynamic country that I had known only a few months earlier had plunged into total chaos.

After we had finished, the principal members of the MAAG were mustered. They included the Chief of the MAAG, Major General Gast; Air Force representative Brigadier General George Kertesz; and Navy representative Rear Admiral Frank Collins. All absolutely first-rate officers. I was updated on the Iranian military and the MAAG's dealings with them. Each man expressed the same opinion – that the whole country was out of control. Because of the strikes, oil production was shut down. The banks were closed, the news media out of action, and the civil air control not functioning. Some food stores were open for short periods, but all other stores were closed. They had been threatened with violence if they opened for business. The shortage of cooking and heating fuel was a grim ordeal at the height of a Tehran winter. Every form of construction had stopped, and many buildings had been gutted by fire.

Our meeting ended at dusk, and I was taken to General Gast's quarters. Nerve-shattering sounds filled the night air as I began my first night in Tehran. People shouted '*Allah akbar!*' (God is great) from nearby rooftops, and every call was echoed from another area. Automatic weapon fire ripped through the darkness, reminding me of the front line in Korea. The electricity was cut off for a couple of hours every night, starting about 8.30 pm, as a form of harassment by the opposition forces. General Gast's house soon felt the winter's chill, and blackness filled the rooms.

Gast and I walked out on the veranda to listen to the sounds of the human jungle. Masses of people had congregated in the streets, chanting back and forth to each other. Fires had been lit, both to create a threatening effect and to keep away the winter's cold. They smelt of burning tyre-rubber.

We spent the rest of the evening discussing the situation. The chanting and gunfire continued until well into curfew, which ran from 9 pm to 5 am. It was not till midnight that the crowds finally dispersed and an uneasy peace descended. I spent a sleepless night.

Friday, 5 January 1979

The next morning I woke tired. After breakfast I was driven to the American Embassy to meet Ambassador Sullivan. The drive went off without incident, but crowds were gathering and tyres were flaming. At the Embassy the big iron gates were secured with heavy chains, and additional guards were standing watch. We were admitted on personal recognition.

When I checked in with Ambassador Sullivan he almost immediately handed me a wire he had received from Secretary of State, Cyrus Vance. The message directed that I ignore all previous instructions. It seemed I was not to make contact with the Iranian military leaders as originally instructed. I was to do nothing until I received further word from Washington. This was not a good omen. It made me realize there was not much unity of effort in Washington. It was obvious that the State Department had one view of the situation and the Department of Defence and Executive Branch another. One would have thought that by this time the men in charge would have reached some agreement about my mission. The Ambassador expressed no opinion about the sudden change of plan, but it did not seem to upset him.

I went into limbo, and spent the rest of the day talking with Sullivan. I told him what my original intentions were, and sought his counsel on how I should proceed. The conversation was less than encouraging, as he had made up his mind that the military had already decayed to the point where they were incapable of doing anything. He felt that the Shah was finished, and should leave the country as soon as possible. He also said it was futile for Mr Bakhtiar to try to establish a government. Sullivan had been living with the situation, so I thought it was prudent to listen. But I found it difficult to accept this prediction that Mr Bakhtiar would fail, when he had not yet even taken office.

Having had experience of the Ambassador's strong will, and his belief in his own personal convictions, I knew our differences of opinion were going to complicate my task. It seemed strange to me that I should arrive in Iran with orders from the President to make every effort to help Mr Bakhtiar, only to hear the President's permanent representative talking of defeat even before the game had started. In fact, the Ambassador was arguing that we should just skip the Bakhtiar interlude and move on to a Bazargan government. (Mehdi Bazargan was head of the National Front and had established close contact with Khomeini; I am sure he believed that he would be in charge if Khomeini returned, expecting the Ayatollah to stick to the role of religious leader.) I listened to Sullivan, but I knew that if I was authorized to proceed with my mission, I would have to draw my own conclusions. It was obvious that he had had major disagreements with Washington. This must be why I had been put into cold storage on arrival.

I told the Ambassador that should I be instructed to proceed I would strictly follow my instructions as I understood them. I would only have contact with the military, while he continued to handle the civilian side. I have since come to regret this strict division of responsibility: one of its major defects was to prevent me making contact with Mr Bakhtiar, either to consult or to inform him.

After a long day of discussions with the Ambassador, General Gast and I returned to his residence. Our night's rest was again disturbed by a highly orchestrated choral and percussion accompaniment.

Saturday, 6 January 1979

The next morning I woke to a bright sunny day. It was a welcome change, for the sunshine would warm the thousands of people suffering without heating oil – not to mention my own selfish need for a psychological lift. General Gast and I were driven back to the Embassy to see if further instructions had arrived. Even though Saturday is the first day of the Iranian working week, the streets were almost as deserted as they had been the day before.

At the Embassy I was told that General Toufanian, the Iranian Vice-Minister of War, had called. He knew I was in Iran and had left word that he wanted to see me. Evidently my arrival had not been as secret as I had believed. There was another message from Washington. It was from Secretary Vance, and said that I was to proceed 'as previously instructed'. I should establish contact with the five top Iranian military leaders, and pass on to them the assurances sent by President Carter. At this point I reiterated to Ambassador Sullivan that my only contacts would be with the military. Throughout the period of my mission I continued to assume that his actions would be planned to coordinate with my own.

Iran's military leaders, the central actors in my mission, were a remarkable and varied group. Most of them had been given political office when the Shah installed a military government the previous November. They had been gradually replaced by civilians, and when the government fell at the end of December, all of them had gone back to exclusive military duty except for General Gholan Reza Azhari, the Prime Minister. Formerly Chief of the Supreme Commander's Staff, Azhari had suffered a heart attack while serving his final days as Prime Minister and was still bed-ridden. Because of this he was unable to resume his military job, and a replacement for that post had not yet been designated. I was told that two men had been considered for it. One was General Abbas Gharabaghi, the Shah's Commander of the Gendarmerie. The other was General Djam, a former Chief of Staff, highly respected by the military, who had retired several years earlier and had been out of the country for some time.

Another key vacant post was that of the Shah's Chief of the

Army. Its previous occupant had been General Gholam Ali Oveissi, but after serving as the Martial Law Commander in Tehran under the military government he had fled to the United States when it collapsed. General Gharabaghi was in the running for this post too.

The Chief of the Air Force was my old friend General Amir Hossein Rabii, who had held this appointment for about two years. There was a very close bond between us, and he called himself my little brother. General Rabii was a brilliant, 'gung-ho' fighter pilot who had received much of his training in the US Air Force. Since most of the officers in the Iranian Air Force were trained by the US and their equipment was nearly all American, and they used the English language to operate, Rabii was running something of a miniature US Air Force in his own country. His units were patterned on those of the US Air Force, and even their squadron buildings were of American design.

The Chief of the Iranian Navy was Admiral Kamaladdin Mir Habiballahi, and he too had held his job for more than two years. He seemed to have a better understanding of Western values than any of the other military leaders. He spoke excellent English. I believe he could think in English as easily as he could in Farsi. He was an excellent officer. Most of his training had been hand-in-glove with the US Navy, so he had close ties with America as well; and he too had just sent his wife and children there for safety.

The Minister of War was yet another vacant post. General Toufanian, who had been the Vice-Minister of War for years, was handling the job. He was a human dynamo, running constantly at 110 per cent performance. Toufanian was respected all over the world, not only as a brilliant soldier but also as a most capable businessman who ran his own large ordnance factory in Tehran. He was the only Air Force officer who had been able to break into the upper ranks of the Shah's personal advisers – most of the top positions were held by Army Officers – and he was very proud of it. But he was somewhat unhappy because he felt that as the oldest, most senior, and perhaps most capable officer in Iran, he should have been made Minister of War. He believed that over the years he had been slighted by the Shah. He thought the Shah should have made him Prime Minister, not Azhari, when the military government took charge in November 1978. Failing that, he felt the least the Shah could have done was to make him Chief of the Supreme Commander's Staff.

These four men – Gharabaghi, Rabii, Habiballahi and Toufanian – were very close to the Shah, and each believed he had a better personal relationship than the next man. They almost worshipped him. Their intense loyalty was sharpened by the Shah's method of organization. He always dealt separately with each of them. It was only on social occasions that they would all be together with him in the same room. This helped the Shah maintain absolute control.

Each of the military leaders seemed to approve of this method of operating. Over the years, I had discussed with them the advantages of joint meetings, but they all seemed to prefer the one-to-one audiences. They enjoyed the challenge of individual competition for the Shah's favour, each constantly trying to outdo the other. For example, when a piece of information had to be delivered to him, whether good or bad, they would rush to be the first messenger. The Shah made all decisions, no matter how trivial – even those that in most military organizations would have been made by lieutenant colonels or colonels.

In other countries, the Chief of the Supreme Commander's Staff would have had a *joint* staff, made up of a balance of members from each of the armed forces. But the previous April, when I was reviewing the Concept of Operations and Operational Doctrine with the joint staff, I was surprised to see that all but three of the 2,000-member staff were from the Army. This was due simply to the fact that General Azhari was Army, and chose all his own personnel. I strongly recommended that he correct this bias fast. If he intended to have viable plans for all three forces, he needed better representation from the Air Force and Navy. At that time he agreed to take the necessary steps, but on my return visit in January I found only about a dozen positions had been filled by Air Force or Navy personnel. The rest were still Army.

During the Shah's many years of rule, he and his senior military leaders had concentrated mainly on external threats, in particular from Iraq and the USSR. They had not foreseen – or maybe they had not been prepared to consider – that there might be internal problems which could threaten the functioning of the armed forces. Consequently they had neglected to make contingency plans for a shortage of important items such as fuel, assuming that their people would produce enough to fill the country's needs in an emergency, and never envisaging supplies being severely cut by internal disorders and strikes.

This gaping weakness probably reflected the Shah's feeling that he had absolute control of his people. His instrument of internal security was Savak (the Farsi acronym for National Security and Information Organization). It combined the function of the American CIA and FBI with others of a more brutal kind. As well as gathering intelligence, it used methods which did not stop short of torture and murder to intimidate would-be opposition and repress the Shah's enemies. In its final throes, Savak seems to have stepped up the tactics of repression on every level of society at the expense of gathering reliable information. I believe that the Shah was careful not to know too much about the shadier side of his security forces, whose methods differed very little from the standard practices of that region of the world. He preferred not to give direct orders, but allowed his unspoken wishes to be interpreted and ruthlessly enforced.

Through discussions with the MAAG and Embassy personnel, I heard strong rumours that a group of senior Iranian officers were working on highly secret plans to stage a coup d'etat. No one outside it knew who the individuals were or what their plans might be, but it was thought that they would only act under two circumstances: if the Shah took a holiday (he had done that in 1953, during the Mossadeq crisis), or if he completely lost control.

Underlying the differing personalities of Iran's military leaders was a powerful common characteristic: personal pride is a universal weakness, but I have never seen more of it than in Iran. Persians often seem to believe that they can do no wrong: if something was done correctly, then 'I' did it; if incorrectly, then 'you' did. This appeared to be a driving force in their decision-making processes. Another characteristic was their reluctance to take responsibility. This reflected a fear of making an error in the Shah's eyes, or maybe was brought on by the Shah's procedure of personally handling every detail. The only leader who did not share this professional nervousness was General Toufanian. He handled nearly all Iran's military purchases, ran the munitions plant and negotiated with other countries for industrial development in Iran; and he never shrank from taking full responsibility.

I immediately got down to making appointments with all these

men, and on the first day we arranged to meet Toufanian, Rabii
and Habiballahi. (I had made a decision that Major General Gast
would accompany me on all my meetings with the Iranian military.)

General Toufanian was very eager to meet me. On arrival at his
lavish headquarters, we found that security had been sharply
increased. He greeted me as a close friend, in true Persian style,
with a sincere hug and a kiss on each cheek. Yet I sensed that his
embrace had a certain need in it – a feeling which told me that he
wanted to share his troubles with somebody who could act as a
confidant.

He opened up with a warning. I must not travel round the city in
uniform. Neither he nor any of his senior colleagues did so. He
himself wore a civilian topcoat to cover his military dress, and he
always travelled armed. In the Embassy car we did carry a pistol on
the floor, but none of us was armed. Ambassador Sullivan had laid
down the rule that guns were not to be carried by individuals; he
believed they might cause more trouble than they could prevent.
But I took heed of this advice about travelling in civilian clothing,
and my security people had me wear a bullet-proof vest and carry
one in my briefcase, which I was supposed to use as a shield in the
event of an armed attack.

Toufanian spoke very frankly. Although he knew that General
Azhari was a very dear friend of mine, he said he had been an
exceptionally weak Prime Minister, had accomplished nothing,
and could not make decisions or direct the military. (I don't know
if this was the fault of Azhari or the people directing him.) I got a
whiff of jealousy as he told me that he himself would have been a
far better man for the job. I believe that the Shah kept a very tight
rein on Azhari, and that his very dedication and subservience to his
King caused him to lose his effectiveness.

General Toufanian was convinced that the troubles were
Communist-motivated: if the Communists were controlled, the
religious factions would begin to support the constitutional government. I thought that the Communists were probably an influential
factor, but was not at all convinced that they were the driving
force. I was to hear this suggestion many times in the future, and it
often occurred to me that it might derive from the strong Persian

pride – a refusal to admit that fellow countrymen were deliberately rebelling against His Majesty. Toufanian also believed that Khomeini would have to be silenced before things could be brought under control. He was worried about the Shah's possible departure, and feared that the military would disintegrate if this happened. Opposition spokesmen were accusing several of the senior military leaders of corruption, and on this account their lives would be in jeopardy either from the opposition forces or from their own military subordinates. I found the latter suggestion hard to believe, as I had always observed good discipline in the military, and a subservient attitude towards the senior officers – almost as strong as those officers' attitude to the Shah.

These preambles launched Toufanian into a lengthy monologue on the 'purity' of all his own business transactions. He kept assuring me that nothing could ever be proved against him, although it seemed he had been targeted as the most corrupt of the lot. As he paced the floor, repeating his words, he gave the impression that he was trying to convince himself of his own innocence. He then told me of his concern about the opposition forces – primarily the National Front and Khomeini's supporters – as they had blueprints of all the country's fuel, power and communications systems, and had already taken control of them.

I decided to question Toufanian about the rumour that a group was planning a military coup. He categorically denied the existence of any such group. I pressed him again: Was there any planning for a coup going on? He repeated, 'No,' but I could rest assured that the military would never allow the Communists to take over the government. I realized I was treading on very sensitive territory, and did not press him further.

We discussed who should fill the vacant military positions. He was a good friend of General Djam, but believed he was a disturbed man; his only son, a child prodigy, had gone to pieces from constant use of heroin, and Djam had been badly shaken. He would probably not want to take another position in Iran, since he had been away a long time, and was now an old man. When I mentioned Shahpur Bakhtiar, the designated Prime Minister, he said he would offer his full support to whoever held that position, even though disappointed at not having been chosen himself. He had been impressed with Bakhtiar's first press conference, in which the Premier expressed his need for military assistance.

Toufanian was clearly worried about his own safety. He wanted to leave if the Shah did, otherwise he was certain he would be killed. But he also wanted to help his country deal with the turmoil, and he was anxious to avoid mass bloodshed. So far the military had only used rubber bullets (he walked over to his desk and pulled out a handful) and teargas. They had ordered and were expecting delivery of fire-engine riot-control water trucks from Germany. They were doing everything they could to prevent injury to innocent people.

When I asked him if the military leaders planned to make contact with any of the opposition leaders, he simply said that the opposition did not have legal status. He asked me if I was going to see the Shah right away, and I said I did not think it prudent: since the public had expressed such hostility to the Shah, I felt it would be more productive to deal with the military for the moment.

At this point I passed on President Carter's assurances, carefully emphasizing the points of the message. He was extremely pleased to learn of this support, but he countered with an outburst against Ambassador Sullivan. It was Sullivan, he said, who had persuaded the Shah to leave Iran. I defended the Ambassador by saying he had been a tremendous friend to Iran, and had personally helped to establish many of the military programmes pursued by General Toufanian.

I had seen him use similar intimidating tactics in many business negotiations. He became blustery and domineering, and strangers often concluded that he was an excitable, nervous man. It seemed to me that he was simply trying to gain the upper hand. He immediately began making requests of me. Could the United States supply oil experts for work in the Iranian fields? The exodus of foreign oil personnel had caused a serious drop in production. On the other hand when I asked if he thought the military could take control of oil production – including pipelines, refineries and storage – he said he thought they could.

He then asked 'Why can't the "big" United States silence Khomeini?' This was a question which I would hear repeated many times in the next few weeks. Then, 'Cannot the US silence the British Broadcasting Corporation's Farsi broadcasts?' He told me that all Iranians, young and old alike, carried transistor radios. Since Iranian radio stations had been shut down by the opposition forces, the only news available came from BBC bulletins transmitted from the island of Masirah, off the coast of Oman. He considered that the news was slanted, supportive of Communism and Khomeini, and that it was extremely detrimental to the Shah and his government.

The BBC Persian service was set up during World War Two in order to help destabilize the regime of the Shah's father, who maintained friendly relations with Nazi Germany. Iran's military leaders, and the Shah himself, probably had this in mind when they protested against the role of the BBC during this crucial period of the late 1970s. Middle Eastern governments exercise strict control over their own media, and they felt that the British government must be conniving in the BBC's coverage. Certainly the Persian people themselves assumed that it represented an official attitude. It was not so much that the BBC was hostile to the Shah's regime, as that it interviewed and quoted the Shah's opponents as well as his supporters, and reported events which the regime would have preferred to keep quiet. From that point of view, the generals were right about the damage these broadcasts were causing.

The General now told me that he believed that the military was going to have to take control of the country. He would want to accomplish this without causing harm to innocent people; it could be done by arresting members of the opposition. I interrupted to remind him that the military had had a chance to show that they could run a government from November on, and they had failed.

Next came a dissertation on patriotism, and duty to one's country. He said that one reason why he seriously considered leaving Iran if the Shah departed was the vast amount of knowledge he carried in his head concerning sensitive US equipment and technology. 'If I stay in Tehran after the Shah leaves, I could be forced to give information that the US would not want to have fall into the wrong hands.' He was also afraid that the Shah would be unable to return when he had ended his vacation. I told him that the military should accept the responsibility of preserving the country for him. They were the only real power in the country, and they only had to take strong enough steps to re-assert the royal authority. General Toufanian replied, 'The Shah is not just a man. He is the *country*.'

I felt I was making little headway; his most important consideration was, clearly, how to save his own neck. But at least he now knew that I considered him very important in helping his country back to stability.

We discussed General Toufanian's fellow officers, and he told me that either General Jeffrian or General Gharabaghi would be appointed head of the ground forces in the next day or two. He thought General Rabii was an extremely fine officer, and also spoke highly of Admiral Habiballahi. This surprised me, because I had noted a tendency among senior officers to disparage their colleagues in an attempt to gain an advantage with the Shah. I could not figure out General Toufanian's motive for all these compliments, and could only hope that he was being sincere.

He repeated his full support for Bakhtiar. He had received a list of the twelve Cabinet members in the new government, and four of them were close friends of his. But for himself, the time had come to retire. He was sixty-six, and had served forty-five years in the Air Force. Most of the armed services loved him, but because of his forceful ways he had made some enemies. I put it to him straight: 'As father of the military, how could you consider leaving Iran? With two newcomers occupying top positions, you could certainly provide the necessary continuity and leadership.' I did my best to persuade him to stay.

Eventually I felt I was making some headway, because he began to agree on some points. He repeated that he would do all he could to preserve his country for His Majesty's return home. He then told me of an approach he had received from a close friend who came from a very rich family in Isfahan. The friend had asked Toufanian to join the National Front, which was pressing the Shah for reforms. At first Toufanian declined, but he then decided to test their true motives by telling them he would join if the Shah was made the axis of the National Front. This promise was not forthcoming, so he felt sure that the National Front now wanted a great deal more than just the reforms they had advocated in the past.

I asked what the government had done to break the strikes and restore order. As best I could make out, the only thing the government had control of was the military and its installations. I told him: 'As long as the military holds together and remains on the side of the legal government, you have the means to control the country.' General Toufanian replied that the armed forces were short of certain vital supplies, and therefore could not realize their full potential. He knew I was aware of their fuel problem, because I had provided pumps and bladders for their C-130s for hauling fuel from Saudi Arabia.

The General spoke about his relations with the Saudis. He had warned them that if Iran went down the tubes, it would be because of the Communists; so it would be their turn next, and they had better provide all the support they could. At first the Saudis had told him that the only oil they had available was crude. Yet it turned out they were quite capable of supplying as much refined fuel as the Iranians could haul in the C-130s. In the event, they got enough for their immediate needs, but it did not provide any reserves. Toufanian wanted my help in getting more.

Toufanian was very glad of the assurances expressed by President Carter, but he warned that too much vocal support for the Bakhtiar government by the United States could be counterproductive. Khomeini had developed a hate syndrome toward the Western world, with the US at the centre of the target. Bakhtiar would be damaged if he inherited the Shah's close ties with the US.

It had been a valuable meeting, but I did not really believe I had persuaded Toufanian to remain in Iran if the Shah left. However, I had gained his confidence. His departing embrace sent a bolt of electricity through me. He was a man who did not express affection easily and it was obvious that he felt the need for support.

General Gast and I then headed out to Doshan Tappeh Air Force Base, the home of the Air Force headquarters, which lies inside Tehran, to meet my good friend, General Amir Hossein Rabii. At the gates there was none of the customary ceremony: just a small reception group of military and security police. Rabii greeted me in his usual cordial way, then before I could say anything, he burst into a lacerating attack on the United States. This really shocked me. He had been trained in America, had always loved the country, and had many times expressed his desire to retire there. He had close friends in the US Air Force and was highly thought of there. It was obvious that this diatribe was the product of sheer frustration.

Rabii's first target was Ambassador Sullivan, on whom he placed the whole blame for the Shah's intended departure. He wanted me to do all I could to prevent it. The military had decided to put a stop to it, and planned to tell him so at a meeting the next day. I told Rabii that I felt he was being rather harsh about Ambassador Sullivan, because I understood that plenty of other people had urged the Shah to leave. He would not have it, and burst into another violent tirade against the US. Why had it not put some pressure on Khomeini? This was essential for the success of the new government, but the US had done nothing.

Like Toufanian, he lambasted the British Broadcasting Corporation's radio news transmissions in Farsi, claiming that the BBC were broadcasting a great deal of false information through their maximum-output antennae. He gave an example. The previous night the BBC had falsely announced that Rabii was planning to retire. This lie, heard throughout the country, had caused panic among civilians and military alike. He had been swamped with telephone calls accusing him of quitting just when the going was getting tough. Why had the US not brought the broadcasts under control? America had close relations with Britain; why couldn't we demand a stop to these transmissions?

Here was a highly stressed, defensive man. In true Persian style, he thrust the blame of Iran's predicament on others. He was deeply embarrassed at the military's loss of control. He could not accept blame for the situation.

Finally the storm passed. The moment had come for me to explain why I had come to Iran. I gave him President Carter's message of support and tried to instil the feeling that the United States intended to stand behind him and his colleagues. He listened intently, and appeared to understand. But soon he broke out again. If this was true, why had our Ambassador encouraged the Shah to leave? Why hadn't we done something about Khomeini?

Very firmly I told him not to be so emotional. I promised I would talk with our government about the BBC, but he had to understand Western news methods. 'I am certain you understand the West's free press, if you'll just stop and think. You have heard and seen enough Western news reports in radio, television, newspapers and magazines to know what I mean. Western media try to express all sides of a problem, thereby allowing readers to draw their own conclusions.' This had to be said. At the same time, I must admit that from what I had heard, I too was beginning to believe that the BBC news was probably slanted.

I said I would discuss with Ambassador Sullivan and Washington the possibility of establishing direct contact with Khomeini. Rabii said he believed Washington did not understand who was actually manipulating the opposition forces in his country. Khomeini was leading the so-called 'religious faction', but to his way of thinking, it was not all that religious. The mullahs had enormous influence, and attendance in Iran's mosques was much higher than it had ever been; but the mullahs were not the real leaders. Rabii was convinced that the planning was being done by Communists. He believed that no one in Iran's religious circles had the ability to lay on demonstrations with the precision of those being currently carried out. The careful timing of the strikes and the seizure and closure of critical Iranian nerve centres had the impact of choking the nation to death. Immediate action had to be taken to rectify the situation.

We talked about the rumoured plans for a military takeover if the Shah left or the current government failed. As an old friend I was able to ask him straight out about the 'Board' that was said to have been formed for the purpose. He confirmed that the Board existed, but its functions were highly secret. It had certainly discussed a military takeover. I asked if the Shah knew of its existence. Apparently all he had been told was that some officers were thinking of forming such a Board.

General Rabii named the Board's members: Admiral Habiballa-hi, General Toufanian and himself. General Khosrodad, who was Chief of Army Aviation, and a tough soldier, had also been a member until the others threw him off. Khosrodad wanted to move too quickly, and he was not discreet enough to keep the Board a secret. Also, although the others believed it was essential not to let Bakhtiar know about it, Khosrodad had discussed it with the Prime Minister. In consequence the other three had told Khosrodad that the Board had been wound up on the Shah's insistence.

I asked Rabii for his opinion of Bakhtiar. Rabii thought him a strong man. Although he was from the opposition National Front, he had been designated by the Shah, so Rabii would offer his full backing. Reverting to the Shah's departure, he said that since he would be providing the aircraft, he would know all the details of the operation. Meanwhile the military had made plans to protect the most sensitive equipment in Iran as well as themselves. When I asked if these had been put in writing, he said No, they had only been discussed.

Our talk was interrupted by the telephone. It was a call coming in on the 'hot line'. He spoke in Farsi, but there was little doubt that the caller was the Shah. (Each Service Chief had a hot line to the Palace.) The conversation was brief, but with every second that passed, Rabii's voice rose in volume and excitement. He was obviously hearing something very upsetting. When he hung up he told me, in a very shaken voice: 'His Majesty has directed that I prepare plans for his departure.'

Rabii was distraught. He declared emphatically that he would have to go too. If he were to stay behind his life would be worth nothing. Public opinion falsely regarded him as the most corrupt of all the Shah's officers. He said the West had no feel for Iranian standards. 'You take the most honest merchant in Iran,' he said. 'He will have been trained from childhood to be a good nego-tiator.' When buying a pound of cheese, you could rest assured that if you were looking at the scale, you would get something like a pound. If you were looking away from the scale, you would get something less. But in neither case would it be a full pound. He also explained that Iranian males were brought up quite differently from those in the West. 'Boys in Iran are looked after to a much greater extent in childhood, so they are more dependent on others. In the United States, boys become more independent at an earlier age.' In my own mind, I linked his remarks with the lack of initiative our military observers had sometimes found among the Iranian lower ranks; without strong central leadership their atti-tude could lapse into one of passive caution.

I asked Rabii about the current capability of the military. He thought its weaknesses had been exaggerated: the Navy and Air Force had many subordinate officers fully capable of taking over the reins, if necessary. But this was not true of the Army. The officer corps did not have the same depth, mainly for lack of proper training. The Iranian Air Force and Navy had worked more closely with the Americans. The Air Force was like a miniature US Air Force, often communicating in English, and it was much the same with the Navy. The Army had not enjoyed these intimate links. Though they had received good guidance from the US Army at high levels, they were a much more dispersed and non-English-speaking organization.

Rabii admitted that there had been no proper contingency planning for the current situation. The Shah had only expected external threats. As a result, the oil strike had caught the military with greatly depleted reserves. The only fuel for the Army and Air Force was by airlift from Saudi Arabia, which was both difficult and expensive. Rabii had anticipated this, and laid in about ten days' supply for the Air Force. The Army was not so lucky. Nor had anyone given thought to diesel and gas for automobiles. I suggested they should put some diesel gas in reserve as well, because fuel for vehicles and support equipment would be vital if the military were to take the necessary action.

Rabii said another delicate element was intelligence. If Mr Bakhtiar was finally installed as Prime Minister he must have not only the support of the military forces, but also that of the Savak as well. But he did not want Bakhtiar to gain control over the military. If this happened, Rabii would be placed in an extremely sensitive position, as he could not divorce himself from loyalty to the Shah. I detected in his whole attitude a deep-seated reluctance to accept a civilian head of government.

By this time I had covered everything I wanted to discuss. I had made a diligent effort to persuade Rabii to remain in Iran when the Shah left, and to support Bakhtiar. I knew I could not hope to convince him then and there, but before leaving I tried one last tactic. I told him I had been visiting General Toufanian, and gave him a very extensive debriefing of our conversation. This frankness shook him: previously we had never talked about discussions with other generals. I explained that it was absolutely vital that we work closely together. There could be no secrets between us. I further suggested that we hold joint meetings with the others. Rabii and Toufanian were both in the Air Force; I advised Rabii that I planned to show the same courtesy to Admiral Habiballahi, and would debrief the Admiral on my discussions with him and Toufanian. This seemed to bother him a bit. He asked if we could meet the following day to pursue some points we had not fully covered that afternoon.

To sum up, I felt that my visit had done some good. Rabii, poor man, needed to express his feelings and vent the emotional strain he had been suffering for many days. I could tell from his appearance that the tension was nearly unbearable for him. He was not sleeping at nights and kept a gun at his bedside.

My next stop was to see Admiral Habiballahi, whom we visited at
Navy headquarters. I told him I had been sent to Iran by our
President, and passed along Carter's assurances and expressions of
gratitude. I also detailed the guidelines the US was offering for
future support.

The Admiral, a man of quite different temperament from Rabii
or Toufanian, was calm. He expressed his appreciation, and then
launched into a pessimistic monologue. He too was sure that the
Communists were executing an elaborate plan to take over Iran,
using Khomeini's eloquent followers as a cover for their machinations. He echoed General Rabii's assessment that the planning
must have been done by outsiders, because it was much too
sophisticated to have been thought up by Iranians. It was the
Communists who had deliberately created a fuel shortage so as to
paralyse the military. He himself had outsmarted them by laying in
a reserve supply for the Navy, as well as a full year's supply of
rations. He boasted that he was far ahead of the other two forces.

Like the two generals, the Admiral was very worried about the
Shah's impending departure. His office had received hundreds of
protesting calls from Navy personnel following the Shah's
announcement. If the Shah had to leave for a vacation, he ought to
take it in phases. He might go to the south of Iran for a while.
Later, perhaps, he could go abroad. At the very least his departure
should be postponed for a week or two. Habiballahi was convinced
that the military would collapse if His Majesty left for good. All
the senior officers would have to leave, including himself, because
their lives would be in jeopardy without the Shah's protection.

For the third time that day, I explained why all the senior
military leaders should stay behind. I talked about how we, in the
US military, always put our country first – 'People come and go,
but the country always remains.' I gave him recent examples of
transitions from one leader to another in America. One President
had been assassinated: yet we made the switch to the Vice-
President without missing a step. On another occasion a President
resigned from office: it was a shock to the nation but we managed
to carry on. 'The same must be done in Iran,' I urged. 'As military
leaders, your responsibilities are not to defend one person, but all
the people of your nation.'

I felt pretty sure that the Admiral would understand this
argument better than the others, for his thought processes were

quite different. But it was not going to be easy. Though he spoke highly of Bakhtiar, his willingness to support him did not meet my hopes. He said: 'As long as the Shah is in the country, I will support Mr Bakhtiar.' I replied, 'That won't cut the mustard, Admiral. There must be direct interface with Mr Bakhtiar.' I explained why. The Shah was going to establish a Regency Council to act on his behalf during his absence. The Prime Minister would be the principal action man in the council, so the military had to support him. 'Perhaps your relationship with Mr Bakhtiar won't be as strong as it has been with His Majesty, but you must offer your direct support so that he can call all the shots.'

It was something that my arguments were not rejected out of hand by the Admiral, as they had been by Rabii and Toufanian. I certainly succeeded in starting him thinking again about the future.

I then asked about the Board, telling him that Rabii had briefed me about it but Toufanian had sidestepped the question. What did he have to say about it? From the Admiral's reply it was clear that planning was too embryonic to expect any results. There seemed to be no detailed plans at all. They had discussed what positions each of the officers would hold on the Board, but nothing had been decided about regaining control of the country or putting the economy back on its feet.

I told the Admiral about Toufanian's distress at not having been given greater responsibility by the Shah. Habiballahi thought Toufanian was a good man, and it was vital that he should remain in Iran. 'He's the man with the corporate memory, outside contacts and the ability to get whatever supplies the forces might need.' He was the only man who could make good the military's failure to stockpile war reserves. He thought all the Board members were good people – 'plain people', who could be trusted. He thought General Gharabaghi would be made Chief of the Supreme Commander's Staff. For Chief of the Army he did not expect Jeffrian, as Rabii and Toufanian did, but General Abdul-Ali Badraie, a former commander of the Imperial Guard, the Army's elite unit and the best-trained troops in the country.

At this point I had a brainwave. If these men could work together on planning as a 'Board', perhaps I could get them working together in the same way in joint support of Mr Bakhtiar. As a first step, I suggested that the Admiral should work out a strategy for regaining control of the country's industrial elements and material assets under Bakhtiar's leadership. This had to be done, and it seemed to me a much better bet than a straight-out military takeover. I made it very clear that if it should be necessary for the military to take control of the country this same planning process must be accomplished. Admiral Habiballahi responded positively. He felt he was in a good position to help because his senior Navy officers had greater depth than those of the other two services, particularly the Army.

I suggested that the Board might evolve into a council, consisting of the Chief of the Supreme Commander's Staff and the Service Chiefs. He liked this idea. He even seemed agreeable to working with the new Prime Minister through such a council. What I really wanted was to establish an element similar to our Joint Chiefs of Staff to work with unity. Thus I felt I had been able to accomplish more with the Admiral than with the other two. He seemed to accept that the Shah might leave, and was reconciled to the need to stay behind if such a moment ever came.

By the time we left it was too late for any other Saturday afternoon appointments. General Gast and I called it a day and returned to his quarters, where we reflected on the day's events over a quiet drink.

The first issue to be faced was the Shah's proposed departure. We had to try to guess what each of the leaders might do when this happened. Washington had been correct in its assessment of the situation: our first task, in keeping with the President's guidance, was to stop them leaving. They must help to stabilize the government and regain control of the country.

The second issue was their undisguised reluctance to deal closely with Bakhtiar. Their loyalty to the Shah was so strong that they seemed unable to contemplate any new allegiance, and they lacked trust in Bakhtiar. I could understand their fears. Bakhtiar was a member of the National Front opposition, and each man feared that his arrival could mean his own demise. They were all worried that Bakhtiar might have heard about the Board, because if so, he might eliminate them as soon as the Shah's back was turned.

The third issue centred on a programme of priorities for the new Prime Minister. Comprehensive plans were needed to recover control of the situation and set the economy in motion. They should cover the nation's water and food supplies, oil, banks, customs, power and the news media. Action had to be taken to counter the psychological warfare being conducted by Khomeini. Gast and I spent most of the evening brainstorming these ideas.

I had scheduled an appointment to meet General Gharabaghi the next morning. Although we had met before, I did not know him nearly as well as the others. So I telephoned Rabii that evening to ask if he would be good enough to give me a rundown on his colleague. He told me that the French-trained Gharabaghi was a good man, but somewhat apprehensive of foreigners, and I could expect him to be very cautious during our first meeting. 'Sometimes in the midst of strangers, or those who he does not know very well, he is reluctant to speak anything but Farsi. He is capable in English, but he's not as good as some of the other officers.' When I asked if he thought I would need an interpreter, he said it might help. I asked Rabii if he would accompany me, and he said he would be delighted. I also called General Toufanian, who confirmed most of what Rabii had said.

After an excellent dinner, cooked by Mrs Gast, we went out on the deck to listen to the bizarre sounds of the night. Sharp reports of automatic weapons were interspersed with religious calls from the surrounding rooftops. The crisp air seemed alive with threatening forces. Then, at midnight, almost as if a master-switch had been pulled, everything stopped. The rest of the night was filled with a deathly silence.

Sunday, 7 January 1979

After breakfast the next day, I called General Gharabaghi's office to ask if he minded General Rabii sitting in. I was told this would be acceptable. During this conversation I learned that we were to meet in the office of the Chief of the Supreme Commander's Staff (SCS); Gharabaghi had just got the job. This news helped us to plan for our meeting.

During the drive we wore civilian clothes, but took our full military uniforms for the meeting. We were glad to see that, though the lines at the gas stations were still long, they were definitely moving; clearly some source of fuel had been discovered. Also, though stores and shops were still closed, newspapers were being peddled on street corners. It had been two months since a newspaper had been published in Tehran, so I was extremely anxious to get to the office and see what had been printed. I was prepared for the worst, because I could not believe the 'good guys' were running the presses.

The SCS compound covered several city blocks right in the middle of Tehran. Completely enclosed by a ten-foot red brick wall, it had four or five entrances controlled by guard-houses. The huge, black iron gates were tightly closed, but we were admitted upon proof of indentification, and then thoroughly searched.

The headquarters were designed in an 'H' shape, with three storeys above ground and six below. The underground area was Iran's Command Centre. It had been built for survival and was equipped to be self-sustaining on the lines of the US Strategic Air Command at Omaha. The US military offices were located on the third floor. General Gast and I went straight there, and exchanged our civilian coats for military coats.

While we were waiting to be received, Major Ray Burnette, General Gast's Executive Officer, came in grinning from ear to ear. I realized he must have witnessed some victory, and indeed he had. He held up two English-translated newspapers – The *Tehran Journal* and the *Kayhan* – the first international versions to appear following a crippling sixty-two-day strike. The *Kayhan* headlines read: 'On The Road To Democracy'. The accompanying article said that Prime Minister Bakhtiar had presented the Shah with 'a cabinet lacking the stains of association with the period of repression'. Mr Bakhtiar was quoted as having said: 'The Shah will reign and we will rule.' The *Tehran Journal* proclaimed rather more sceptically: 'Bakhtiar In The Hot Seat'. The main article reported: 'A new fragile era of hope dawned on Iran yesterday when the former Deputy Leader of the National Front took over as the country's fourth Prime Minister in five months.'

Then my eye caught an article at the bottom of the *Journal*'s front page. 'Top US Military Officer Here', it declared. Its author had speculated that I was in Iran either to reduce the number of US advisers or, as the BBC had broadcast, to impress on Iran's generals that Washington was firmly backing Prime Minister

Bakhtiar, and that they should do so as well. I immediately picked up the *Kayhan* paper and, sure enough, in the middle of the back page in heavy black print it read: 'US General In Talks With Military Heads'. The article read much the same as the one in the *Journal*.

The media could certainly not be called inefficient. I had been on the move in Tehran for only one day under what I believed to be highly secret conditions, but obviously they had me well covered.

General Gharabaghi gave us a cordial but rather formal greeting. He was a very cool, calculating man, standing about 5ft 10ins tall and weighing some 175 pounds. He had very clean features, with deep brown eyes and light brown hair rather thin on top. He looked immaculate in his uniform, just the way I remembered him when he served as Commander of the Gendarmerie.

'I have not been extensively briefed on why you are here,' he said, 'but I have some idea.' General Rabii, who had arrived earlier, greeted me with a warm 'Good morning!' and appeared pleased to see me.

I told the Chief: 'The reason I am here is to deliver a message from our President. I had meetings yesterday with your Service Chiefs. I am sorry I did not meet with you first, but it was not clear what your position was at the time. Your appointment as Chief of the Supreme Commander's Staff had not been announced until last evening.' General Gharabaghi accepted my explanation and asked me to proceed.

I expressed, point by point, those things President Carter had asked me to pass on: the assurances; our confidence in the military leaders; the need for them to support a new government; Washington's intentions to lend full support. Several times Gharabaghi would interrupt and talk with Rabii in Farsi. When I had finished, he reviewed each of the points for clarification. He seemed very sincere in expressing his appreciation.

He then wanted to know what else I had discussed with his Service Commanders. I spent the next three hours debriefing him on each of my conversations and explaining my relationship with each of the leaders. I went on: 'I think we have reached a point where, instead of relaying back and forth what one has said to another, it would be far better for all of us to gather as a group in your office and conduct open discussions. Being Chief of the

Supreme Commander's Staff, you would orchestrate the meetings. We should all work toward one common goal: success.'

Gharabaghi agreed that 'something along that line might be necessary'. But he then reverted to his primary concern: the Shah's proposed departure. 'You should immediately pass word to your President to have him call the Shah and ask him to stay in the country.' Gharabaghi said he could not hold the military together if the Shah left, particularly at such short notice. 'He just cannot leave.' Eventually, however, his tone changed and he conceded: 'If the Shah must go away, it would be best for him to take his vacation in phases.' Echoing the views of the other leaders, he said: 'The Shah could travel to Kish Island or some other remote spot in the south, remain there for a period of time, and then take a vacation abroad if necessary.'

Then came the predictable bombshell. 'When His Majesty leaves, I would want to leave with him.' This triggered off another lengthy exchange about the responsibilities of the military to their country and the Shah.

Gharabaghi then began dilating on the Iranian temperament and work habits. 'You should understand that things are very different from your country. If you expect an individual to accomplish something, you have to give him a specific order. Once the order is given, the person then has to be constantly supervised, otherwise you see no progress. People of my country have been trained that way for hundreds of years.' He contrasted this mentality with that of the Americans who had come to help his country. 'An American officer could be sent to Iran by himself. If you dropped in while he was alone in his room, you would find him working diligently on the things he had to get done. He would be recapping one day's work and planning for the next. This would never be true of an Iranian officer. You would have to give him specific orders, and then watch him to be sure he kept at it.'

At the next opportunity I casually brought up the subject of the Board. 'Are you aware of any actions along that line?' I asked. He said he had some knowledge of its existence, but I really believe he was pretty much in the dark. I told him what I had learned about the Board – that it appeared to have done no real planning. I watched Rabii very carefully as I spoke, but he offered no reaction.

I said I thought it was highly desirable to have plans in case the government failed, or if for other reasons it appeared that military action might be necessary. I argued that the Board's success would be directly proportionate to the amount of planning it had done and suggested that the best option would be to work as a group, with Prime Minister Bakhtiar as the leader. 'Plans could be made to break the strikes and get control of the oil, power, customs, communication grids and all the critical elements necessary to bring Iran out of its present paralysis. Unless there is progress along these lines, and fast, I am afraid the Bakhtiar government is destined for failure.' General Gast, being a superb planner, weighed in very heavy in this conversation. Gharabaghi would not entirely accept our argument. 'If the United States took the appropriate action, more could be accomplished than through any method we could come up with,' he said. Here it came again – the same complaint that I had got from his Service Chiefs.

Gharabaghi went on: 'The United States should move at once to pressure Khomeini to cooperate. There is just no way Iran can do it. Such a move would be totally unacceptable in Iran because Khomeini is a religious leader, protected by Islamic Law.' Inevitably he fired his second barrel: 'Why can't the US silence the British Broadcasting Corporation?' Its transmissions were thoroughly disruptive since nearly the entire population of Iran listened to them.

Then he introduced a new topic which shocked me. He said the whole Western world was lined up against the Shah and his regime, and was working to undermine it. I could not accept this, so I pressed him for a definition of 'the Western world'. He started ticking off the names of various nations, and I noted that he excluded the United States. I pressed him again. 'Why do you feel the Western world is against you?' He replied, 'There have been pressures from Great Britain to have the Shah leave Iran, which they have said will help restore stability. Khomeini is in France, where he is not being kept under control. The French are allowing him to pass out damaging information and work directly with Moscow and the Communists. Furthermore, our requests for help from Western countries have gone unheeded.'

I denied this, since I had been sent by the President of the United States with specific instructions to help. At that he became very emotional. I was extremely surprised because I have been told he was always as cool as a cucumber, even under fire. Again he blasted the French and British. He said he did not consider the Germans his friends, either. I contested this last point. Toufanian had spoken highly of the Germans' offer to help, and before leaving Stuttgart I had been advised that the German government was firmly behind the American effort to help.

I then asked if he had given any thought to asking his Muslim brothers for help: Kuwait, Turkey, Saudi Arabia, and even Iraq. He admitted that the idea was absolutely new to him, although Iran was already receiving some fuel deliveries from Saudi Arabia. I reminded him that it was the US which had provided the bladders for the C-130s in which the fuel was being hauled out of Saudi Arabia.

Gharabaghi agreed that it was vital to work with other countries, because if Iran were to crumble, the next one to go would be Turkey. 'Turkey and Iran are the pathway to the Mid-East, to the warm-water ports and the oil,' he said. 'I believe there has been no change in Soviet motives for centuries, and that they will go to any lengths to control both countries. I think the methods the Communists will use will not be overt, aggressive actions, but covert, destablilizing techniques. Once a country is shaken, they can move in their leaders.'

'The US has been concerned along exactly these lines,' I replied, 'and that's why our government wants you to support Iran's new government.' Gharabaghi did not understand how the military could support a civilian government. His incomprehension shed a lot of light on the main problem confronting us. If the military leaders felt this way, it was obvious why no planning had been done, and why they had no appreciation of the methods by which they could be used to regain control.

This provided me with an opening to discuss the planning that had to be done. I presented my complete concept on how plans should be developed to include Bakhtiar's involvement in all the military leaders' work. 'In addition,' I said, 'you should establish a national security council to help advise the Prime Minister on when and how to get things done.' General Gast again fortified my thoughts on planning.

Gharabaghi seemed to like the idea of having the Prime Minister shoulder the overall responsibility, but he felt the military just did not have the capability to plan, and he did not know if they even had enough people they could trust. I could see what was coming next. He wanted the United States personnel to do the planning for them. This would have been wrong. Any plans would have to be understood and executed by Iranians, so that Western planning would be inappropriate. I also thought it was about time for the Iranian military to measure up to their responsibilities. So I told him that the US would provide assistance and advice, particularly in the form of a question-asking mode, to help stimulate the thought processes of his own people; but from there on, they should develop their own plans.

It seemed as if the Chief was fighting the problem. He said I should not forget that there were Communists in the military ranks and at high levels in the Iranian government. Clearly, all the generals felt they could get my attention better by stressing the Communist threat, and they themselves had been trained to see a Red ghost behind every tree. Whereas I was sure that it would be foolish and unsafe not to assume Moscow's ambitions and influence in Iran, nevertheless at this point, I had about reached the conclusion that any officer who disagreed with the military leaders was branded a Communist. 'If you know who these individuals are,' I said, 'they could be excluded from the planning actions. I also can't understand why you don't just put them under arrest.' Of course, one reason was that Mr Bakhtiar had announced that day that he was going to release all political prisoners.

Gharabaghi explained that they had little experience in planning because the Shah had formulated all the plans single-handed. They were now missing the detailed guidance which they had been accustomed to getting. 'Our background has more to do with our capabilities than perhaps you realize. It is not simply our training that affects our performance, it is something even deeper: Persian tradition.' He said I could not be expected to understand this tradition, which explained why they wanted to leave Iran with the Shah. Their established priorities were God, Shah and Country. I knew what he meant, but there were times when I thought that their real priorities were Shah, God, self and country.

I offered a suggestion, 'As new Chief of the Supreme Commander's Staff, I recommend that you change the whole image of this post. You should bring the Service Chiefs together and discuss all the issues openly. You will then be their spokesman, reporting to the Prime Minister on all military matters.'

We had been talking for four and a half hours by now, so I

thought it was about time to bring our first session to a close. I was disappointed that Gharabaghi had not shown greater enthusiasm for writing plans to break the country's strikes and organize the military to regain control of Iran. He fully agreed on the need for emergency action, but gave absolutely no sign of getting down to it.

I had found the General to be much as I had been told. He was apprehensive, with reservations about foreigners. I also realized that he felt as strongly as the others about leaving Iran if the Shah did, and was furious about the pressures to quit exerted upon the Shah by Ambassador Sullivan, as well as the British Ambassador, Sir Anthony Parsons. He saw the future as totally hopeless. He believed that Khomeini, the BBC and the Communists would prevail in one way or another, and there was nothing he could do about it. He was clearly afraid of the threats made by the opposition. At the same time, he believed that there was nothing the US could not do, even at this point.

The tasks ahead of me were clear. I had to get the planning going. I had to change the military leaders' thinking. General Gharabaghi had no objections to what I had told his Service Chiefs, but we had not really come to complete agreement on future joint meetings where ideas could be shared openly.

I told him that I would inform the highest levels of our government of his requests for help in dealing with the BBC and the Ayatollah. In turn, I wanted him to establish contact with his country's religious leaders to try to persuade them to change their attitude toward the military. I also stressed that I had been instructed by Washington *not* to try to influence the Shah one way or the other on the question of leaving Iran – that was to be his personal decision.

Finally, I gave him my opinions of Iranian habits. Their reluctance to put plans in writing had to be changed. To sit back and expect miracles such as Khomeini's evaporating into thin air was foolish. Plans had to be made. 'Everything must be planned, and then executed in small but positive steps each day, if one wants to maintain unity and enjoy success,' I said.

It was now approaching evening, so General Gast and I left the SCS compound and were driven straight to his residence in north

Tehran. We agreed that it might not be too healthy for us to be caught in the open after dark. Already groups of people were starting to form in the streets, although this was the quieter part of town compared to southern Tehran, where a near-total breakdown of law and order made it ten times easier for a passing foreigner to get himself killed. I never really understood why the crowds chose to wait until after dark to begin their chanting sessions, unless it was to add a mystical aura which only the blackness of night could provide. If so, they were certainly right.

On our return we had a game plan session. We now had a good foundation to start from. The consensus of the Iranian officers was clear on at least five points:

1) the Shah's departure had to be stopped;
2) if he left Iran, all of them wanted to go with him;
3) the US should influence the Ayatollah;
4) it should also do something about the BBC broadcasts;
5) Iran's current unrest was the result of a Communist conspiracy. This we found difficult to accept, as the majority of the opposition appeared to be the National Front and pure Khomeini supporters now working together.

Our problems were now crystal-clear, but finding solutions was going to be a lot tougher. The one ingredient still missing was first-hand knowledge of Mr Bakhtiar's opinions.

While we were chewing over our next move, a call came through from General Toufanian saying that there was a dire emergency, and he had to see us right away. We agreed to meet him at his own home as quickly as possible. It was only two miles away, but I was glad of our escort. We passed a large crowd chanting round a blazing fire, and the sight and sound sent a chill up my spine. I wondered if they really understood what the crisis was about; these were people who stood to benefit from the Shah's programme, yet they were trying to get rid of him. It seemed a clear case of cutting off their nose to spite their face. The Shah had created his own dilemma: the education he had provided for his people caused them to become dissatisfied with an absolute monarchy, yet His Majesty was unwilling to make the transition towards a more democratic form of government. There is no doubt he had improved his people's living standards, and had the country en route to becoming a twentieth-century industrialized nation, but he refused to modernize his methods of ruling.

We turned off Pahlavi Avenue into a narrow, dark street. My first thought was, if we are blocked on this street, our only hope will be to shoot our way out. As we approached General Toufanian's house, we saw some men standing outside his gate. They were dressed in dark, drab clothing, which allowed them to blend into the night. They seemed to know who we were, and gave some crisp orders in Farsi. The house was surrounded by a high fence. We were admitted through a large iron gate which shut with a clang as our car passed through. We were escorted to the front door, where we were greeted by Toufanian. The general's physical appearance was alarming. His face was drawn and his eyes looked wild.

It was a magnificent mansion, fairly new, with elegant furnishings and breath-taking Persian rugs everywhere. In contrast with this luxurious grandeur, however, was the acute cold caused by the lack of heating oil. As if to cover his embarrassment, Toufanian asked if we would like to see the house. His reception room was fabulous. The floor area must have been about 50 by 50 feet, the ceiling 25 feet high. To call it ostentatious would be an understatement. Many mementoes were on display, no doubt gifts from around the world. He was an avid hunter and a lover of beautiful guns. One group of shotguns was the most astonishing collection I have ever seen. Each of the stocks was etched with hunting dogs, geese, ducks, pheasants, or doves, and all were heavily inlaid with silver and gold.

Our host then led us to a tiny study just off the kitchen. He apologized for its modesty, explaining that it was the only warm room in the house. I had seen this high-strung man acting nervously before, but this time was different, almost touching. Here was a distinguished senior officer in something approaching a state of frenzy. When we sat down, I asked him what was up. He said: 'I received several telephone calls today. Each caller told me I was on a "wanted" list, and that I must get out of the country immediately. They not only threatened my life but threatened to torture and decapitate me,' he exclaimed. As I had learned on earlier visits, the thought of death to a Persian was not all that frightening, but the notion of torture or decapitation was totally different. It was the ultimate threat. This may partially explain why the Savak came to adopt their notorious torture methods.

'The situation is hopeless anyway,' he said. 'General Djam has turned down the War Minister's job. Prime Minister Bakhtiar and I pleaded with him to take it for two or three weeks – just long enough for us to use his name – but he still turned it down. I told Djam that I would even take full responsibility and do all the work myself if he would do it, but it was no use.'

Toufanian then came clean about the Board, apologizing for having denied its existence. He described in detail all its discussions, and admitted that it had done no planning. I told him: 'General Gast and I talked with General Gharabaghi today about the Board, and we suggested that planning be started immediately. General Gharabaghi agreed with this.' Toufanian replied: 'Then I will do all we can to get things started. But,' he was extremely agitated as he talked, 'I must tell you my main concern. If Khomeini returns to this country, I am finished. There is no way I will survive. I must make plans to get out of the country.'

I tried to talk to him about his duty to his country, but he was too preoccupied with his own troubles to listen. He began to meander, telling us the story of his life – how he was brought up, how he had made his money, how much he had, and where it was banked. He named his friends and enemies. He talked about his relationship with the Shah; he said he had the reputation of being as close to the Shah as two people could get, but this was not true. They merely had a mutual understanding based on their need for each other. The relationship had become a formal business arrangement.

'All this should be obvious to you,' he told me, 'because I have never been appointed as Chief of the Supreme Commander's Staff or Prime Minister. I am one of the most capable people in this country yet I have never even been appointed Minister of War.'

I felt very touched by this emotional outpouring, and tried to comfort him. 'You can play an extremely important part in helping to get Iran back on track,' I said. 'We realize your talent, which has not been properly recognized. There is no one else who can do what needs to be done. This is a very difficult time for Iran. We are playing hardball. A military leader must put his country first, and I know you are the man to pull it through.'

'I am willing to accept responsibilities,' he replied, 'but I also want you to understand about the threats against my life. You must realize how serious they are. The only way I would stay in

Iran is if the military pulled a coup the same day as the Shah left.'

'Are the military leaders prepared to do that?' I asked.

Slowly came his sad, honest answer. 'No. There has been no planning.'

Then he suddenly interrupted himself and asked if I would like to know what the rest of Tehran was like. His son, a medical doctor from Dallas, Texas, happened to be home at the time, and he had been out all day scouting the city to find out the real vibes. The General left the room for a moment and returned with his son. 'I have covered the entire city, from north to south,' Dr Toufanian reported. 'The north side is not too bad. Things seem fairly stable, and there was no real ruckus as I wandered through. Everything seems under control. I saw groups chanting in the streets, but there was no violence. The best I can determine,' he continued, 'is that the people on the north side [by far the most affluent part of Tehran] have food, but they are suffering from a shortage of heating and cooking oil. Automobile gasoline is in short supply as well.'

The southern part of Tehran was completely the opposite. 'It's a downright jungle,' he declared. 'People are burning cars in the streets. The entire area appears to be unstable in every way you can imagine. There is no fuel or food, and people are beginning to look desperate.'

Curfew was fast approaching, and General Gast and I had to think about our trip home. We said farewell to the two of them, and asked the General to give full consideration to what we had said. We assured him that in one way or another he would be protected.

Our drive home was uneventful. After a couple of hearty nightcaps I slipped away into the first good night's sleep I'd had since my arrival.

Monday, 8 January 1979

I woke up very early, my thoughts on yesterday's meeting with General Toufanian. It gave me a heavy heart to see such a dynamic man so deep in depression and fear.

At breakfast, General Gast and I reviewed the meetings we had held during the past two days. We felt we had made very clear the message which President Carter had directed me to deliver. If there was to be progress in establishing stability, the military were a very important ingredient in the Prime Minister's game plan. They were the only visible support he had, and it was apparent that he must gain authoritative control to break the strikes and take over and protect key installations and locations.

With this in mind we decided we had three tasks for the day. First, we should inform General Toufanian and Admiral Habiballahi of yesterday's exchange with General Gharabaghi. Second, to ensure unity and common thrust to their activities, the military leaders must meet *as a group*. Third, they must be made to understand that we had no objection to a military coup, if necessary, but it was our opinion, and that of our government, that the best option was for the Prime Minister to use the military to gain control of the country. It was an absolute necessity to prepare workable plans for both options.

We decided to go by the Embassy first, to debrief Ambassador Sullivan on our activities and to tell him our game plan. I felt very strong about keeping him fully informed, so that he could close the loop on the political side. When we arrived, the Ambassador was in a meeting, so I reviewed some of the press. The most interesting article in the Tehran papers was one on the Shah's intentions. It quoted him as saying that he had no intention of leaving Iran permanently. He planned to return, and would retain full control of the military. Though he would withdraw from politics, he would be the head of a 'Constitutional Monarchy'. I was afraid this report could complicate our efforts to swing the military behind the Prime Minister.

The *Washington Post* reported on my meetings with the military leaders, and said I had been pressing them to support Mr Bakhtiar. It also said that I had got hold of several million dollars from the paralysed banking system, which would go towards paying the United States for the military equipment Iran had purchased. This was a gross overstatement, as General Gast and his people had put much effort into getting some payment before the banks were completely tied up. We had received two further checks on 7 January. The *New York Times* had an almost identical article, except that it also reported on my first meeting with General Gharabaghi. This was rather surprising, as I had not communicated to anyone in the United States about it, and we had only just finished the meeting a few hours back.

I was handed a message from General David Jones, Chairman of the Joint Chiefs of Staff in Washington, saying that he and the Secretary of Defence would appreciate a comprehensive report on my activities thus far.

When Mr Sullivan ended his meeting we proceeded to bring him up to date. He agreed that we had adequately delivered the President's message to the military leaders, but did not share our enthusiasm about getting the joint group meetings and the planning started. I told him that once I had some confidence that the military would get on with these two tasks, I was going to request a release to return to Stuttgart.

We left for Doshan Tappeh Air Base to see General Rabii. We got a cordial reception and immediately started reviewing the previous day's meeting with Gharabaghi. We pressed hard to see what their discussions in Farsi had been about. The areas that seemed to be bothering them were the group meetings and the planning. There was acknowledgement of the need for both, but for some reason there was reluctance to get started. We were given a lot more rhetoric on the grievances he had already raised – the Ambassador's desire to have the Shah leave, the BBC, Khomeini, and the need for the United States to show more support. Rabii seemed convinced that if Washington would just wave the magic wand, Iran's troubles would vanish.

Before leaving, we again stressed the urgency of unified action by the military. He said he would give it some deep thought, and keep in touch with us.

We next went to see General Toufanian, and then on to Admiral Habiballahi. We covered the previous day's meeting with both of them, and pressed hard for their support on the two central tasks. Both recognized the need, but neither showed much enthusiasm.

The Admiral brought up the report about the Shah's intention to keep control of the military, and asked if I didn't think this ran counter to my recommendations for the military to support Mr Bakhtiar. I disagreed; if they did not put all their support behind the Prime Minister, the Shah would not be able to return. I suggested that if he really thought I was off-base, he should discuss the subject with the Shah.

We went to General Gast's office so that I could get to work on my report to the Secretary of Defence. On arrival, we had Ray Burnette inform General Gharabaghi's office that we were in the vicinity, having just visited Rabii, Toufanian and Habiballahi. I hoped this would tickle his curiosity and he would ask us to come over and see him. Sure enough, I had just about finished writing my report when I was told that Gharabaghi would like to see me for a few minutes. He was alone, and very cordial. I thought this was super, because it meant he was beginning to lower his nationalist barriers, and to converse in English. We covered our meetings with the other officers, and pressed him for immediate action on the group meetings and planning. He too was lukewarm about both, so I suggested that he discuss them with the Shah. This was a shot in the dark, but I felt sure the Shah would agree with us on both counts.

After a lengthy rehash of yesterday's meeting with him, the General thanked us and we returned to our office. I finished my report and had it transmitted to Washington.

We decided to call it a day, and left for General Gast's quarters. There were larger crowds than before, and they had started gathering earlier. As we passed, we received some less than friendly gestures and many raucous shouts.

It was a cold and noisy evening outside as I prepared for bed. My prayers that night were that the military leaders would understand that their country's problems would not just vanish, and that they must see the wisdom of getting together as a group to plan the future. I also included a few words hoping that Ambassador Sullivan would enjoy success in the political court.

Tuesday, 9 January 1979

We had breakfast and discussed our tactics. Our objective was to bring the group of leaders together in a joint meeting. Having received only half-hearted encouragement from General Gharabaghi or anyone else, we decided to have another meeting with my dear friend, General Rabii. Perhaps he could help organize things. It was still early when we drove off to Doshan Tappeh Air Base.

We were cordially received by Rabii, but the minute we sat down his whole personality changed to that of an absolute tyrant, with violent outbursts and a venemous attack on the United States. 'I asked you to take certain actions and you have failed in all of them,' he exclaimed. 'You haven't shut up Khomeini, the BBC is still broadcasting, putting out very bad information; the US Ambassador is still pressing the Shah to leave Iran! President Carter started the whole business with his human rights programme, and now our country is suffering! You are not fulfilling your responsibilities by helping us to get out of this deplorable mess!'

I then laid down the law quite severely, but carefully, and tried to explain what the US had and had not done. 'What about the tremendous support our Ambassador has given your country? He has seen to it that you have received all the things you've needed. What about the amount of attention that I have personally given you from the US-European Command? President Carter is giving you an extremely large amount of his time right now, and has sent a very senior man to work with you. You had better settle down and get things into perspective right now.'

He was very startled by my attack, but it seemed to bring him to his senses. He sobered up a little, although he kept repeating: 'Iran will fall apart when the Shah leaves. We as leaders have no alternative but to pull a military takeover just as soon as the wheels are in the well of his airplane.'

'That's all well and good,' I replied, 'but, once again, tell me how you're going to do it.' My query, of course, left him speechless, so I continued: 'There is no way I can agree that it is good logic to try to pull such a scheme unless you have a plan of action.'

Rabii finally replied that it was a waste of my time visiting him.
'If the Shah is going to leave as soon as he has said, and if you are
not going to stop him, then I will just have to go with him.' With
this, I decided to try the shock treatment. I called him a 'gutless
deserter', a man disloyal to his country, and not thinking in mature
terms. I told him I thought he had better face reality.

Again he seemed extremely shocked. He was silent for a time,
then looked at me, shrugged, and said: 'Well, I guess you're right.
Maybe I'd better take a different view.' He then apologized, saying
he hoped I realized how much strain he had been under. I asked
him if he was willing to put pressure on the other leaders to meet as
a group, so that we could talk openly about the situation and see if
we couldn't get some action started. He agreed, but reminded me
that the Shah had not yet appointed a Chief of the Army. 'I think
it's less than likely that General Jeffrian will be made Chief of the
Army because I've heard talk of other people being considered.
Because of this, I think it might be well to postpone any joint
meetings until that post is filled.'

I heartily dissented; General Gharabaghi was with the Army and
he was perfectly able to represent that branch of the service. 'I
don't think we can afford to delay. We must move quickly,' I urged,
and Rabii finally agreed. He excused himself to place a few
telephone calls in private. When he returned it was obvious his
conversations had been productive. 'I have scheduled a meeting
for later this afternoon. You will be meeting with General Gharabaghi, General Toufanian, Admiral Habiballahi and me. You will
have your first joint assembly.'

Now that we had gained the results that we had been hoping for,
we adjourned and left for General Gast's office, where Gast and I
had an early lunch and reviewed the message traffic. I had received
a call from General David Jones in Washington, with instructions
to take extra measures to protect the newest and most sensitive
equipment shipped to Iran – particularly the F-14s and their
weapons. The message read: 'It would be well to discuss this with
the Chiefs of the Air Force and Navy.' The message was very
timely. I would be able to discuss the matter that very afternoon.

Shortly after midday, the Iranian liaison officer announced that
the four senior military leaders had assembled in the Chief of the
Supreme Commander's Staff's Office and that they were requesting our presence. This meeting signified a major move forward,

and General Gast and I were quite excited about it. Except for
social occasions, there was no way we could tell how long it had
been since all the Service Chiefs had met with the Chief of the
Supreme Commander's Staff. Certainly this would be the first joint
meeting of these particular men.

When we arrived at General Gharabaghi's office, all four of
them were present and standing: Gharabaghi himself; Toufanian,
Vice-Minister of War; Rabii, Chief of the Air Force; and Habiballahi, Chief of the Navy. Gast and I were received very warmly. The
atmosphere was strange but lively.

After brief exchanges about the cold weather and the suffering
of the Iranian people, I opened the meeting by saying that I
wanted to bring out into the open all the views that had been
expressed to me thus far. I also wanted to give each of the Service
Chiefs an opportunity to correct anything that I might not have
understood. 'My overall goal,' I said, 'is to try to bring the group
together as a team. It is of primary importance that we speak with
one voice, and that we offer our combined support to Mr Bakhtiar.'

General Rabii interrupted to ask if all this was really necessary
so I became very forthright. 'Based on my own observations,' I
said, 'I have come to the conclusion that you have all been
operating in something of a vacuum. You've never worked as a
team before. I have personally watched the US Joint Chiefs of
Staff discuss, as a team, items of grave importance. "More heads
are always better than one," and for the United States, such joint
efforts have proved to be the most constructive way of doing
business.' I also intimated that some of the Service Chiefs
appeared to have been trying to cut one another's throats to gain
favour with His Majesty. I saw some flinching and eye-shifting at
this, yet to my surprise, there was no counter to my accusation.

I then reported on my meetings with each of them. As I spoke,
they all appeared amazed at the similarity of each other's views,
even though they had never exchanged ideas before. They were
certainly of one mind on three major issues: keeping the Shah in
Iran, influencing Khomeini, and stopping the troublesome BBC
broadcasts.

Next, I decided to put my imagination to work. I deliberately
took some liberties by embellishing the view they had expressed to
me. My object was to produce a collective reaction. 'I appreciate

your dedication to His Majesty and your individual concerns about his intended departure,' I said, 'but I was extremely pleased with your change in attitude when you said you recognized your responsibilites to your country. It seems you have all accepted that if the Shah leaves on vacation, his absence will be only in body; the important thing is that his spirit will remain here. His Majesty will need a country to return to after his time away, and it is important that all of you have seen fit to remain in Iran to keep it stable for that purpose. I think we have to develop more ways in which to work with Mr Bakhtiar to achieve our objectives. But at least you have expressed willingness to work on the problem.'

My calculated deception was far better received than I had anticipated. The expressions on all the leaders' faces indicated approval. Although I was well aware that this was a fragile situation, I still felt rather proud of the progress of the past three days. In my individual meetings, all of them had emphatically expressed views quite opposite to those I had outlined, but my hope was that these tactics would generate a more positive outlook in each of them.

I told them that if they had truly decided to help the Prime Minister, they should continue meeting as a group. 'I have no intention of dealing with any officers below this level,' I said. 'When we meet in joint assembly, we will all have the same knowledge of all the important issues. If I can avoid discussions at a lower level, I believe we will be able to establish a chain of command, and you will each serve as the spokesman for your service.'

My motive was not simply to observe the formalities. I wanted these men to accept their responsibilities. They could not be constantly leaning on someone above them, which had been the Shah's role for years. It was absolutely necessary for them to stand on their own feet, to maintain continuity in their service, to get the right word out to their men, and to sustain discipline and morale. The chain of communication had nearly ground to a halt. The Shah was no longer putting out information, so nothing was getting through to the men. I told them: 'Your forces must be updated on the situation and made to play an active part in the nation's problems. We must also set up two-way communications so that the commander can get reports from his people. I suggest that each of you hold officers' calls, to meet and talk with your men, which I realize has never been done in the past.'

At this point General Gharabaghi created a small distraction by pushing one of the buttons on the telephone next to his chair. He uttered a few words in Farsi, then hung up. Servants came in with coffee. The pause enabled him to start afresh, and he took advantage of it to launch an almost desperate plea for the United States to influence Khomeini and silence the BBC. Though I was getting pretty tired of this refrain, I was rather relieved to see him showing some assertiveness. But my relief was short-lived. As soon as he had finished, he asked General Toufanian to back him up. It was clear that his idea of leadership was to lean heavily on others.

Toufanian duly backed him up, but added a new worry of his own. 'We have an urgent need for warm clothing,' he said. He was right. His troops must have been suffering acutely, particularly those on the northern border standing guard against Russia. 'If the troops are to be effective,' he said, 'we must give them warm clothing. We don't have any. We would like to have the US send us a supply as quickly as possible.' This seemed a strange request, as the same troops had endured previous winters, but I saw it as a ploy to test the strength of our support, so I did not challenge him. 'I will take this up with Washington,' I told him. 'I am sure we will do all we can to have supplies shipped, and we recognize the lack of fuel for heating.'

Toufanian went on: 'We know you recognize our problem with oil, gas and diesel fuel shortages. We will continue to work towards a better allocation for the military now that production has increased, but I must admit I don't have much hope of success.' Next, I told them: 'You must support Mr Bakhtiar so he knows he can count on you when the chips are down. You will have to put every ounce of energy behind the Prime Minister. You must bring things back under control, get rid of the terrible paralysis that is gripping the country, and rebuild Iran for the Shah's return.' I was glad to see greater agreement on these issues among the leaders, though I was unable to tell if this was simply due to a sort of group confidence. At last it seemed we were headed in the right direction. My first objectives, as directed by President Carter, were well under way. The military leadership would remain in Iran, and were ready to work together.

I moved on to the next item. 'This group should produce a

written plan of action. You must get away from the one-day military action concept. You must start planning much further ahead. We must work out a way to counter the psychological war being waged by the Ayatollah. It is obvious he hopes to take over the country without firing a shot. We have a whole machine at our disposal, yet it hasn't been used in months.'

After an exhausting give-and-take, they finally agreed to begin writing plans. But now I had two new problems: to convince them that they had the ability to do it; and to get them started. I realized it could take hours to get the wagons rolling. They all asked for help and guidance, but they actually wanted us to write the details for them. I refused. 'You must do the planning yourselves so that you can get the detailed information you'll need concerning the oil and power systems. You must create your own strategies. That way you can understand them sufficiently to execute them,' I said.

They were appalled. They said it would take at least a month to get the work done, and it could be calamitous if the Shah left before it was completed. If they were to do the planning themselves, Washington must explain to the Shah what was happening and insist that he remain in Iran. I now delivered a broadside I had prepared and thoroughly memorized. 'Washington has no intention of becoming involved with the Shah's proposed departure. That will have to be His Majesty's own personal decision.'

After a pause, Gharabaghi asked how long I planned to remain in Iran. Before I could reply they all chimed in with the same question, Toufanian the loudest.

I replied: 'I have delivered the message that President Carter sent, and I believe you have a thorough understanding of the US's intentions to stand behind you. I deeply appreciate your individual changes in attitude towards staying in-country to offer your support. By working together as one body, you will be able to provide a backing that will greatly enhance Mr Bakhtiar's chances of success. Knowing that you are fully capable, I think I can be most help by returning to my own headquarters in Stuttgart. From there I can ensure the proper logistical support you need. Consequently, I plan to leave tomorrow.'

This detonated an immediate, high-charged response. 'What could you possibly do better from Stuttgart? You have direct communication with Washington from Tehran!' exclaimed one. 'With your presence here, you are immediately available to us for guidance! Don't you want to see us through the crisis of the Shah's departure?' asked another.

Rabii broke in: 'If you expect us to write and implement plans in support of Prime Minister Bakhtiar, you won't be able to provide all the expertise we need from Stuttgart! You certainly can't leave until it is finished!'

It seemed they were still thinking of their own skins and the Shah's impending departure. My own concern was that the longer I stayed in Iran, the longer they would take to pick up the reins and shoulder their responsibilities. Trying to reassure them, I said: 'I will certainly present your views to Washington. I will press Washington to contact Khomeini, and the British government regarding the BBC, and I will request immediate delivery of warm clothing for your troops.'

Then, speaking directly to Rabii and Habiballahi, I began to discuss in some detail the need to protect the most sensitive weapons. Both of them immediately agreed that greater security was needed, and said they had already implemented special precautionary measures. I said we should also have as much of the equipment as possible in a ready-to-use status. 'That way, if we have to move it rapidly, it will be ready to go. When our men are not flying in the United States we concentrate all our efforts on getting everything in tip-top, flyable condition. Your men haven't been doing much flying due to the fuel shortage, and when airplanes are not being used, they have a habit of going out of commission unless you pay close attention to them. Another reason for working on them would be to put the idle hands of your airmen to work – so it could double as a morale boost.'

With that, it was time to adjourn the meeting. I felt that some degree of progress would be made now that a spark of team effort had been generated.

General Gast and I went directly to the American officers in the SCS compound. I wanted to discuss the day's events with Ambassador Sullivan, and checked with the Embassy that he would be free to see me right away. I also wanted to touch base with the Ambassador before sending my reply to Chairman Jones's message. Gast and I prepared a draft reply, to the effect that extra protection of sensitive-military equipment had already been put in hand, and that additional safeguards were to be added immediately. We also decided that this might be the proper time to approach Washington about my return to Stuttgart, so I added: 'My intent is to leave Tehran tomorrow about noontime on a C-5 that will be passing through and heading back to Stuttgart.'

With message in hand, Gast and I left our office. En route to the Embassy we saw a new build-up of activity. Crowds had been growing each day, but today we encountered several very large groups, and decided it was time to switch our tactics for moving about the city. It was clear that as a result of the publicity I had received in the Tehran and US newspapers, as well as statements pumped out by Russia's Tass, *Pravda* and Radio Moscow, I had become targeted. It seemed prudent to take proper precautions right away. The accuracy of the Russian media's reports on my own movements and actions raised questions in my mind about the nature of their involvement. They were far more correct and detailed than either the Tehran or US media. Subsequent information has thrown doubt on the role of Major General Fardust, who was working in the Supreme Commander's immediate staff and probably reporting to the National Front. He became Chief of Savma, which is Khomeini's successor to Savak, and in December 1985 was arrested for being a Soviet informer.

As soon as we arrived I debriefed Bill Sullivan on the day's events. 'I am pleased with the progress you seem to be making,' he said, 'but I don't think you should be too optimistic. The mood of the Iranian people can change from day to day, and the psychological warfare being waged by the opposition is gaining rather than losing momentum.' We agreed that with the reappearance of newspapers and the continuation of the BBC broadcasts, everyone was getting more information every day.

It was clear that Ambassador Sullivan thought any effort to promote Bakhtiar was a waste of energy. This was extraordinary, because the policy from Washington was unquestionably to give all aid and comfort to Bakhtiar. It was obvious that the Ambassador had a very low opinion of the military, a view which I could not share.

This disagreement between myself and Sullivan derived partly from our judging them from a different platform. I had watched them build their capability over the past ten years from the lowest element to the top. The US military in Iran that monitored and worked with the Iranian forces had worked directly for me for the past three and a half years. I had made frequent visits to Iran to check their progress and inspect the units. In the overall evaluation, they were highly disciplined, well-trained professionals. Based on standards of US or UK forces, they had one major weakness. They were not trained to act or solve problems on an individual basis. They had to have strong leadership, and they had that under the Shah. Even though to our minds this is an unacceptable standard, it is not unusual. For years we have talked about the great military capability of the Russians, yet until the 1980s, when they started to change their training philosophy, they operated on the same principle. That is one reason they established the skip echelon command control to ensure that orders came from the top. Pilots who defected to the West told us they could not start even a one-to-one air-to-air attack without orders from higher authority.

It is a bad idea to think for others, and I should know the hazards of such speculation because dozens of other writers have done this for me on my Tehran mission, with false conclusions in many cases. But I cannot avoid the conviction that Ambassador Sullivan, and many other creditable writers who disagreed with my assessment of Iran's military capability, evaluated them against a set of purely Western standards. In my opinion, this was wrong. The capability was there with strong leadership, and that is one of the main reasons I pressed hard to have that leadership emanate from Mr Bakhtiar. I believe until this day that had he given an order to act, the military would have reacted in a professional manner. But Bill Sullivan and I were always completely frank with each other, so we both understood that we were operating from a different base-line.

I told him that I hoped to leave the next day. As I understood it, Washington had only meant me to stay for two or three days – just long enough to get the generals' attention, pass on the President's assurances and extract some kind of commitment that they would stay and support the new Prime Minister. 'All these things have been done,' I said, 'though perhaps not as conclusively as I would have liked. If I stay much longer, they may become dependent on me. They must learn to stand on their own feet if they are going to function when the Shah is gone. It's obvious they are looking for someone to lean on, and this has got to change.'

After reviewing my message to General Jones, the Ambassador agreed with it, and also with my plan to leave the next day. I sent off the communique, and General Gast and I made tracks for home. Snow started falling shortly after we arrived, so we built a fire and thawed out over a cocktail. We now felt some degree of confidence that if the Shah left, the military leadership would face up to their responsibilities in Iran. They now saw the need to develop a plan by which they could take control of the country, by whatever means they chose: either on their own, or in support of Prime Minister Bakhtiar. We also had the feeling that they might now adopt the second course, even though there remained an undisguised wariness on both sides.

That was about the state of play that night, as the evening chorus of *Allah akbar!* (God is Great) filled the air, and gunshots shook the city. Knowing how much the military needed a leader, my final thought for the night was a prayer that Ambassador Sullivan would work more closely with Mr Bakhtiar.

Wednesday, 10 January 1979

The snowstorm continued all night, and next morning a six-inch crisp carpet covered the dreary brown earth of Tehran. I checked with the airport about the chances of getting to Stuttgart. I already knew that the C-5 would not be coming in that day. Now I learned that no one would be at Mehrabad Airport to clear the runways of snow, and no air traffic would be moving because of the air controllers' strike.

Having drawn a total blank, General Gast and I decided to get to the US Embassy to catch up on the day's news. We also wanted to try to fix up another meeting with the military leaders. We had to wait awhile for the snowbound roads to become passable, and eventually reached the compound about mid-morning. As we arrived, the Ambassador's secretary anxiously handed us a copy of the *Tehran Journal*. Its headlines shouted at us '*US POLICY SHIFT ON IRAN*'.

The article read: 'Officials in Washington announced that in a policy shift the US has decided to advise the Shah to temporarily leave Iran . . . Top officials in Iran are reported to be infuriated by the "colonial" interference of the US in the crisis, especially after the arrival of the US Air Force General Robert Huyser in Tehran to specifically tell Iranian Generals to back the Bakhtiar solution.' It went on: 'Informed sources say that nowadays there is no love lost between palace officials and US Ambassador William Sullivan. The US has been dropping hints at the policy shift for two weeks, but this is the first time it has made it official.' To complicate matters, the papers carried an article reporting the Shah's fears that if he were to leave the country, the Bakhtiar government would fail.

I felt a deep sense of responsibility for this, and began to think the night's snowfall had been providentially sent to keep me in Iran to deal with the problem. But I realized I would have to face a group of men who would now be less than rational on hearing the morning news. I knew they would all believe it – particularly the bit about US policy toward Iran – because Persians always seem to believe anything in print. I realized the progress I had made with the military leaders was far from irreversible. Yet I still hoped that these events might spur them into developing their plans.

Meanwhile Bakhtiar was having troubles of his own. No progress had been made in forming a government. Meetings of Iran's parliament, the 'Majlis', were constantly being postponed. There was uncertainty as to whether or not the new members of government would serve. There were reports that the opposition was putting pressure on them, with threats of bodily harm.

I telephoned General Gharabaghi's office to reconnoitre the chances of a meeting with the leaders that afternoon. Much to my surprise he said they had anticipated my call. They knew the snow had cancelled my departure and were anxious to meet again. Could I be at his office at 4.30 pm? Gharabaghi also told me that a new Chief of the Army had been appointed. He was General Badraie, who would also be at the meeting.

That afternoon General Gast and I reported at the SCS compound. I knew the minute we walked into Gharabaghi's office that it would be like poking a stick into a hornet's nest. The Group of Five greeted us: Gharabaghi, Toufanian, Rabii, Badraie and Habiballahi. (In my conversations with Secretary Brown on the secure phone, I called them the Group of Five; but on a few occasions we were joined by General Jamshid Fathi Moghaddam, Chief of Savak. They then became the Group of Six.) It was immediately apparent from the long faces and aura of defeat that they had read the newspapers. Not for the last time, I noticed how temperamental the Group's mood could be: they missed the leadership that the Shah had provided, and they had a tendency to lean on me rather than to produce strong initiatives of their own.

The storm struck as we entered. The first to speak was General Rabii. He shook the newspaper at us and shouted: 'You must have read what this says!' He lashed out at Ambassador Sullivan. 'Your Ambassador is forcing our Shah to leave his country! The newspapers said he was just a messenger, but we know that he *is* the problem!'

I tried to reassure them, but the leaders ignored me and angrily demanded that something be done to reverse the new US policy. I said I knew nothing about the source of the articles, and had not been officially informed of any change in policy. 'My government have always told me that the Shah's departure was to be at his own will. It is to be his own decision. If pressures have been exerted by Washington, it is news to me.'

I then revealed that I planned to accompany Ambassador Sullivan on an audience with the Shah the next day. 'We have scheduled a visit, and I will probably be given more detail about his departure plans at that time.' I was surprised to hear that each of them had had separate audiences with the Shah that day. None of them would give the purpose of their visit, other than to say they had discussed the situation in some detail.

'Did the Shah give you a departure date?' I asked.

'He talked about a new flight route,' volunteered General Rabii, 'but . . . ' Suddenly he was cut off in Farsi by General Gharabaghi. I believe he was about to give me the date, but he had been sharply censored. I also believe that all the others knew the date, because they looked as if they were carrying the whole world on their shoulders. They had finally come to grasp that he was actually going to leave.

Suddenly General Rabii spoke up again. 'There are no alternatives! America's attitude has changed! The Shah is going to leave! The Shah himself said that Bakhtiar would fail – so what alternative do we have but to leave when His Majesty does, or else pull a military coup!'

I immediately challenged him, becoming pretty rough. 'I think you had better settle down! This is a very serious business. Your country is at stake. How on earth do you think you are going to pull a coup? Do you have plans? Are there plans that you have never told me about? Is there something that I don't know about, which will enable you to take control? What are your plans if Mr Bakhtiar calls on you to take over the customs, or electricity, or oil, or any of the other elements essential to the economy? How will you respond? Who will be your leader?'

All of them wore the same blank looks that I had always received when asking such questions. I therefore pressed harder, because I wanted to reach the bottom line – to find an answer to the one question that had nagged me ever since my arrival: Did this group have secret plans for a coup that I did not know about?

At last I had found the answer I was looking for. Iran's military leadership was in a totally helpless state. The Group had nothing.

My line of questioning, however, proved productive. General Gharabaghi said they all understood the seriousness of the situation. 'We must get on with it,' he said, 'we are ready to start today, if you are ready to start today.' It was thus that the Chief of the Supreme Commander's Staff, in true Persian fashion, tried to thrust the burden back on to my shoulders. The Iranian leaders were ready to start if we could come up with our own advisers right away; so if there was any delay in starting, we would be to blame. Happily that was no problem. General Gast and I knew who our key people were when it came to helping them to work out their plans. 'We are ready to meet this evening,' I told the Group. 'Let's be on with it.'

We both sent out messengers to start assembling the teams. It was now that I began to see some of the progress we had hoped for. I had a strong feeling that if we got the planning started, we could get to grips with several of the country's problems. We would be tackling three areas: breaking the strikes; cementing relations between Mr Bakhtiar and the military; and taking precautions against a collapse of the civil government. The only alternative I could visualize at this point was for the military to make a strong stand – firm martial law. The masses had cooled off in November when they faced the same prospect: why not now? The role of our own people would be to define the kind of detailed information necessary in order to make military action work. They would make sure that the Iranian planners had identified the key people in the opposition, and knew the location of essential equipment and installations, whether these could be bypassed, and how vulnerable the oil and power lines were. What sized force would be needed to protect them? What proportion could be sabotaged before the system became inoperable? What facilities were available for repairs?

Having made these preparations for the evening's meeting, the group settled down again, and Gharabaghi volunteered some new information. 'You should know that I have discussed the need for planning with Prime Minister Bakhtiar. He suggested appointing a National Security Council.' However, Bakhtiar did not see how he could get a new Council together in less than three days. On hearing this, the Group of Five – not exactly models of organization themselves – grew quite critical of the Prime Minister's lack of urgency.

Gharabaghi went on: 'Mr Bakhtiar left no doubt that he intends to run the government. He knows it will be slow going, but he intends to start the economy moving just as soon as his government is approved. His Majesty has assured him that confirmation of his government will be forthcoming within a few days. In the meantime, he intends to take whatever steps are necessary to maintain control of the country, and is ready to ask the military for help if necessary.'

This was good news to me. Because of Gharabaghi's distrust of foreigners – almost xenophobic – he had never told me much about his dealings with Mr Bakhtiar. So it was real progress when he started opening up on the subject.

In this delicate military-civil relationship, a critial appointment would obviously be that of Minister of War. Since General Djam could not be persuaded to take the job, the Prime Minister had appointed another man; but none of the senior officers would tell me his name. Through another of Toufanian's outbursts – in which he threatened to resign – I learned that the new Minister was junior to him. I allowed Toufanian to vent his anger and then said: 'We have talked about this before, General, and it's good for you to get your feelings out in the open. But now I hope you are ready to re-enlist.' He looked a bit sheepish and then said Yes, he understood. He could certainly stick with the Group for the present.

As the discussion progressed, all of them were agreed that Mr Bakhtiar would be able to do very little. He was 'just a man with a desk and a chair'. He had no staff; there had been no progress in confirming his government; and the opposition was using force to stop people from reporting to work. How could he possibly succeed? I told them I thought they could give him enough backing to get started. 'The military has a very firm structure,' I said. 'Even though there have been desertions, my observation is that the organization is strong. If you could establish close enough ties with Mr Bakhtiar you could fill in a lot of gaps. It is true that he will eventually have to fill the other areas of his government, but the individuals could be found, and placed in position, if you could give him enough protection to do so.' The suggestion went across very well, and this raised my hopes. I was looking for the firm leadership which could give direction to the military. That was essential if they were to enjoy success.

Then they pressed me again for more help from the United States. 'Your country has to be solidly behind us all the way!' they kept saying. They seemed to be overreacting to the morning newspapers, which had made it perfectly clear that Washington was ready to support Mr Bakhtiar to the nth degree.

Finally General Toufanian took the floor. He started out by asking: 'Why are we together as a group? What are we doing? Why are we discussing these things?' Then he answered his own questions: 'We are here to plan, and if we do things properly, we could get a strong and lasting civilian government. Mr Bakhtiar is a brilliant man and a capable leader. All he needs is the proper support. If we can do all the planning, he could secure power without sacrificing a great number of lives. All our planning efforts should be directed towards minimizing bloodshed and ending the turmoil and strikes.'

This short speech was a welcome departure from the position taken up by the Group a few hours earlier. But they wanted to be sure of a strong American back-up, such as would be needed, for instance, if Bakhtiar decided to take over the oilfields. I assured them that if they did their utmost to support the civilian government, they could count on American support, even in the event that a military takeover became unavoidable.

They then brought up the eternal threat. They had intelligence that there was a Persian-speaking Russian division just across the north-west border. They also believed that in addition to massing forces there, the Russians were lowering the fences and taking other steps to prepare for an invasion. I said this was news to me. Our own intelligence did not show any such activity. There were forces there, but there was no abnormal movement.

They pointed out that under the bilateral treaty of 1921, the USSR had the right to send troops into Iran if a third power intervened in the area. The agreement still existed, and even though the Iranians had declared it void, Moscow had refused to terminate it. Their fear, which I had to share, was that Moscow would not hesistate to invoke that clause if the opportunity arose. However, President Carter had warned the Russians that the US would resist any incursion onto Iranian soil by whatever means were necessary.

The Group said that Washington must get the free world radio system to support their government, and warn the world of the danger of Soviet intervention. Their intelligence sources – which I could not verify – indicated that Khomeini probably had direct telephone links with Moscow and had been working with them. They were convinced that the US could sever that link and force Khomeini to collaborate with the Bakhtiar government. I frequently puzzled over their claims about Khomeini's links with Moscow, but although their fundamental principles differed so much, I recognized that Khomeini was likely to accept whatever help he could find – financial or material – from whatever source.

The bottom line for the day, in the Group's view, was that Washington must repudiate the reported change in policy and try at least to persuade the Shah not to leave abruptly. If he had to go, he should do so in a phased programme. He should first go to Bandar Abbas, or Kish Island, and stay for a month or so; then take his vacation from there. An abrupt departure would be catastrophic. It was obvious that they were apprehensive about shifting their obedience to Mr Bakhtiar, yet I felt they knew in their hearts that they had to have a leader, someone who could harness the armed forces' power to a viable political strategy.

It was now getting late, and we had to respect curfew, so we made a quick check to see if the teams had started planning. We found that they had, so we took our leave. Before doing so, I telephoned Bill Sullivan and briefed him on the day's activities. He

told me a message had arrived saying that Washington wanted me
to remain in Iran indefinitely.

We went home, but had only been there an hour when the
Ambassador called back. It seemed that Secretary of Defence
Harold Brown wanted to speak with me on the secure telephone
as soon as possible. Since the only secure telephone was at the
Embassy this meant that I must go downtown. It was curfew time –
no drivers, no transportation – so I was not exactly sure how to
proceed. The nearest car belonged to Brigadier General Kertesz,
the Air Force Section Chief. We called him and he said no sweat,
he would be there in a few minutes. He drove us across Tehran,
but it was a hair-raising journey – through pitch-black, curfewed
streets. Navigation was so difficult that we overshot the Embassy
and strayed into South Tehran, where in daylight your life wasn't
worth a dime. When we got to the Embassy, General Kertesz said
he would go straight back to his quarters. This startled me, and I
asked him to spend the night at the Embassy. But he told me his
wife was home alone, and no way would he leave her by herself.

Ambassador Sullivan had alerted the Embassy guards and the
secure operators, so all was ready for me to talk to Secretary
Brown. They had the old-type secure telephone, which leaves
much to be desired. When operating at peak performance, you
sound like Donald Duck and need an interpreter. Then, just as you
think you have established contact, it goes out of synchronization,
and you have to start over. When we finally got linked with
Secretary Brown, he had many questions. He wanted to know
what happened that day, and I told him. He wanted to know what I
thought about the Bakhtiar government: could it succeed if the
Shah decided *not* to leave? I explained the degree of hostility
toward the Shah and said I was not sure this could be pacified if he
stayed. Mr Bakhtiar must be given his head, and the public must
be left in no doubt that he was in charge.

I said I was inclined to agree with the military that if Ayatollah
Khomeini was not brought under control or persuaded at least to
indicate some support for Mr Bakhtiar, life was going to get very
unhealthy. If he maintained his present tempo and kept sniping at
Mr Bakhtiar, the chances of success were not high.

Secretary Brown wanted to know if I thought there was enough

military capability to protect the oilfields and power plants, break
the strikes and regain control. I gave him an unqualified Yes; I
thought the capability existed, given the necessary central control.
The missing ingredient was the plans; and the planning had started
that day. I had hopes that we would be able to get something on
paper which would identify the country's logistic systems – especially where the nerve centres were – and then determine the
procedures to control and protect these essential elements. I said I
thought it would be necessary for Ambassador Sullivan to have
instructions to work as closely with Mr Bakhtiar as I was doing
with the military, since the Ambassador was not inclined to do so
on his own.

I said I thought I had made significant progress in convincing the
senior military leaders that their loyalty must not be only to the
Shah, but also to the nation. They seemed ready for closer ties with
Mr Bakhtiar. Most important, they now seemed to realize that
they were incapable of carrying out a coup because they didn't
have the necessary plans or information.

I again talked about trying to establish some relationship with
Khomeini. I suggested that the US should take the initiative and
work directly with him. Secretary Brown seemed sceptical about
this. I was not sure why, because I had always been trained to find
out as much as possible about the opposition. Both Ambassador
Sullivan and I believed that direct contact was the only answer. If it
failed, we could not see how we would be any worse off. As it was,
Khomeini was driving more nails into Mr Bakhtiar's coffin every
day.

Secretary Brown wanted to know if I thought there was any
chance of drawing the masses away from Khomeini. I did not think
there was, because emotions had become so strong; there were
pictures of Khomeini everywhere and the crowds carried posters of
him and chanted his name wherever they went. Much the more
promising approach was to sound out Khomeini to establish his
terms for cooperation. I told him that I thought only about ten to
fifteen per cent of the population supported Khomeini, but they
were the active element, and made more noise.

I said the outlook was not all black. This was the first time I had
seen any unity of effort among the military, and I believed after
our last two meetings that this unity was very solid. The Group
seemed to enjoy working together, openly expressing their views,

and even supporting one another. The real cause for alarm lay in the increasing polarization of power: the line-up of a Khomeini-religious faction against a Bakhtiar-military faction was extremely unhealthy. It gave the other factions the chance to operate with almost total immunity – in particular the Tudeh element. If there could be some understanding between Khomeini and Bakhtiar, it would close this gap and leave little room for these third-party elements to operate.

Secretary Brown wanted to know about progress on the Regency Council. He was happy to hear that the names were filling up and the selections almost complete. He wanted to know my thoughts about having a military man on the Council. I said I had pressed Sullivan and the Council hard to get General Gharabaghi included, and thought he would be accepted. It was certainly important to forge closer links between the military and the government. I reported that a new Minister of War had been appointed but I did not know who it was. He wondered if they were still hoping for General Djam to change his mind. I said I thought not.

Secretary Brown asked about the Ambassador's appointment with the Shah the next morning, and wanted to know if I was attending. I told him I was, having received instructions to do so from the Secretary of State and from Secretary Brown himself. The same instructions gave me permission to accompany Ambassador Sullivan on any missions he might have, although he was not to accompany me on my own missions. Sullivan expressed no reservations about this, but I did not particularly like it. My background had taught me that teamwork was the proper approach to a crisis, and I hoped we were trying to work out the same problem with a common objective. Here the Ambassador and I were agreed. We may have had differences of opinion, but nonetheless I hoped that our objective was the same. At all events, I briefed him to the maximum degree on all my activities, including those with the Iranian military and the US Secretary of Defence. He seemed fairly open with me in return. With hindsight, Secretary Brown's instructions should have set me thinking about what they implied for my relations with Sullivan, but if Washington did have any doubts about his activities, they were never made explicit to me.

Secretary Brown said he would like to have a daily report from then on. I suggested if I was going to do this, I would much prefer, for security reasons, to report by secure voice, and not put it in print; that way we had absolute control of who had access to the information, and duplicate copies could not be made. This was agreed, with the provision that for any special items I would put the information in a message.

I spent the night in the Ambassador's residence. It had been quite a day.

Thursday, 11 January 1979

At breakfast I discussed with the Ambassador my report to Secretary Brown. I told him this would be a daily assignment, and I would be calling in every evening to report the day's happenings. Ambassador Sullivan recognized immediately that he had acquired a star boarder. He graciously offered me a place to stay, which I much appreciated. So, from that day on, my billet was with the Ambassador and his wife.

Next we discussed our plans for the audience with the Shah, which was due at 11.15 am. I explained I was anxious to check with the Group of Five to see how the planning was coming along. I would meet with them first and then return to the Embassy to accompany the Ambassador to the palace.

General Gast and I made our way to Gharabaghi's office, where the Group was already assembled. At once I asked about the planning, but on my way in, I had already heard the worst. None of the Iranians had reported for work. This was Thursday, which is the Iranian equivalent of our Saturday; and in spite of the urgency of the situation, and the importance of every minute that went by, they did not feel that anything should interfere with their weekend. I told them what I thought about this pretty clearly. I said we all had too much at stake to accept this irresponsible behaviour. After some cavalry language along these lines, they elected to call in their people and get the ball rolling. Gharabaghi said they would go on a full seven-day week with extended days, until the planning was finished. This was vital because the torrent of Khomeini tapes, leaflets, pictures and demonstrations was increasing every hour. Either we got some movement or we were going to be lost, and lost soon.

Having kick-started the machine, I returned to the Embassy to join Ambassador Sullivan for our trip to Niavaran Palace. I had not seen His Majesty for several months, and I was struck by his obvious exhaustion. Stress and concern were written all over his face. He was dressed in a dark civilian suit, in contrast with the military uniforms I had often seen him wear. He opened the discussion with some light talk, and then asked me the purpose of my mission. I knew full well he had been briefed up to the hilt on it, but duly went through the instructions I had from our President, and brought him up to date on the latest developments with the Group of Five. I went into the plan we had initiated in great detail. He seemed very interested, and agreed that it was badly needed because there just hadn't been any planning. Their only plans were for an external threat. They hadn't given internal threats a second thought, and their war reserves were quite inadequate for an internal operation.

He then brought up his departure. He said he felt the need for a vacation; he was tired, and he thought his absence would also stabilize the situation. He asked our opinion on when he should go. Ambassador Sullivan said that as soon as possible would probably be the best for all concerned. I registered an objection, knowing that this would not sit well with Sullivan. I was not sure we yet had the military completely reconciled to the Shah's departure. His ties with the generals were deep. A few more days would make a difference. Even though I knew it was skating on thin ice, I suggested that he might help on the Bakhtiar-military relationship: his armed forces would need a leader to follow.

He then switched gears and talked about flight planning. He wanted to know what route I would suggest, and said he wanted to stop in Egypt to see his good friend President Sadat. He would like his next stop to be in either Morocco or Spain, for fuel; and then he would like to go to Andrews Air Force Base in Washington, and from there to Palm Springs. His destination in the US was the Annenberg Estate at Palm Springs. The US government had completed all the arrangements for the estate, including security.

I had already discussed the Shah's route with Secretary Brown, so I suggested that it might be more secure if he chose some other place than Andrews Air Force Base to arrive in the States. Other bases would provide much more security. Charleston Air Force Base in South Carolina, or one of the north-eastern airfields such as Pease, Plattsburg, Loring or Westover, would all provide better security and fewer problems. He agreed, and asked me to get together with General Rabii to work out the details.

I reminded the Shah of what he had said to me the previous summer: that I shouldn't be too concerned, and should continue to work on his Command Control programme, because even if he fell from grace with our President, he did not intend to lose control. I asked him: 'What happened Your Majesty?'

He turned and stared at Ambassador Sullivan for what seemed like a very long time. He scratched the back of his head several times and then started to change the subject. I said: 'Your Majesty, I asked a question.' He turned and looked at me with a very solid stare through his thick glasses. Finally, he said, 'Well, you really don't understand.' He went on, 'Your Commander-in-Chief is different from me. I am a Commander-in-Chief who is actually in uniform, and as such, for me to give the orders that would have been necessary . . . ' He stopped and asked: 'Could you, as Commander-in-Chief, give the orders to kill your own people?' I said: 'Your Majesty, we are not talking about me, we are talking about you.' At this point he changed the subject, and I never received an answer.

It is still something of a mystery to me as to what had happened to him. I have given considerable thought to it, and have read most of the books and articles of people who thought they knew the answer. I don't feel satisfied by any of their explanations. But I will offer a couple of thoughts.

I don't think anyone who knew the Shah would question his respect for, and dedication to, the United States. He had every reason to feel grateful. Would he have been on the Peacock Throne at all if it were not for the Americans and their help in 1953? The US had steered him through the 1960s before he had the means to help himself, and once he had got the means, Washington had gone that 'extra mile' to satisfy his desires. I believe too that he had a deep love and concern for his own people. He subsidized commodities which they craved, and which were too expensive for them to have without help, such as sugar. He paid the tuition fees and provided expense accounts for students to study abroad. As he said to me five months earlier: 'The people that were to benefit have rebelled.' I am sure the Shah's physical condition must have influenced him. He knew he had cancer, and he was taking medication for it. This, coupled with the almost unbearable pressures on him, would be enough to snap anyone's mind. Whatever the reasons, he certainly did not take the actions necessary to maintain control, so that the country progressively degenerated into a state of complete paralysis by January 1979.

The Shah now reverted to the plans the military were working on. He said he wasn't clear as to who would execute them. I explained that the hope was to put them into operation under the leadership of Prime Minister Bakhtiar, but they would be written in such a way that the military could act unilaterally if necessary. This served two purposes. First, though his generals had talked about a military takeover, they had no idea how they were going to do it. Second, the planning might heal the distrust between Mr Bakhtiar and the generals.

The Shah, to my surprise, told me I was getting a little too strong in my support for Mr Bakhtiar. He then talked a bit about the doctrine and the concept which I had developed for his forces. He said that it was certainly valid, but it needed to have strong central control to keep the power of the armed forces properly balanced. I wondered if he was thinking about the plans we were currently developing. When I was working on his concept and doctrine, he had been extremely sensitive to the possibility of a military takeover.

He went into a lengthy 'what-if' analysis of the present outlook. The principal speculations were: what if Khomeini would not back away? And what if Bakhtiar failed? This led him to talk about the Regency Council. He said he had been working very closely on it with his people. He wanted Mr Bakhtiar to be Chairman, and it should include two or three Cabinet members. There would be three others: a representative from a religious group, General Gharabaghi from the military, and a third whom he failed to designate. He wanted a balanced slate of people which would ensure representation for all. I'm sure he advocated this collective formula so that no one man could gain the backing to replace him.

He wanted action to limit the suffering and bloodshed during this period of chaos. The breakdown in the economy had to be turned around and brought under control. This was a major cause of suffering among the people. The customs bottleneck on the Turkish frontier had put a stop to the trucks packed with foodstuffs which were badly needed in Iran. Obviously he had the situation in perspective and knew what needed to be done. The question was, why hadn't he done it?

The Shah expressed very deep disappointment that the US had not gone directly to Khomeini to persuade him to stop the suffering in Iran. He said there was no chance of progress if Khomeini withheld all support from the Bakhtiar government. He couldn't understand Khomeini's attitude – after all, Mr Bakhtiar was from the opposition party. But the approach to Khomeini must not be indirect, he believed. Like Bill Sullivan and myself, he wanted a clear-cut US initiative.

It was essential to know where Khomeini stood; this was the key issue for all of us on the Iranian end of the chain. We should be able to find out because Ambassador Sullivan and his people had been doing a lot of homework with the opposition. (I frequently wished they had put forth the same effort on the Bakhtiar side.) My contacts were strictly on the other side of the fence, and I had no relations with the opposition forces. In fact, I had specific instructions not to have contact with them except on a case-by-case basis, and then only after clearances from Washington.

The Shah now revealed that he would leave Iran in his 707 with his crew. He would use the routine call-sign and fly the aircraft himself. He would stop at Aswan to see Sadat, and then refuel in either Rabat or Madrid. He agreed to use a base of our choice on the US east coast for refuelling, and would not disembark there but merely refuel en route to Palm Springs. He said he was determined to leave the country in an orderly manner. He did not want to give the impression of fleeing from chaos; he was merely taking a vacation. He thought he could not leave until the Bakhtiar government had its vote of confidence from the Majlis, which was scheduled for the coming Saturday. He could be ready to go in six or seven days.

Ambassador Sullivan promised to discuss this with our President. The Shah said he would wait a day to get a US reaction, but he would like to plan on leaving not later than the following Wednesday, 17 January.

We had been with him for two hours. For me, it had been quite unlike any previous audiences because of the Shah's obvious exhaustion. He accompanied us to the door, where we parted with an extremely warm handshake. He thanked me profusely for being there, and for working with the military. He said he had high confidence in me, that his military had too, and that he hoped I would keep a proper balance in my support for Mr Bakhtiar. He was glad I was getting the military together collectively. This was rather enigmatic, because he had never chosen to do so himself; even yesterday he had met them all individually.

Immediately outside his office a guard took me by the arm and led me off to a side room saying: 'You are wanted here.' Then another guard started talking to Ambassador Sullivan. When I entered the room, there were General Rabii and General Toufanian, both in a high state of emotion. They obviously wanted to know about the Shah's departure.

Sure enough, the first question was: 'What did you say to His Majesty about departing?' At that moment Ambassador Sullivan came to the door, wondering why I had been filtered off so abruptly. This immediately cut off the conversation, because both Toufanian and Rabii were convinced that Sullivan was behind the Shah's departure. They quickly asked when they were going to get some cold-weather gear, and what about the BBC and Khomeini? I told them we had a meeting scheduled that afternoon, and I would talk to them then.

Sullivan and I went back to the Embassy. On the way I told him about the generals' questions, and also what I intended to do at the afternoon meeting with the Group of Five. I principally wanted to be sure the planning was under way, because one could never tell from day to day when it would be needed. Time was rolling by with few positive results. The Shah would be gone in a few days, and progress on the new government had been practically nil. There had been a few encouraging features – the newspapers back on the streets, more gasoline and fuel oil, a relaxation of the curfew – but we needed to crank the economy and build up the Bakhtiar government. We also had to get more pro-Bakhtiar press to offset the opposition propaganda.

The anti-American campaign had reached a new tidemark. The chanting in the streets was depicting the United States as the Satan of the Persian people. The threat level against American personnel was increasing, and we had to get all non-essential Americans out of the country. We were already moving wives, children and some others out of the country.

When we got to the Embassy, I immediately put on a civilian topcoat and prepared to make the two and a half miles' drive to the SCS compound. As I was leaving I was handed a wire from General Jones, giving me explicit instructions on the sensitive equipment – the F-14s, Phoenix air-to-air missiles, and associated equipment. He wanted me to have the Iranians move them to more secure bases in the south, and to protect them there. The Iranian officers were sensitive about this. They felt they had bought the equipment, and it was theirs. So the pressure I was getting from Washington looked as if it was becoming counter-productive.

At the compound, the Iranian liaison officer in the US office told me that my presence was requested immediately. In Gharabaghi's office the whole Group was waiting, plus a new ingredient: General Moghaddam, Chief of the Savak. They were on tenterhooks to know the answers which I couldn't give to Rabii and Toufanian at the palace. I told them first that the Shah was all in favour of the planning, and wanted us to get something in print as soon as possible. This pleased General Gharabaghi, who said I would be happy to know that the planning had really started and was progressing well.

That was true, as I confirmed when I stopped at our office. They had reached the point of deciding which military elements would handle which tasks. The Army would be responsible for food, water and communications. The Navy would look after the oilfields; they had the technical capabilities to run much of the system, and some of them were working in the oilfields at that moment. The Navy would also be responsible for psychological warfare, leaflets, posters, etc. The Air Force would be responsible for the electrical power and the water systems. All three services had started on the plans, and though they were still only outlining requirements, it was certainly progress.

I dodged their questions on the Shah's departure, as this was still undetermined. I confirmed that the Shah wanted to leave and to do so in an orderly manner, but I told them he did not foresee a phased departure, such as they had been talking about. I was pretty sure General Rabii knew all about the Shah's flight planning, but I was not sure about the others: the old habit of one-upmanship was not easy to break.

They were still steamed up about the external threats – why, I did not know, because we had no new indicators. They were absolutely certain that Russia was stirring the pot, aiming to break down one or two provinces and separate them from the rest of the country. They said they had evidence of attempts to split the military. Certainly there were a number of defections from the Army to the Khomeini forces, but for a force numbered in hundreds of thousands the rate was low – maybe a hundred a day. We had received reports of these desertions, but many of the men involved were young draftees, and they did not represent a significant drain on Iran's military strength.

I told the Group I wanted them to concentrate one hundred per cent on the internal problems, and the United States would take care of any external threat. I had talked to Washington about this and felt I was on safe ground; we had discussed making the appropriate dispositions – moving naval forces into the Indian Ocean and F-15s into Saudi Arabia – to show that we meant business.

I believe the Six were satisfied that we would take care of any external threat. But they came back at me very hard with their chronic complaints about the BBC and the lack of direct contact with Khomeini. They also complained about the newspapers in the US, and would not accept my explanations of how American newspapers work. I did ask Secretary Brown to discuss with President Carter the possibility of persuading the BBC to moderate its reporting of events in Iran. Also, I believe that a Savak representative went to London to lodge a protest. But nothing came of these efforts to approach the BBC.

I was able to tell them that the first planeload of cold-weather gear was already en route. The Secretary of Defence had responded magnificently: in fact, the first loads were delivered to Tehran even before I could get a letter of understanding signed. When we discussed the lack of war reserve materials, particularly fuel, they said that though fuel production had increased, they were not getting their fair share of it. I told them that by one means or another they must syphon off more as production increased. In the meantime, I would refer this problem to Washington. I felt sure the US could work out some solution, if necessary by bringing in a tanker. This was a good way to start getting results even before the plans were complete.

Another area where I thought we could get early results was the psychological battlefield. We should be turning out leaflets and posters which would put some backbone into the forces of law and order. This was overdue; with the increase in traffic, the situation on the streets was getting completely out of control.

Again, I suggested they look very carefully at customs, which were now letting in large numbers of guns – for onward routing to the mosques – while virtually paralysing the entry of foodstuffs. I emphasized how upset the Shah was about the hardship this was causing to his people.

The customs problem was a good one to tackle because it combined a necessary step to re-establish the government's control with the humanitarian function of relieving the artificially created shortage of food. If the Group could handle this relatively straight-forward job, it would improve their morale for some of the harder work ahead. The oil situation was equally urgent, but I was told that the National Front had a grip on the National Iranian Oil Company, and that Mr Bakhtiar thought he could take care of restoring supplies by means of his own political connections. If the military did have to move in, it would be the Navy who would take over the oil system, because of their experience with the major refineries, which were situated close to the country's tanker-loading facilities.

Once again the Group returned to the Shah's departure. They felt certain that Mr Bakhtiar would be overwhelmed and that, therefore, their only hope was an immediate military coup the day the Shah left. I said this only made sense if they had done all the necessary planning in advance. How often did I need to keep on saying this? We should quit talking about it and get on with it.

I pointed out that the Shah had told me there would be a wide national representation within the Regency Council, including a military member. Gharabaghi reported that the National Security Council had now been established and its members designated; but it would not be meeting until Saturday afternoon, two days away, so he thought the Prime Minister was taking the Council a bit too casually.

Then came a surprise. Gharabaghi looked straight at me and asked how much I thought he should tell Mr Bakhtiar about their plans, if anything. I said that he and the Prime Minister should work together on them, and there should be absolutely no secrets between them. Again I thought how helpful it would be if Ambassador Sullivan would close the loop on the other end with Mr Bakhtiar. I had provided the Ambassador with all the details about each day's meeting with the Group. He was fully aware of my concept of regaining control of the commanding points of the country, and knew that the military had to have orders from some unquestioned leader.

My even bigger concern at this time was that there was absolutely no dialogue between Bakhtiar and Khomeini. The Khomeini elements were still condemning Bakhtiar and rejecting any form of negotiation with his government, doubtless because they reckoned they held all the cards. I had a 'gut' feeling that there were millions who would support the legal government, given some encouragement, but they were all silent.

I spent a long time trying to stiffen the Group, but it was hard going. At least they now seemed to have resigned themselves to staying in Iran; but they were still dithering with the half-baked idea of a coup the moment the Shah departed.

At this point, just as the meeting broke up, General Gharabaghi turned to me and said that a new Minister of War had been appointed. He was General Shafaqat – a man comparatively junior in rank but of good reputation. They all seemed to trust and respect him. I felt he was a good choice if they were not going to appoint General Toufanian. I looked at Toufanian, and he smiled and said: 'That's okay, that's okay. I understand, and I will work with him. In fact, I'll do his work for him, and let him get the glory.' He had intended to leave with the Shah, but now seemed prepared to take my advice.

Then a very startling thing happened. Gharabaghi said: 'There is one thing we should tell you. The Shah ordered us to listen to you, to trust you, and to work with you.' I asked them when this had happened, and they said it was during their meetings with the Shah. I could only assume that those were the meetings of the previous day; or perhaps they had been called immediately after my own audience. At all events they were quite definite, and all agreed that those were their instructions.

This was gratifying. But I had to be careful. It was clear that they were hungry for leadership, they needed it, and somebody had to supply it. In the strictly military context that was the job of General Gharabaghi, not me. I had worked very hard to get him into the leadership role, since he was the senior man. But the person who had been assuming that role was General Toufanian; he had just marched in and taken over. As I have already indicated, I could see a gradual transition taking place; Gharabaghi seemed to be taking the reins, but as yet not very firmly. In the broad political context it was clear that they needed an overall leader, and in my book if we were going to enjoy any success that had to be Mr Bakhtiar.

I told them I appreciated what the Shah had said, and my only desire was to be of service to them by my advice and guidance. If at any time they thought I was of no further use, I would ask my government to withdraw me. Until then I would give them all the counsel I could. But, of course, it was their country, they had to take the actions and their leader must be General Gharabaghi. I told them there was no way I could be optimistic about the future. But they had a good civilian leader, and if they would fully support him and get the plans complete, that was much their best hope. The greater their progress the greater the chance of success.

With that we bade each other a warm and cordial farewell. I got a feeling of real sincerity on their part. Maybe that was wishful thinking, but I felt now that their intentions were sound. My concern was whether or not they would shoulder their responsibilities.

General Gast and I went back to our office, where I reviewed the messages, traffic and intelligence reports, before returning to the Embassy residence. I had dinner with the Ambassador and his wife and debriefed him on the day's play, going over all the points I intended to make in my nightly report to Secretary Brown.

I asked the Ambassador if he had yet got an appointment with Mr Bakhtiar. He said he had made himself available, but the ball had been left in Mr Bakhtiar's court. He did not wish to force the pace for fear that, like the Shah, the Prime Minister would get the stigma of being a US puppet. One of his greatest assets to us was his independence, as a member of the opposition. The press reports indicating full US support for Bakhtiar cannot have been wholly welcome to him. I felt that if the Ambassador could really

get alongside Bakhtiar, we might at last get the necessary cooperation out of the military. My opinion was obviously not shared by
others, possibly people in the State Department, because this was
not the route we were going. Sullivan and I had agreed that each of
us would stick to our own territory, political or military, so
anything I wanted conveyed to Mr Bakhtiar had to go through the
Ambassador. Throughout my mission I never met the Prime
Minister and was never in direct contact with him.

Ambassador Sullivan and I exchanged impressions of our audience with the Shah. Both of us felt he had expended all his useful
energies. It would be counter-productive for him to remain in Iran
as a target of increasing public uproar. Our only disagreement was
on the timing of his departure. I felt we needed a few more days to
ensure that the military would stay in-country, and would not go
off at half-cock on some futile putsch. Also, things would go better
once Bakhtiar was confirmed by parliament. The military had
often expressed reservations about working with an unconfirmed
group.

The Ambassador and I believed the Shah meant what he said: he
was not planning to leave the country permanently, and there was
no question of abdicating the throne. He was leaving, under the
guise of a vacation, in order to give the Bakhtiar government a
chance. I felt he planned to return as soon as things settled down,
or if the military attempted to take over. Many people were
guessing that he would go to Aswan, that the military would then
pull a coup, and that he would come right back again. As I saw it,
the Shah wanted no part in a coup, because of the bloodshed it was
bound to cause. He had refused to get tough at a time when the
carnage would probably have been less. Now he was far less
prepared for a rough-house, either mentally or physically, than he
had been in the past. Besides, what would a coup prove? The
military had tried to run the government and had failed. What was
needed was strong martial law enforced by the military under
effective civilian direction.

When we established contact at 10.30 that night, I gave Secretary Brown an extensive report on our audience with the Shah. The
Secretary then carefully read me the instructions which had been
dispatched to Ambassador Sullivan on 28 December, and to myself
on 4 January. That really shook me; I had a feeling that Washington thought I was not following these orders. This was a mystery to

me, and I couldn't imagine where I had tripped over my shoelaces.
The only thing I could think of was a number of tendentious news
articles. I had heard of one which quoted General Khosrodad as
saying that if the Shah tried to leave, the military would not allow
him to do so, and should he succeed, they would then have to seize
power. I had also heard that the front page of the *Tehran Journal*
carried a report that the Shah had called in his generals and told
them to listen to me. Was this what was bothering Secretary
Brown? Was he worried that I was edging myself into a position
which was more than advisory?

I listened intently as he read the instructions. There was no
change: he read them exactly as I had received them. He then went
into a monologue to the effect that the military must give the
civilian government one hundred per cent support if they themselves wanted the US government to support them. If that failed,
he said we must be prepared to take whatever action was necessary
to ensure order.

I began to feel I was walking a tightrope. I was to expend every
possible effort to get a civilian government which was friendly to
the West – and not just any civilian government, but the Bakhtiar
government. The tightrope part was that if that government
collapsed, then at exactly the right moment, I was to see that the
military took action. This was not at all the same as my previous
guidance, which was that I was not to give directives, just advice. I
put this view to Secretary Brown and once again he gave the clear
instruction that I was to remain an adviser, giving only recommendations.

Trying to dissect the fine print of Washington's latest thinking
was not easy on the antiquated secure phone, which at the best of
times was one or two notches below satisfactory. For this reason, I
thought I should quote back my own understanding of my instructions. I told the Secretary that I clearly understood the high
priority which Washington attached to getting a civilian government which was friendly to the US. If it looked as if that
government was going to be unfriendly, or if it appeared to be
about to collapse, then I understood that military action was
appropriate. I said I had been playing this song right down to the
final note. The Iranian military understood that they must throw
their full weight behind Mr Bakhtiar or I could not guarantee them
US support for their military needs.

Secretary Brown asked if the military were going to prepare themselves for possible intervention. This puzzled me because I had discussed their plan with him only the previous night. Just to be sure there could be no misunderstanding, I went through the planning arrangements in minute detail. I also warned him to expect some hefty applications for support, as the Army did not have war reserves. The immediate need was for motor gas and diesel fuel for the Army. I asked if Washington could take a look at how we could satisfy this requirement. Maybe there was a tanker on the high seas which we could divert to an Iranian port.

I again very directly called his attention to the unfortunate effects of BBC radio, and told him I would appreciate some action. The Chairman of the Joint Chiefs, General Jones, intervened to say that this had been discussed at the highest government level, and approaches would now be made to the British. But he said they were not at all hopeful about what could be done.

I again pressed them on direct contact by the US with Khomeini. I told them I believed the military were ready to get behind Mr Bakhtiar and give him their full support. As of this moment they were now resolved to stay, if the Shah should depart; but when that day came their reaction might be less predictable. With this we brought our conversation to an end.

What a day! The crowds had increased, and with them the security threat. I had had two meetings with the Group of Five, an audience with the Shah, a long and elaborate report to Secretary Brown, and then, to put the frosting on the cake, Secretary Brown had thought it necessary to read me my instructions, and implied that he didn't know about our planning effort.

I was really exhausted, and went to bed expecting to go out like a light. Not so. I was still puzzled about Secretary Brown's comments. I had only scan-read the *Tehran Journal*, as I'd been very busy all day, so I got up and found the paper. Sure enough, the main front-page article reported Bakhtiar as telling General Khosrodad to cool it; he was not going to stand for Khosrodad trying to order him or the Shah around. If the Shah wanted to leave, that was his business and it was probably the best hope of Bakhtiar's success.

The next column said that Khosrodad had been posted to Kerman. This seemed to be tantamount to being 'limoge'. The same article said the Shah had advised the generals to listen to US

Air Force General Robert Huyser, who was in Tehran to strengthen American backing for Bakhtiar. It went on to say the Shah
had agreed to endorse the American – and British – proposed
Bakhtiar solution.

Among other news items the *Wall Street Journal* reported that
Iran's new leader feared a military takeover. It quoted Bakhtiar as
saying that he was 'trying my best to prevent a military coup d'etat
by officers loyal to the Shah'. (Both the *Washington Post* and the
New York Times carried similar stories.)

ABC News had addressed the subject: Barry Dunsmore reported that Secretary Vance denied the US was interfering in Iran
to protect America's vital interests. With reference to the Huyser
mission, Vance said that I had not only discussed technical
matters, but had also urged the military to support the civilian
government. Dunsmore suggested that I was using a good deal
more than friendly persuasion to talk the generals out of a coup.
He said I was softening them up by guaranteeing US military
equipment in spite of the fact that Iran's banks were closed and
there was no money to pay for it. He said this could prove
sufficient incentive but, like the decision to drop the Shah, it might
have come too late.

It seemed to me that Washington might have thought that these
reports emanated from some contact of mine with General Khosrodad. In fact I had been careful not to do business with him at all,
for although we were close friends, he was well known as a rapid
mover and not too reliable on protecting information. Also, I felt it
might cause animosity with the Group. But I don't want to
disparage him, because he was an extremely fine officer, with a
first-class brain and unlimited courage. In fact things might have
gone a lot better had he been Chief of the Supreme Commander's
Staff.

My last thought on returning to bed was that I would send a
written message to Washington first thing in the morning; I felt I
should document the whole situation for future reference, so that
there could be no misunderstanding between myself and the
leaders of the US government.

I went to sleep trying to count the credit items on the ledger. We
now had a carrier task force steaming into the Indian Ocean. Plans
were being made in Washington to put F-15s into Saudi Arabia.
We had the cold-weather gear en route to the Iranian Army. We

had the military finally starting to plan. We had a new level of solidarity among the military leadership. We had good reason to believe that, should the Shah depart, they would stay. The question was how they would react when he did. Would they play the situation as it developed, or out of a clear blue sky try to pull some kind of military takeover which, in my opinion, would be futile.

Friday, 12 January 1979

I rose at six o'clock, which I found necessary in order to beat the crowds in the streets, now growing larger every day. With the publicity spotlight beamed on my presence, the threat level was getting higher all the time, and I had to take greater precautions. We increased the number of personal bodyguards and used a different car and different routes each day – Iranian, not American, and dilapidated enough to be inconspicuous. But we had to be sure it would not break down in the street, because there were plenty of people who wanted to get their hands on me. All this involved a routine by which, between the call to Washington and the early morning start, I could not get more than three or four hours' sleep a night. Little did I realize that this would go on for nearly three more weeks!

When I checked in at my office in the Supreme Commander's Staff compound I was told that General Gharabaghi was due to see Mr Bakhtiar so he would prefer to have our meeting in the afternoon. This did not bother me, as I wanted to get down to clarifying my position with Washington. Just as I was getting started I had a call from General Rabii. Could I come to see him at his headquarters at Doshan Tappeh Air Base? This was tricky. I had established an unwritten rule not to meet with the military except as a Group. But on hearing the anxiety in his voice I thought it might be better to see him. My security troops considered Doshan Tappeh by far the most dangerous assignation in town. They called it the 'Little Bighorn'. I was 'General Custer' and my chief security man, Frank Johns, was 'Major Reno'. I was not too happy about this as, in Custer's Last Stand, Major Reno was the one who lived. I must add that Frank Johns was one of the most dedicated, loyal and thorough men I had ever met. I have frequently thought he was responsible for my survival.

My security men made a fast check with the base, and there were reports of gatherings, but none that seemed to be violent or out of control so we headed out. When we got to the area we encountered large crowds, and our motorcade drew considerable attention. Several attempts were made to stop us: people stood in our way and threw themselves on the hoods of our cars, and vehicles swung into our path. We got through eventually, and were met by General Rabii at the front door. The moment we entered his office he came unglued at the seams. He said the day of the Shah's departure was getting closer, and he now had it from very good sources that all generals, down to and including major generals, were to be put on trial immediately. I asked him what on earth would they go on trial *for*, and he said the main allegations were corruption; but they also had indications that anyone who supported the Shah or Mr Bakhtiar would go on trial.

I said this could only happen if Mr Bakhtiar failed, and the Khomeini forces took over. He tried to confuse the picture by saying he thought that under the circumstances, if the Shah departed, he would be likely to be put on trial.

I frequently thought that one qualification for my task should have been a degree in psychology. I worked on him very hard, and pointed out that if he really got his shoulder to the wheel and bolstered the civil government, he would be safe, and so would all the other generals. Since Mr Bakhtiar had been selected by the Shah, I could see absolutely no jeopardy for any of the military men.

He said he knew I had been pushing Washington hard to get a meeting with the Ayatollah Khomeini to find out what his intentions were, and try to get him to cooperate. He said he had advocated this himself, but he now considered it futile to try to get any sense out of the religious leaders because they were infiltrated by Communists. He had learned of one who had been trained in Russia some fifteen years earlier and sent to Iran to bide his time. This was a technique I had noted several times in the extensive planning done by the USSR. I believe many people are a little naïve about the lengths to which the Russians will go, and the time they are prepared to wait to achieve their objectives.

Once again we went over the same ground. General Rabii repeated that if he did not leave with the Shah, the only alternative was an immediate coup. I repeated that the more steam they put into the planning, the sooner they would be prepared to take such action, but that Washington wanted them first to give the civilian government a chance. However, I was not opposed to a military takeover in principle once the plans were complete. In fact, if the situation dictated it, I would highly recommend such action.

Rabii once again fulminated against the United States, saying that with all our muscle we could easily control Khomeini if we really wanted to. At least we could bring enough pressure to cause him to stick to religion and keep out of politics. I explained that Washington might have done that sort of thing in the past but it wasn't going to happen today. If the military felt so strongly about Khomeini, I could not understand why they were reluctant to act on their own account – almost anything could be done for money.

General Rabii quickly answered that. Iranians could not take this type of action against a religious leader: the Islamic law would completely rule it out. It seemed strange to me that it was all right with Muslim law so long as you got somebody else to do the dirty work.

The phone rang and Rabii was told that His Majesty was calling. Gast and I volunteered to leave the room, but he said it wasn't necessary. No doubt he felt that he would give away no secrets if he talked in Farsi, which he did. When he hung up he started ranting furiously. The Shah had requested him to get busy on the flight plan. The time was approaching; he needed the flight planning to be done, the crew alerted, and the aircraft prepared.

General Rabii's state of mind was shocking; he was almost raving. They couldn't let the Shah leave. If he tried to take off, they must prevent him by blocking the runway. If he got airborne they must shoot him down. He had to be delayed or stopped. They needed his leadership. He was the only man who could hold the country together. This went on for some time. I just let him get it off his chest and then I got hold of him in no uncertain way with some straight jabs. This was getting to be something of a habit in my dealings with Rabii, but there was no doubt that it worked. I had to start again from square one, stressing that our only hope was to give Bakhtiar a fair shake. If that failed, then the military must take over; someone had to break the strikes and get the country moving again. Once again he agreed, and again seemed a little ashamed of himself.

We were interrupted by one of his orderlies, who said I was wanted on the phone. It was General Toufanian, who had learned that I was with General Rabii and wanted to see me before the afternoon's meeting. It was, he said, a personal matter and I agreed to see him. As I left, Rabii gave me a hug and a warm Iranian cheek-to-cheek embrace. He was under great stress, because there was now no question that the man he loved so much was about to vanish from the scene.

It occurred to me that maybe they were beginning to break ranks by seeing me individually. If so, I thought I could keep it under control; but I must bring it right out in the open at the afternoon meeting. The others knew I had long been close to Rabii and Toufanian, and I did not want them harbouring any suspicions. Particularly I did not want the situation created by the Shah, of playing them off against each other.

We found General Toufanian very nervous and uptight. He tried to hide his feelings and to show calm, but it was just a matter of when he was going to blow his stack.

I started by reporting on my talk with General Rabii, and said I felt he was back on track and willing to support the Group. That triggered Toufanian. What had stuck in his craw was the appointment of the new Minister of War. He was hurt, professionally and personally; his pride was damaged. He just could not understand why the Shah had left him in mid-air. He had never crossed the Shah, and he had never been corrupt; he could not see why he had not been given a job commensurate with his capabilities.

I had to agree that the title of Vice-Minister, which General Toufanian had, was not commensurate with either his capabilities or his duties, because he actually functioned as the Minister and took care of all the decisions. He said the only explanation he could think of was that people wrongly thought he had been on the take, syphoning off a percentage from foreign military purchases and from his own manufacturing for the government. He said it was quite true that he had a lot of money, but he had made it legally.

Toufanian was also bitter about the Shah leaving. If this happened, he said, all was lost. He himself would be brought to trial, and at best, would be killed, and at worst would be maimed and tortured first. If the Shah left immediately, Bakhtiar would fall apart. It would be pointless to try to shore him up. They must pull a military takeover within hours.

I bounced right back and said that if that was their decision they had better get their thinking a little straighter than it had been up to now. It was not easy for me to get tough with General Toufanian, as he was about eleven years my senior, had ten years more service than I, and was a superb manager and a fine man. But at times it seemed there was no other recourse than to raise my voice to shock him back to reality. On this occasion I let him have it loud and clear.

More rationally, he asked me what we had done about the BBC. I told him I had heard from the highest levels of our government last night that they would approach the British government to try to get some action. He then switched to Khomeini and said that if he were eliminated, it would solve a lot of problems. He thought there must be a way to curb him, perhaps by having the French government cut off communications. The mosques were putting out very up-to-date tapes, which must be coming in over a telephone system. This should be controllable. I told Toufanian that the Group should be making a plan to gain control of communications in Iran. They would certainly need it if they were going to run the country. I also stressed the folly of losing all control of the customs, which could explain the entry of Khomeini's tapes as well as that of the guns and ammunition. He got this message very clearly, and we agreed on the need for high-pressure planning sessions.

Before leaving, I told him I wasn't going to have any further meetings with individuals, only with the Group. We must work as a team, one hundred per cent behind Mr Bakhtiar. Should Mr Bakhtiar fail, then we must decide *as a group* how to address the next step.

As before, General Toufanian radiated a real feeling of affection beneath an outward brusqueness. This time I got a similar feeling from the people in the outer office: a lingering need for friendship and warmth. Even the guards, as I went down the steps, conveyed that mood through their gestures, their physical contact and their good wishes. It gave me a strange sensation. These people must have felt they were pursuing a desperate cause; yet they had not completely given up. They needed leadership, they needed warmth and friendship. This put quite a weight on my shoulders.

We met the Group of Five about 2 pm. I opened the discussion by telling General Gharabaghi of my one-on-one discussions with Rabii and Toufanian. Then Gharabaghi reported on his meeting with Mr Bakhtiar that morning. He said that each of the Group and Mr Bakhtiar had had sessions with the Shah. The Shah had said he would definitely be leaving for a vacation, and had told them to close ranks behind Mr Bakhtiar. He had also reiterated that they were to listen to me and trust me. He endorsed the need for early planning.

There would be a National Security Council meeting on Saturday; General Gharabaghi would attend, and possibly the whole Group as well. I said I thought that was great; it showed progress with Bakhtiar, and looked like an expression of confidence in the military; they should push for all of them to attend. Gharabaghi said he would like to have the Group meet with me before the National Security Council meeting, and again afterwards. He brought up the need for warm clothing, and I was able to tell him that the first aircraft was already en route – super-fast action by our government. General Toufanian had promised to get on with drawing up a letter of agreement.

Gharabaghi thought it was time to get some petroleum products available for the Army. They just didn't have any, and they still had not succeeded in persuading the National Iranian Oil Company (NIOC) to give the military a better quota. This refusal seemed to be a deliberate decision designed to drain the Army's gasoline reserves down to zero, and thus keep them paralysed. I told them I felt sure that Washington would take action very soon. We would bring a tanker in, and they would have to be ready to offload it and distribute the cargo where it was most needed. I thought this job should be given to a special task group with priority over all planning. It seemed that the other planning was now in high gear and really moving along. The Iranians were taking good initiatives, and our own people were functioning strictly as advisers. They were just asking questions and letting the Iranian staff officers come up with the planning. Gharabaghi had paid them a visit, which I thought was good.

I then talked a little about the departure of the Shah. I thought he should leave with dignity and not as a man fleeing his country. There should be a televised ceremony at Mehrabad Airport with full honours. Bakhtiar should be wired in and given credit for being the leader in charge of the country.

At this session I started the process of nudging General Gharabaghi into the lead, ahead of Toufanian. His legs were still a little shaky, but I felt sure he could fill the job. I now pressed him to take the lead with the armed forces as a whole, and make them understand what they could do for their country. Good leadership would probably cut down the number of desertions: though this was small, we could never be sure whether we would wake up and find the dam had broken. New political initiatives would probably have to come from the military, and General Gharabaghi was the man to produce them and present them to Mr Bakhtiar.

We had been together for over four hours, and decided to call it a day. It was time for me to straighten out the wires with Secretary Brown. I still wasn't sure why he had re-read the guidance to me. I certainly had no desire to deviate from that guidance. I was already becoming concerned about the divergence between my own operations and those of the State Department. If there was now a feeling in Washington that I might be starting on a third road, I wanted to clear that up before I went any further. So I decided to draft a telex to Secretary Brown telling him exactly what I was doing, step by step.

My instructions were that it was vital for Washington that Iran should have a strong and stable government friendly to the US. The Iranian military had deeply impressed our President, and he wanted them to throw their full support behind a strong and stable civilian government. The only gloss I had given to these instructions was that anything we did should be aimed at minimum bloodshed; this had been implied to me by Washington on many occasions. Also, that the Iranian military must stand squarely behind Bakhtiar if they were to retain full US support.

In my statement I suggested that Bakhtiar could use the military in three ways. First, with their support, he could succeed in exercising constitutional rule. Second, if that collapsed he could introduce martial law, plus military control of essential services. Third, if that looked unworkable he could invite an outright military takeover.

I didn't want Washington to think I was claiming to be an expert in the field of forming governments. My job was to work with the military. Nonetheless they should know what my thoughts were on the political options. Since the Shah was definitely leaving, Option A would be the best available – a successful Bakhtiar government. Option B would be for Mr Bakhtiar to succeed for a period, but eventually fail. This would not rule out another civilian government, but it would need to be one more acceptable to Khomeini and the religious faction and sympathetic to the West. (It was far from clear at this point whether Khomeini would accept any cooperation with the West; after all, it appeared that he was using all factions to support his cause. Mehdi Bazargan was the most likely man to implement this option.)

If Option B failed, Option C was a military coup with decisive action to break the strikes and regain control of the country. The only other options would be (D) an Islamic Republic under Khomeini, and (E) a Communist government. I did not rule out this last possibility, then or for any time in the future. In fact I thought that if Khomeini did take over, the situation would probably deteriorate to the point where the Communists would take control. One of their classic tactics for gaining a foothold in a country is to foment international unrest and cataclysm and then to move in trained leaders to solve the problem.

I felt I should document the feelings of Toufanian and Rabii. I reported both of them as calling for a military coup the moment the Shah left, on the grounds that otherwise they could not predict what would happen to the armed forces. I passed on Toufanian's fears that if he were captured, a lot of Western technical secrets could fall into the wrong hands. I also reported Rabii's view that the day the Shah left, the military would just collapse, and all the young people would go over to Khomeini. I said I did not believe this for one minute, because in spite of all the anti-American razzmattaz, whenever I walked through the troops in my American uniform they all jumped to attention enthusiastically and saluted me. They weren't obliged to salute a foreign officer, and it was strictly a show of goodwill. So I did have a feeling that there was real discipline, and things were not just going to fall apart the day the Shah departed.

I told the Secretary of Defence that I would do my best to keep the generals in Iran, and solidly behind Bakhtiar. There would not be a military coup until they had at least given him a chance. But as the departure of the Shah got closer, we had to be prepared for any eventuality.

Meanwhile it was not all bad news. Though there were still large demonstrations in the streets, there was not the same violence and destructiveness as there had been earlier. This could be credited to the sagacity of the military in issuing permits to demonstrate on strict conditions of moderate behaviour. In the mosques, though people were being urged to demonstrate, they were also told not to be destructive. We knew there was going to be a super-demonstration on 19 January, a special Khomeini command performance, but he had passed the word to keep it peaceful.

Having written my report, I took it with me back to the Embassy compound, where I wanted to go over it with Ambassador Sullivan before dispatching it to Secretary Brown. When I did so, my differences with Ambassador Sullivan became more apparent than ever. Mr Sullivan actually thought a Khomeini Islamic Republic would be preferable to a military takeover. He had no faith in Bakhtiar and thought we should work directly towards a Khomeini government. I respected his opinion but he did not change my mind in the least.

During dinner, Sullivan told me that the United States had now approached Khomeini, but indirectly through the French. This really infuriated the Ambassador. He said that both his recommendations and mine were being ignored. He couldn't understand why the President was being so timid about making direct contact. He had sent a wire to the Secretary of State deploring the government's refusal to make direct contact with Khomeini, and saying that he and I both agreed that this was a very stupid decision. I wasn't too sure I was ready to call the President 'stupid', because he might well have more facts than we did, but I certainly agreed on the need to have direct contact. I added a paragraph to this effect to my own report. Just how it should be done was out of my expertise and above my pay grade, but I was convinced that the most disastrous option now would be for the Ayatollah to return to Iran without our having even tried to reach an understanding with him first. Up till then, his supporters had been taking a mainly peaceful line: it was not till later that Khomeini removed that mask.

It was getting on towards midnight before I was able to make my secure phone call to Secretary Brown. Concerning Khomeini, he told me that the US had approached him through France in an effort to enlist his support for the Bakhtiar government, or at least a degree of tolerance. Khomeini's response had been negative. Maybe he would be more accommodating in the future. Secretary Brown was certain that when the Shah left, Khomeini would return, probably at once. I told him this was still an almost unthinkable subject to the Iranian generals, but they were now at the point of discussing options such as eliminating Khomeini on his return or diverting him elsewhere. My own view was that if anything happened to Khomeini on his return, we would immediately have a civil war. Emotions were just too high, and they would erupt into open warfare.

The Secretary brought up the possibility of a coup. I reminded him that any sudden seizure of power was diametrically opposite to what I had been told the President wanted, namely a legal civilian government; but we must keep the option open for two reasons. First, if the civil government failed, a coup was better than any of the alternatives; second, the opposition must always be kept aware that the possibility existed. The element with the military power held most of the cards. It could force the issue, break the strikes and take charge of the country, even though this could be a very bloody affair. I strongly shared the President's desire that bloodshed be kept to an absolute minimum. But what was a minimum? Five or ten thousand lives now might be the price of avoiding a million dead later. This had happened in history before, and one must try to maintain a balanced judgement.

I signed off and reviewed the US news clippings for the day. A very interesting *New York Times* article reported in great detail on differences of opinion between Dr Brzezinski and Secretary of State Vance. This could explain the apparent lack of unity which Ambassador Sullivan and I had observed. It reported, quoting State Department aides, that when I was sent to Tehran I had been told by the White House to bypass the US Embassy. This was not true. I was told no such thing. I would never have accepted orders to bypass the Embassy; I believed then and continue to believe that the true representative of the President overseas is the Ambassador. But the White House had certainly implied that I was on my own.

The article developed this theme by alleging that Dr Brzezinski was dealing directly with the Iranian Ambassador to the US,

Ardeshir Zahedi, who was working closely with the Shah. This would mean that Bill Sullivan was being bypassed, which seemed more than possible, and later turned out to be true.

In fact, I was never too sure exactly where Ambassador Sullivan was getting his guidance from. The people he said he was talking to were David Newsom and the Iranian Desk Officer, Henry Precht. I always assumed that he had a direct line to the Secretary of State, or even to the President, as I had to the Secretary of Defence. My own instructions were coming directly from the top, and the information I was feeding in went straight back to the top undiluted.

Other news reports showed that inside Iran there had been a lot of activity. During the day there was a large anti-Shah demonstration in the southern city of Shiraz, with a violent attack on the Savak building. The mob took over the building, fired it, and seized everything that could be used for future reference, such as personal records and techniques of torture. These were removed to a mosque for use as exhibits in future trials.

A number of developments were reported among the groups of strikers in Iran. The bank employees said they would return to work, part-time, on 13 January, but would not handle foreign exchange transactions with Israel, the US or South Africa. They had been on strike for two months, in response to a request by Khomeini. Mr Bakhtiar announced that no Iranian oil would go to Israel or South Africa. This had been one of the chief demands of the striking oil workers, so it could open the way to an increase in production. The striking customs workers said they would admit essential and humanitarian goods into the country but nothing imported by the diplomatic missions of the US, Britain, Israel or any other country hostile to Iran's revolutionary movement. Perhaps this would release the log-jam of food trucks on the Turkish border.

And so to bed for three hours' sleep. Tomorrow we would have the first meeting of the National Security Council.

Saturday, 13 January 1979

At breakfast I told the Ambassador that I had pressed Secretary Brown the night before on direct talks with the Ayatollah, but did not receive much encouragement. I left immediately for the office, as the volume of street traffic had picked up considerably and, due to all the press publicity, there was no question that I was a marked man. We checked in with General Gharabaghi's office because he had said he wanted to see me before the Security Council meeting.

To my surprise the only person there was General Rabii. He said that all the others were busy, and he had been designated as spokesman for the Group of Five. Rabii started with another of his diatribes. He said they had all agreed that when the Shah left, the armed forces would disintegrate unless the leadership took immediate action. Again, I found it necessary to get a bit terse with him. I said the military must first give Bakhtiar a chance. I was getting very irritated indeed at having to go through this same old song and dance.

During our conversation the Shah called and told Rabii to have an aircraft standing by, as he was now planning to leave earlier than he had intended. (His original intention had been the following Wednesday.) Rabii tried to dissuade the Shah by telling him there was no way he could get clearance. The Shah had told him to get the aircraft ready, and said that he would take care of the clearance himself, which would present no problems as he only planned to cross Saudi Arabi and land in Egypt. I thought this might be just an exercise by the Shah to keep the Air Force on its toes. It certainly shook up General Rabii, and later the others, who thought he was now going to leave on Monday.

I took the opportunity to press Rabii very hard to see if any of the Group had made contact with any of Khomeini's followers. I thought it unlikely, and he denied it. But I asked if he did not think it could be productive. They must know some of the mullahs and ayatollahs personally. Would it not be wise to develop their relationships in an effort to break down the barriers of mistrust between the two factions? He said that none of them seemed to think it would. We ended up where we always ended up, with Rabii promising to stand by his post when the Shah left.

Later in the day, after the National Security Council meeting, they called and asked if I would come on down to Gharabaghi's office. On arrival I found them all there except for Gharabaghi, who was said to be working with the Shah on the presentation of the Regency Council. They were a little bit fuzzy about which of them had attended the Security Council. It could have been all six, as General Moghaddam was present this time. I concluded that at least five of them were there.

The principal item on the agenda had been the problems arising from the Shah's departure. They had passed on to Mr Bakhtiar our Group decision to keep the military in garrison so that we would know where they were. Also, they might well be needed if the opposition tried to take over government offices.

Mr Bakhtiar had told them he would go on television and lay down the ground-rules, and take full responsibility for maintaining order. He was prepared to revive crowd control measures, including rubber bullets and teargas. The military warned him that they had not worked very well in the past and there might have to be more stringent measures. The demonstrators had got wise to bullets being fired over their heads, so that something more lethal might be needed. Bakhtiar said they would meet again the following day and defer final conclusions about riot control till then.

I was glad that Bakhtiar was prepared to discuss these crucial matters openly with the military, but I was frustrated that there was still no real contingency planning. I spent much of the afternoon working out the options of maintaining order. We had to plan each move step by step. I told them we must develop sufficient solidarity to survive the fall of Bakhtiar if necessary. They were quite apprehensive about this. Bakhtiar had told them that what he really needed was time; if he had thirty to sixty days he could make his government secure, but if Khomeini came back too quickly it could be disastrous. The Group urged that the United States intervene to block Khomeini. Couldn't we work with the French, and get them to keep him in France for a bit longer? I said I had repeatedly pressed Washington to do so, and they were doing what they could.

I asked why Bakhtiar felt that Khomeini's return would be so catastrophic. Was he afraid it would prevent him from getting the economy going? Was he unsure of the military? I got no answer. I pointed out that progress had been made: the newspapers had started publishing, there was more oil, the bankers were going back to work, and customs were beginning to relax. We needed greater progress, but it was a start.

Still, it was all too clear that the Five were not moving nearly fast enough. One problem was Gharabaghi. When Toufanian was in charge, as he was on this occasion, things fizzed along. It was obvious that he was respected as a leader by the others. This did not happen with Gharabaghi. Somehow he must contrive to inspire the same confidence and dedication. Time was against us; I myself couldn't stay there forever, and they must develop their own momentum.

We left Gharabaghi's office and went straight to the Embassy, where I immediately debriefed Ambassador Sullivan on the day's activities. We got straight on to the thorny topic of contact with the religious groups. I now learned that Sullivan's people were having extensive discussions with them. For his own reasons, he had never told me about this before. Even so, it was not clear just who they were contacting, and they certainly were not in touch with Bakhtiar's people. Sullivan liked the idea of my military friends contacting the religious opposition and strongly encouraged me to pursue this approach.

Later on, from the Chancellory, I made my nightly call to Secretary Brown. He said they had received my wire, and it greatly clarified the situation. It had been submitted to the President and I would be getting any feedback or comments in due course. He repeated, without much confidence, that they would try to get the French to delay Khomeini's return, and again asked why I thought this mattered so much. I told him we just weren't far enough along. His return would have an electrifying effect, since Iranians reacted quickly to a bullhorn, and needed to attach themselves to a power base. Khomeini's arrival would bring hundreds of thousands on to the streets. If there were a little more time for Mr Bakhtiar to build up his authority, more people would rally to him as their leader and be less apt to jump the traces.

Secretary Brown then repeated his instructions of 11 January – we were absolutely not to pull a military coup until we had attempted, in every way possible, to establish a civilian government; if the worst came to the worst the military must be prepared at any moment to take over; and I was to keep them psychologically and physically in a state of readiness for it. Again, I was a bit mystified by Harold Brown's tone, because I thought he knew this was what I was trying to do.

General Jones brought up a question about the military sales programme, to which I replied that things were truly paralysed; we really couldn't even discuss the subject in a normal and rational sense. Iran's needs would have to be specified on a daily basis. He did not seem to appreciate that all the banks were locked up and the country was in a complete state of stalemate. We must provide immediate needs like the cold-weather gear; I would try to get a memorandum of understanding and we must just hope some day to be reimbursed.

Secretary Brown wanted to know if I had any more information on General Djam. I told him I really thought that this was a dead issue, and the Shah thought so too. He hadn't been that good when he was on active duty, and this was one reason he retired. He would probably be even less effective now because of his deep worries over his son, who had turned out to be either a drug addict or an alcoholic. To the best of my knowledge he was back in London, and I had dropped him off my computer.

Next, the Secretary wanted an evaluation of the military desertions. I said they should not be exaggerated. The Army was some 450,000 strong, and even if they were deserting at the rate of 1,000 a day, which they were not, it would take some time before this made much impact on their capability. I actually thought the figure was more like a hundred a day, greatly inflated by the press. (Here the Group's assessment was confirmed by my own military and Embassy sources.) The more junior military could be infected by their daily contact with the religious factions and other political elements, but I was sure that the Army still had a tremendous capability. All that was required was the leadership and the direction, and they would do the rest. This had been demonstrated on several occasions and in different parts of the country when it was necessary to protect key elements such as government offices and military installations. We told them to get serious about it, and they did. But I reported that Ambassador Sullivan took a different view. He believed that the day Khomeini came back the military would completely disintegrate. I could not agree.

I asked the Secretary if he had received Ambassador Malcolm Toon's report from Moscow, but he had not seen it. I told him it was headed: '*Pravda* sharpens attack on General Huyser', and pointed out that on 13 January *Pravda* carried an article on the subject by V. Ouchinnikov. Under the heading 'What's Interference Then?' it attempted to demonstrate that I had been sent to Iran to persuade the Iranian military to turn the course of events to Washington's advantage. Ouchinnikov described my mission as 'Coordinator of US actions', directed at the maintenance of the present regime, or the creation of a new but equally pro-American one. He dismissed US protestations of 'non-interference' as unconvincing.

The Soviet media had been devoting a great deal of attention to my mission in Iran, and I have to say that they were more accurate, and seemed to know more about my daily movements, than any other news source including US and Iranian. They had put out accurate releases through Tass, *Pravda* and Radio Moscow since the day I arrived. Today's attack was the sharpest yet. This did cause me concern because I knew that it would be not only in the Soviet media but on the BBC and in the Iranian press. That would increase the threat level, and I would have to take even greater measures to protect myself.

After my transatlantic call I had a late-night session with the news traffic. I was informed that a German paper, *Die Zeit/Welt*, had carried an article on me, and so had the European edition of the *Stars and Stripes*. This worried me, since up to now the European press had been rather silent; my concern, of course, was for my family in Stuttgart. The press had been very insensitive, and on several occasions had mentioned the threats on my life, which I did not want my family to hear. They were worried enough anyway, because they knew I had packed for a two-day trip and had already been gone nine days. I knew my wife was praying daily for my safety, and for me to have the proper wisdom to handle the situation.

The final wire I read was one in which Secretary Vance had announced that the Shah was going to leave Iran. This would probably be in the Iranian press, and it was bound to cause me some problems, since the Iranians would conclude that Washington was masterminding his departure.

Sunday, 14 January 1979

The world looked no better, and was even colder, early the
following morning. The tempo of activity was accelerating as the
time of the Shah's departure approached. Today we were due to
get a vote in the Senate on Mr Bakhtiar's government. The debate
had started, and Mr Bakhtiar had got the whip out by limiting each
speaker to no more than thirty minutes.

I made a quick review of the message traffic and noted that the
Russian press was very vocal, accusing the US of causing dissen-
sion and turmoil in Iran. I didn't see any resistance to this in the
US media. The US news was straight down the line, supposedly
giving all sides of the picture: but it appeared to me that even our
own commentators were leaning against the administration. Within Iran this was extemely counter-productive. Iranians could not
understand why our people could accuse their own government of
interference and indecision. Our press was bluntly saying that we
seemed to have two governments in Washington, one ready to
support Khomeini and the other rooting for Bakhtiar. The trouble
was that this was not too wide of the mark.

In Moscow Vladislav Kozyakov put out a very strong warning
that the world was about to witness another event in Iran similar to
what happened back in the 1950s. The Central Intelligence Agency
was moving in, much as it had done in Chile. Washington was
getting to work on the top Iranian officials. We had even moved in
helicopters, teargas and other equipment for dispersing demonstrators. We had stepped up our military presence. We had sent
the Deputy Commander-in-Chief of US Forces in Europe, General Robert Huyser; announced the dispatch of the aircraft carrier
Constellation to the Indian Ocean; and sent a squadron of F-15s to
Saudi Arabia.

The article talked with relish about the attack on the Savak
headquarters in Shiraz and said that the American flag had been
torn down from the consulate. The mob had gained access to
torture equipment which the author alleged was made in the USA.
He referred to an article in the *New York Times* in which a former
CIA agent, Jess Leaf, had said that we had introduced torture
methods to Savak; the CIA had supposedly trained them in Nazi
World War Two techniques.

This type of misinformation was circulated widely, and added
fuel to the fire of anti-US feeling which was blazing higher every
day. Certainly whoever was orchestrating the Khomeini campaign
was doing it with a great deal of professionalism. I wondered at
times if they weren't over-doing it from their own point of view, as
they might trigger off a civil war the moment the Shah left.
Certainly this was more likely than not if Khomeini were assassinated on his return.

After breakfast we left for the SCS compound. The threat level
was clearly higher than ever, and I was conscious of the need to get
the American presence down to the bare minimum, and then to
ensure protection for those who had to stay.

On arrival I found that planning was progressing very well,
particularly in the area of psychological warfare. The US officer
overseeing this area was Admiral Frank Collins, a man of great
initiative and ingenuity. He was getting the Iranians to prepare
posters, leaflets, quotations, sayings, press releases, and radio
broadcasts, together with methods for distributing them.

The planning for oil and power was going more slowly, and that
was understandable because the military had to start from scratch
in identifying the key nodes in the country's systems. This information was not the easiest thing in the world to obtain, with both
systems under the control of the opposition. But at least they knew
what they were trying to do, and they realized that the success of
the Bakhtiar government depended almost entirely on their
efforts. There had also been a swing towards liberalization. Mr
Bakhtiar had released all restrictions on the press, which would
have been great except that the opposition was controlling nearly
all the press. This irritated me. I was all for press freedom, but I
would have preferred it to produce some degree of balance.

In General Gharabaghi's office it was a pleasant surprise to find
the Group of Five bright-eyed and bushy-tailed. There was a
distinctly upbeat feeling, and a sense of accomplishment based on
the progress of the plans. But the Shah's deadline was getting very
close, and much remained to be done if we were to get past that
highly emotional milestone without disaster. So I again brought up
the subject of getting them together with the religious leadership.
While Bakhtiar must continue to lead the government, other

arrangements with the opposition could be negotiable. Ambassador Sullivan had told me that such leading opposition figures as Bazargan and Ayatollah Beheshti were willing to meet with the military leadership; so I brought their names and telephone numbers along with me to try to fix some meetings.

The Group was reluctant, but eventually did make some calls. However, a real problem then surfaced: it became a matter of pride on both sides as to *where* they would meet, each insisting it had to be on their turf. They were so adamant about this that the only solution appeared to be some type of neutral territory. I contacted the Ambassador and, with his concurrence, offered American territory in Tehran, but neither side favoured this solution, because the American image was now that of the bad guys in the black hats. I told the Group that we should all come up by tomorrow with a solution acceptable to both sides. The situation was urgent, as Khomeini might come back at any time.

While we were meeting, there was another call from the Shah, who wanted his aircraft standing by and ready to go. He did not give a departure time. I still believed he would wait until the vote on the Bakhtiar government, which would probably come either today or tomorrow; then he would leave, either on the 16th or 17th.

At our request His Majesty agreed that before he left he would tape a radio and TV message primarily directed to the armed forces. The Shah was aware of the new plans, and he fully understood that only the military could implement them; so his message to the troops should be to stay together, to work for the country and support the new government. He asked General Gharabaghi to come to the Palace and work with him on the wording of the message. We spent the next few minutes rehearsing Gharabaghi with the right type of thoughts, and then off he went. My feeling was that this TV address was crucial. If we could get the troops through the first day or two after the Shah left, there was a good chance of holding them together.

The parliamentary debate on the Bakhtiar government seemed to be going well. But there were some who damned Bakhtiar as being too close to the United States. One deputy, Mr Ghorbani Nassab, complained that Washington had been selling used weapons at exorbitant prices, and there had been no statement by Mr Bakhtiar as to what he was going to do to put this right.

Further, he saw Mr Bakhtiar had virtually denied all knowledge of
the presence of General Huyser in Iran. I was unaware of any such
denial, but it is worth quoting what Nassab said:

> The Iranian people do not understand how the Prime Minis-
> ter can hear about the presence of armed Afghans in the
> streets of Tehran and yet remain ignorant of the presence of a
> US General. For your information I wish to point out that the
> newspaper *Kayhan* carries the following: 'The US State
> Department has announced that the Deputy Commander of
> US Forces in Europe has gone to Iran to advise the Iranian
> military leaders to support the civilian government in their
> country.' As a worker [Ghorbani Nassab was head of the
> Iranian Workers' Organization] I was really disappointed as I
> believed that the Army were our brothers, and more con-
> cerned about our country than this US General. You have
> included another point in your programme which is of some
> interest to me, and that is securing the nation's independence.
> Mr Prime Minister, I must inform you that Iran's national
> independence is shouldered by the Iranian people and the
> Iranian Army. It has nothing to do with General Huyser.

I didn't like this anti-American feeling within the parliament,
but I felt sure the Prime Minister could handle it. Also I welcomed
the sympathy for the military, and thought it might help in our
efforts to get a dialogue going.

One bright spot in the meeting with the Group was that this time
there was very little talk about anyone leaving the country. The
only time it was mentioned, General Toufanian brought up his
own case and asked if he could have a word with me in private. We
talked during a break, and it turned out that he badly wanted to get
out of the country ahead of the Shah. He said he had drawn up his
retirement papers, effective 1 January 1979, but they would stay in
his safe unless things went wrong. I had noted that when he signed
the papers on the cold-weather gear, he had dated them 1 January
1979. No doubt he thought that if he was recorded as having
retired before the new government started, maybe he would not be
blamed if it failed. I didn't get too concerned, as I had the feeling
that he just wanted to vent his frustrations, and really planned to
stay. In any event Gharabaghi was starting to pick up the reins as

Chief of the Military, and was showing that he had the capability; and Toufanian was no longer playing the big horse.

An Iranian enlisted man then brought in a Tehran paper which caused all eyes to widen and chins to drop. They started to chatter in Farsi at the same time, and you could feel the emotional stress building up. I was told that the headlines announced that Khomeini would be returning very soon. As usual they turned on me and asked what should be done if he came back immediately after the Shah left. I needed a way to get them to simmer down, so I told them to take twenty-four hours to work on the problem. I would have consultations with my government on this precise question, and at the same time would see what, if anything, had been done by our government to contact Khomeini.

We discussed the readiness and capability of the forces. I again told them that it was vital that they keep accurate track of their military capability. They should establish an Old Boy net which could be relied on to get the real and ungarbled truth about the troops. You couldn't do this through the bureaucracy because subordinates tended to paint a rosy picture to their leaders. They must establish a personal touch with their troops. There had to be an alerting network which would let us know if we were starting to get in trouble; and we had to know quickly, before we reached the point of no return.

Rabii said such efforts would be futile because when the Shah left, the military would just disintegrate. This called for another rather harsh lecture. I suggested that one way of ensuring discipline was to increase the alert status. They could start this now, and have the armed forces at a fairly high state of alert when the Shah left. This would confine troops to their garrisons and give them the feeling of military vigilance. They could maintain the alert status for a few days after the Shah's departure, at least until they felt they could have some confidence in the future. The troops would be off the streets, and thus have less contact with the religious and political elements. The Group finally agreed with these proposals, though not with great conviction, I felt.

General Gharabaghi came back with the news that there would be another National Security Council meeting tomorrow. This bothered them because they didn't know what would be expected of them and were not sure what to contribute. I told them I thought this was a wonderful opportunity to convince Mr Bakhtiar that they could be of real value to him.

When Gharabaghi asked me if I could provide him with some points which would prompt Mr Bakhtiar to clarify his intentions on using the military, I duly prepared some questions dealing with control of the country's economic elements. They should ask Mr Bakhtiar how he would gain access to the refineries; how he would protect the oil lines from Abadan to Tehran; how he would protect the wells themselves; how he would protect the power lines to prevent them from being cut; and how he would protect the power plants. These and many other questions were designed to make the Prime Minister realize that he needed the military, and without them he was helpless. I suggested that Gharabaghi should be prepared to answer each of the questions himself, which he could do by reference to the new plans. Gharabaghi seemed delighted. He started talking about the planning that would be needed for crowd control in the next few days, what with the Shah's departure, the demonstration due on the 19th and the possible return of Khomeini. On this basis he and the Prime Minister could reach agreement on what actions should be taken under all likely contingencies. By the time we were through, the Group was as pleased about this new opportunity as I was.

Gharabaghi also brought less welcome reports about unrest among the Kurds in the western provinces. They were looking for another allegiance, and some of them might link up with their fellow-tribesmen in Turkey.

The Group were incensed that in one of the demonstrations in the north-west, pictures of Lenin had figured prominently. They blamed everything on the Communists, even though they knew perfectly well that there were many other factions operating in the country. I told them they were missing some important tricks. For example, Mr Bakhtiar had made a dynamic speech arguing that if only unity could be restored, the country's sufferings could be reduced and most services could be normalized. But the speech had not received any publicity. It was ignored by all the media. This had to stop, and they, the military, must stop it. The Group took the point, and promised to discuss it at the National Security Council.

It was getting towards late afternoon, so before we left I recapped the important things we had discussed, and stressed that time was of the essence in preparing for the Shah's departure and Khomeini's return.

I went back to the Ambassador's residence to find Bill Sullivan getting really frustrated about our failure to bring the religious and military elements together. He blamed the military. I didn't feel that way; I recognized that it was a genuine problem to agree on a mutually acceptable meeting-place on neutral ground. If there were press leaks, it would be just as well that the meetings should be known to be taking place in an office associated with the constitutional government. Certainly it would be bad for morale if the senior military leaders were to accept a meeting-place designated by the religious elements.

We discussed the return of Khomeini, and agreed in censuring Washington for its failure to do anything to promote an understanding with the Ayatollah. We felt our government was being extremely timid, and we didn't understand why. We also agreed that a quick return of Khomeini was something which could not be handled, and would cause the whole situation to come unglued.

After dinner, I tramped through the blackness to report to Secretary Brown. I gave him a comprehensive report and said I thought I had made progress. I felt sure that the military leaders were now reconciled to the Shah's departure and ready to support Mr Bakhtiar. The crunch would come when the Shah left and Khomeini came back.

Secretary Brown said the options (A through E: see p.98) that I had sent in were accepted in Washington as the right priority, and the logical way to look at the alternatives. However, there was one concern about my Option B, which envisaged a short-term success for Bakhtiar followed by his collapse. I had conjectured that he might be replaced by another civilian government. Washington was worried that such a government could be more anti-American than the Bakhtiar one, and might even lean towards the Soviets. While these political manoeuvres were going on, the military might lose their unity and loyalty. If it appeared that this was going to happen, we needed to proceed straight to Option C – a military coup d'etat. This was not that far from what I had recommended, as I assumed that any suitable government under Option B must be friendly to the West. But the constant nagging problem I had with a military coup d'etat was who would be the leader of the nation.

Washington was now equally concerned about Khomeini's return; the situation could deteriorate rapidly, and he could overthrow the Bakhtiar government. They had heard predictions that the moment the Shah left or Khomeini returned, the military would just leave their garrisons and disintegrate. I said I didn't believe it; but it was essential to try to delay Khomeini's return, or at the very least to persuade him to cooperate with the Bakhtiar government.

Secretary Brown said the French were now trying to discourage Khomeini from returning too soon. They were warning him that if he did, it could lead to massive bloodshed. I was never sure that this would cut much ice with Khomeini, bearing in mind what the Shah had told me almost a year before about his vindictiveness. I wasn't convinced that he had all that much compassion for his own people; I thought he would put his own ambitions first, and as for anybody else, his signature tune would be 'Que sera, sera'.

I told Secretary Brown that I didn't think we had yet arrived at a need to choose between Option B and Option C. We must wait and see how the vote on Mr Bakhtiar went in parliament. It could be a very close call, but we must exercise patience for a couple of days. The only alternative would be more direct involvement by the United States. I had absolutely no illusions on this subject, because the American press was already scorching the administration for excessive interference. The foreign press, particularly Moscow, were having a field day on the subject. In actual fact the Soviets were interfering far more overtly than the United States. I could see at first hand what they were doing with the Tudeh party – the demonstrations they were promoting, and how accurate they were in their day-to-day information. They were doing everything they could to keep the pot boiling. They would probably have liked nothing better than a civil war, which would have made Iran an easy prey for them. With this in mind I was ready for much stronger support from the US and overt, solid endorsement of Bakhtiar.

In signing off, Secretary Brown was very complimentary. He said that from the President down, including Mr Brzezinski and Secretary Vance, and himself, they thought I was doing a fine job. I think these tributes were sincere, and I was glad of all the encouragement I could get, because the daily cycle of success and failure was very frustrating. The nagging thought was: why didn't they get more direct with the Ambassador?

Back in my room I reviewed the day's happenings, and there were some pluses. The Shah had convened the Regency Council, and it now seemed to be a reality which would act in his absence. He was working to get the vote for Bakhtiar's government. He had called in General Gharabaghi to work on his statement to rally the military. There was to be another National Security Council meeting, which hopefully might bring closer ties between Mr Bakhtiar and the military. And the item which pleased me most was the progress being made on the planning side.

There were some minuses. One was the recent events in Isfahan and Shiraz, where there had been overt demonstrations. Another was a development of which I learned just before retiring, and which spelt trouble for tomorrow. In a television interview in Paris, Khomeini had announced that he was forming a Council for an Islamic Republic, and would install a government on his return to Iran. I knew this would have a disastrous effect on the Group of Five. I could hardly get to sleep that night, trying to work out a game plan to convince them that it was no more than a propaganda ploy.

I also had word from Washington about a piece by the influential journalistic team of Roland Evans and Robert Novak, criticizing my mission. They had already labelled it a failure. I guess they didn't realize that I hadn't even got to the first crunch-point. They dilated on General Al Haig's unhappiness about my involvement. They said the President had picked completely the wrong guy to do a very tough and delicate job. Though I was highly regarded as a military technician with broad logistical experience (I think they had me confused with an Army General, Joe Heiser, who had been a logistician, because I didn't have 'broad logistical experience'), I had no diplomatic or political background. This was not true: I had been through several years of diplomatic experience at a high level. As for the political background, my mission as officially stated to me did not require it: I had been sent to Tehran to work with the military, and we had an Ambassador to handle the other side.

The article also damned the Bakhtiar government as being left-of-centre and liable to lean towards the Soviet Union. I knew this spelled trouble in the Group, as I was not sure I had really overcome their apprehensions about Bakhtiar. If there was any hint of a Communist affinity there, they were going to become uncontrollable. They saw a Communist behind every mosque. And the article delivered yet another blow to their confidence by asking how firm the US administration really was in support of Bakhtiar. It pointed out that Carter had ordered the *Constellation* carrier task force to speed toward the Persian Gulf, and then halted it at Singapore. Just how sincere was he about supporting his friends?

Monday, 15 January 1979

I started the morning by reviewing the message traffic and the press coverage. The most significant item was that the Shah had asked Ambassador Sullivan to notify Egypt that he would arrive there at about 2 pm on 16 January. This meant he would leave Tehran around noon. It was the first indication we had had of a firm time of departure.

There was a recap of yesterday's events in Tehran. The main demonstration had been several thousands strong. It had set a new style, in that it was orderly and peaceful. At the direction of Khomeini, they had launched a new kind of attack on the military, and its weapons were love and kindness. The marchers carried flowers which they muzzle-loaded into the gun barrels of the soldiers, and strewed garlands all over the tank guns. They were extremely kind and courteous to the soldiers, who displayed corresponding restraint on their side. The marches ended on the same peaceful note, with only a few minor incidents during the entire day.

This technique of fraternization was a new threat, especially with the very young soldiers, who might now be attracted to the other side. To set up the programme, Khomeini had sent in tapes to be played in all the mosques. His theme was that Iran's armed forces needed to be 'protected' against infiltration by foreign 'hoodlums': outside influences were trying to pit the Army against the people, and this must not be allowed to happen. The 'illegal' government of Mr Bakhtiar was arming and training the armed forces for a face-to-face confrontation. This must be avoided; the public was duty-bound to show brotherly love and kindness towards members of the security and armed forces, who were equally duty-bound to act in the same spirit towards the public. This message was echoed in the debates in the Majlis on Prime Minister Bakhtiar's government. There were many calls for the people and the Army to make common cause against foreign interference.

The Tehran newspaper *Kayhan* carried pictures of nine of the Regency Council members, including Mr Bakhtiar and General Gharabaghi. It also carried the headline: 'Grinning Troops Greet Street Demonstrators', and reported the cordial attitude of the people towards the military. The demonstrators had been dishing out handbills, plastering them on telephone booths, walls and lamp-posts, blasting the United States for its support of the Shah and Bakhtiar. One of these handbills had asked: 'What could be more disgusting than to buy arms with Iranian money and then use them to waste the blood of Iran's glorious youth? In this manner the United States has taken our money from us, wasted the blood of our people to tolerate these colonial schemes? Shame on any Iranian who obeys such orders.'

The paper said the poster appeared to be a response to reports that General Robert Huyser had come to Iran to urge the military to support the new civilian government. It also carried a front-page article with a Cairo byline saying that the Shah might meet Sadat in Aswan. Obviously this information came from Cairo. The report said that the Shah's mother and his sister Princess Shams, had been staying at the Walter Annenberg estate in Palm Springs, California, where the Shah was due to arrive, but in the face of local anti-regime demonstrations they had sought refuge elsewhere.

With all this in mind I was anticipating a rather rough ride with the Group. They would be extremely apprehensive, with the Shah's departure imminent, and I guessed they would be thrown off balance by the sweetness-and-light approach adopted by the mob, and the reported reaction of the military to it. The event had been blown completely out of perspective by the press, who gave the impression that all the military had fallen in love with the demonstrators. This was quite untrue. We monitored the situation very carefully, and only a very few of them had actually joined the opposition, while a fair number simply decided to fall in with the mood of the crowd. It was a sensible way to make the best of a bad situation. To me, this was a further indication of the troops' good training and state of discipline.

I learned that there had been some progress in increasing oil production, which was now up to 240,000 barrels per day. The expectation was that in another week it would be up to half a million barrels. Tehran had been allocated some 23,000 barrels per day, which was only about 3,500 barrels less than normal. They were even talking about exporting oil again. One of their problems was that they were getting too much heavy oil at the Abadan refinery, and had to dispose of it in order to be able to refine more oil; so they were looking for an overseas market. We discussed helping them, as it was to our advantage to try to get more petroleum produced.

I had asked my headquarters in Stuttgart to see what fuel was afloat in the Persian Gulf area in case we had an emergency requirement for the armed forces. They replied that there was a Navy tanker in the vicinity, but it was loaded with the wrong fuel. It could be offloaded, properly loaded with the right fuel and made available without too much delay.

We reached the SCS compound, and found that the planning was coming along well, particularly in the psychological warfare area. On customs, we now knew where the key nodes were and the number of troops we would need to control them. We were still short of some critical information on the supply points for oil and power. We had extremely good information on the water supply, and also had the communication network pretty well wired down.

On arrival at General Gharabaghi's office we found we had a Group of Six that day, General Moghaddam being present. They needed a full house because the Shah's departure was so close. There was also a strong uneasiness, and I must admit that I had a queasy stomach about Khomeini's new strategy for winning over the military. We had to move fast or we could lose the troops without ever knowing what happened. If the Shah came through with his speech, on television and radio, that would be helpful. But it was also vital to get General Gharabaghi on the air. This was against his nature, and had never been done before. It would break all precedents for a military man to go public with a major policy statement. I now urged him to call Mr Bakhtiar to see if he would have any objection, and went over very carefully with him the kind of points he ought to make. Gharabaghi made the check, and there was no objection from Mr Bakhtiar. No doubt the Prime Minister was aware that his own future depended on a loyal Army.

Speed was now essential. The military had the same information as I did, namely that the Shah would be leaving the next day, 16 January, to arrive in Aswan at 2 pm. So we had twenty-four hours to get prepared for his departure. I asked Gharabaghi about yesterday's National Security Council meeting, and he thought it had been very productive. The Prime Minister had said he would enforce the law and was prepared to jail anybody who obstructed him.

Then we got another alert from the Shah – a repeat of the previous exercise to keep the military on their toes. He wanted his crew and airplane ready for an immediate launch. This was clearly going to be a daily event until he finally left. He wanted to be able to drop everything and leave at a moment's notice, in an orderly way.

Next I got the daily litany about the BBC, the need for pressure on Khomeini, and now a new protest about the unbalanced reports in the American press. I felt that these were partly the fault of Western governments. There had been no counter-balancing statements from the US or any other Western nation to offset what Khomeini was saying. The tempo of his activity had picked up considerably with the open attacks in Tabriz, Shiraz and Isfahan against the Savak headquarters. This, coupled with the new 'hearts and flowers' approach to the military, was a powerful threat, and the Group needed more help from Washington than they were getting. However, there was much less talk about any of them skipping the country. Rabii and Toufanian argued that when the Shah left, they would have to pull a coup, but Gharabaghi jumped on this. He said that it wasn't going to be necessary. He was so emphatic about it that I felt he was excluding it under *any* circumstances and this caused me some concern.

We all agreed on the need for maximum intelligence on the activities of both Khomeini and the Soviets. I told them their job was to devote their full attention to the internal threat; if there was any external threat, it would be taken care of by the West.

The latter part of the meeting was spent helping to prepare

General Gharabaghi for his public statement. We had to be sure it would convey the feeling of confidence needed to bolster the troops' morale and enhance discipline. We then had to decide how to get this message on the air and into the newspapers. We also had to be certain we could do the same for the Shah's message, and I felt we might have to get quite forceful because we would encounter opposition. These were items which we just could not postpone any longer. The planning group reported that their first batch of leaflets and posters were ready to hit the streets, and they would be put out the following day.

During the meeting we were told that another massive demonstration was building up in the streets. The same techniques were being employed: the hand of friendship towards the military, the traffic officers, and the police. They showed almost inordinate affection, hoisting security men on their shoulders, and carrying them around as heroes. We picked up word that the Tudeh party were calling for an armed struggle. They were clearly getting impatient at the conciliatory tactics employed by the Khomeini forces. A shoot-out was what they wanted.

Just as we were getting ready to adjourn, we heard that the Senate had voted 38 to 1 in favour of the Bakhtiar government. This exceeded all our expectations, and gave us a morale boost which we were going to need in the next few days.

I asked Gharabaghi about the chances of a meeting with the religious leaders. Had he had any success? He said it seemed possible that General Moghaddam might be able to meet them. He didn't say where or when, but the object seemed to be to establish some rules of behaviour during the Shah's departure. The Group appeared reluctant to go any further. I said that the Ambassador and I would do all we could to help with the coordination of any meetings.

In the course of the day we had logged some significant achievements. We had worked up the basic ingredients of a speech for Gharabaghi. The Shah had finished taping his messages, and part of them would be released that evening; he would release the rest at a press conference the following day just before his departure. The next thing was to get Gharabaghi's address to the troops into the press.

We went back to the Embassy, where I debriefed Ambassador Sullivan on the day's activities. We discussed at length the danger of Khomeini returning too soon: we still didn't have all the plans ready to take emergency action. Two other developments were wrenching the initiative away from Bakhtiar: the attacks on Savak and the brotherly love campaign in the streets. There was an urgent need for a meeting with the opposition. Sullivan said the religious leaders were still willing, and the military should be ready to meet on religious territory. I told him I would sound them out again.

At about 10 pm I got a summons to go over and talk to Secretary Brown. As I crossed from the residence to the Chancellory I sensed a different feeling in the air. The security had been stepped up. Guards in civilian clothes were lurking among the trees, and there were many uniformed men at the gates. The Embassy Chief of Security, Colonel Holland, knew his job; he was one of the best I had ever seen, a picturesque individual, 5 ft 5 ins tall, stocky, but not an ounce of fat. He kept a 357 Magnum on his hip, about as big as he was, and all the Iranian guards knew he meant business.

At the other end of the secure phone, the Chairman of the Joint Chiefs and the Secretary of Defence had been joined for the occasion by Dr Brzezinski. If you ever want a real test of your faculties you should try to understand Dr Brzezinski on one of our vintage secure phones. Most people sounded more or less like Donald Duck, as I have said, but with Dr Brzezinski's accent and speed of delivery, the end product beggars description.

I gave them the day's activities: the planning was going well, but the Group of Five were pretty uptight. We would soon know whether I had accomplished anything.

Dr Brzezinski asked me whether the military had developed plans for use in the event that Bakhtiar failed. I was amazed at this, because I had only just reported on the subject. However, I just said Yes, we'd been working on them for four or five days, but at this moment we would have to consider them a marginal capability. We were almost ready to go with psychological warfare and customs, but my first priority was to secure the oil, power, water and communications. Only when those plans were complete could the military claim to have a viable capability.

He then asked about the attitude of the middle-level officers.

Did I have any feel for people at that level as to whether they would hang in there, or what they'd do? I said the senior military were working with remarkable unity, and that this was having a positive effect down through the middle ranks. Their good morale was confirmed by the observations of my own officers and of the Embassy staff, which verified the reports of the Iranian military leadership. At the lowest level I reported the fraternization and desertions, but I stressed that the media had greatly exaggerated them. There was no reason to think the military was in danger of collapsing, given that the leadership stayed solid. I then reported that General Gharabaghi was going public, which might not seem much in the United States, but which in Iran was a tremendous step forward because it was completely without precedent.

Secretary Brown asked if I was comfortable with the plans to take control of the economy and maintain law and order. I referred him to the answers I had given to Dr Brzezinski. Though the plans were still incomplete, we had made great progress. Since we had started from absolute zero, and had to contend with a lot of obstruction, this was remarkable. All the groups dealing with power, oil, communications, food, customs and propaganda were really moving in top gear. Though we couldn't yet do the full-scale operation, in a few days I thought we'd be at the point where we could. That was why it would make all the difference to have a few days' grace before Khomeini's return. If the Shah left tomorrow and Khomeini came the next day, all our planning might go down the tubes.

On this point Secretary Brown had some good news. Through the efforts of the US, working with the French, one of Khomeini's men (whom I took to be Ibrahim Yazdi), had urged Khomeini to delay his return by at least a few days. The Secretary thought there was reason to believe the Ayatollah would agree to this. My Iranian colleagues would be delighted to hear it.

Washington did not appear to know that the Shah planned to leave at noon the next day. I told them I thought this was at least ninety per cent certain. He had now got the vote he wanted on the Bakhtiar government, and could leave in an orderly fashion.

I stressed to Harold Brown the need for maximum intelligence on Khomeini's movements. Every available source should be put to work to keep track of him. We couldn't afford to be behind the power curve either on Khomeini or on Soviet movements across the border. I was glad to hear him say that I could tell the Iranians to concentrate on their domestic problems and that the US would look after any external threat. Dr Brzezinski added crisply that we would not stand idle if any neighbour intervened. He sounded very aggressive, as if he would like to see the Iranian military swing into action now. From this short discussion, on top of what I had read, I felt he was sold on Option C, the military coup d'etat, and wanted to be sure we were properly prepared for it.

In this context I pointed out again that our chief constriction was the shortage of gas and diesel for vehicles and tanks, and that I needed immediate help. I told them I had been in contact with my headquarters in Stuttgart, and they were scanning the high seas for available supplies. I was assured by both the Secretary of Defence and the Chairman that they would take immediate action, and I would be receiving support in the near future. I had absolute confidence that this would happen, because I had had nothing but top-notch support from both of them in the past.

Secretary Brown again asked me about troop morale and discipline. I repeated my view that the press was overplaying both the desertion rate and the scale of fraternization. He asked if we couldn't set up a reporting system that would give us a better feel of the military pulse. I said I would pursue this further with the military tomorrow; we already had a system established, but we would try to improve it. I added that one of the things that were really causing us problems was the lack of clear statements from Washington to counter Khomeini's pronouncements. I was told that the US planned to issue a statement when the Shah left. I said I thought that would be a good time. Some people feared that too much US support for the Bakhtiar government could injure it, but I was now hardening in the view that this was misguided, and we should give it one hundred per cent public backing.

Ambassador Sullivan had by now joined me in the secure communications room; he had been summoned to hold a teletype conference with the State Department, and the equipment was in the same room as the telephone main frame. As I had pretty well wrapped up my report, I asked the Ambassador if he would like to speak with Secretary Brown. He took the phone, they exchanged pleasantries, and then Sullivan reported Bakhtiar's view that his greatest threat would be an early return by Khomeini. I was glad to get this confirmation right out of the blue. Mr Bakhtiar had, in fact, told him he needed a clear month before Khomeini returned. Then the State Department came on the line for the teleconference with the Ambassador. After an exchange of greetings the first word from Washington was: 'We hope you are in the secure room alone. This is for your eyes and not for the eyes of General Huyser.' We looked at each other at point-blank range, as I was standing over him and had read the words as they came in. I said I would be glad to leave, but the Ambassador said: 'Well, we're either in this together or we're not, and you are invited to stay.'

Here again was an example of what was, or maybe was not, happening back in Washington. It was a complete mystery to both of us. We thought it was time someone got hold of the system in Washington and straightened it out before we were required to do the whole exercise again in some other country.

While I was waiting for the Ambassador to finish his teleconference I reviewed the late news coming in by teletype. A *Wall Street Journal* article was headlined 'Shah Expected to Leave Iran By Mid-Week But Departure May Cause Further Chaos'. Reporting on Khomeini's announcement of the creation of an Islamic Revolutionary Council to run the country once the Shah had gone, it said that this decision 'further weakened the new civilian government of Prime Minister Bakhtiar who was being supported by the USA. American officials believed it increased the likelihood of bloody civil war between followers of the Ayatollah and the Iranian armed forces.' There was no reason to believe the military would let Khomeini just walk in and take over.

It appeared that the Ayatollah had been on CBS's 'Face the Nation' and had struck a very truculent note. He had said that 'if the US would back off from supporting the Shah and quit supporting Bakhtiar, maybe Khomeini could treat the American people with friendship and justice.' The article said the Carter administration was supporting the Bakhtiar government, and General Huyser was in Tehran to persuade the key military leaders to do so. It said I was charged with trying to persuade the Iranian military to stand together. A split in their ranks would, in the view of American officials, eliminate the last remaining bastion of authority in Iran. All these things put together spelt trouble for our meetings the next day.

The Ambassador finished his conference, and we went back to the residence. It was nice to have company on that rather creepy walk for a change. We both decided we had better get some sleep, as it was already early morning, and I knew that if I was going to be able to get to the office at all I would need to leave the Embassy compound by six o'clock. If the Shah was really leaving, I felt I must be with the Group when it happened.

Even though I was exhausted, and seemed to get more so each day, I was not cool enough to be able to sleep. This was a night of great apprehension. If the Shah did leave, how would the civil population react? Would they call off the strikes? Would things start to settle down? Would the troops desert en masse? Would the Khomeini forces openly attack Bakhtiar? They were preparing for something, but it was difficult to predict their next move.

Tuesday, 16 January 1979

After rolling and tossing and catnapping for three or four hours I got up, and prepared to leave for the Supreme Commander's Staff's compound. General Gast had spent the night at the Ambassador's residence because we did not know what to anticipate at his end of the town, and I wanted him to meet the Group. The streets were surprisingly quiet, which made the trip faster than usual. It was a cold, grey morning, and I felt the entire day would be that way inside and out.

On arrival at the office we found there was no heating. This seemed odd, because there had been a boost in the oil supplies and we were getting used to being in warm offices again. We figured we might have been just too early, so we bundled up in sweaters and topcoats and hoped for the best. I spent the first couple of hours reviewing documents, bringing my notes up to date, and reviewing all aspects of the planning. Were there loopholes? What had we missed? Had we really thought through all the possible contingencies?

At reveille, we watched the troops form up to go through the flag-raising ceremony. They were very precise and sharp. The thing that sent thrills up my spine was their deep-throated shouts of '*Javid Shah*' ('Long Live the Shah').

Between 7 and 8 am the rest of the office arrived, with the

conspicuous exception of Colonel Arthur Heinhott, the Chief Administrative Officer. General Gast ordered an immediate check on his whereabouts, as he was an extremely reliable officer and usually got to work early. We were very sensitive about the safety of our people because of the anti-American campaign being waged by Khomeini. An American civilian employee, Martin Berkovits from San Francisco, had been knifed to death in the town of Kerman two days before. We were not sure of the reason, but they had written all over his walls 'Go Home', so it had all the earmarks of targeting an American.

When the Executive Officer, Major Burnette, came in we dispatched him immediately to the streets to get the morning papers. I was particularly anxious to see if General Gharabaghi's press conference had got a good showing. He came back with both the *Tehran Journal* and the *Kayhan*. I was extremely pleased to see in the *Journal*, on the front page, top left-hand corner, the Gharabaghi article. It was headlined 'Gharabaghi Rules Out Army Coup', and carried a picture of the General. So we had broken precedent: we had got the Chief of Staff into the newspapers. This was a completely new experience in Iran.

Gharabaghi had declared that there would be no military coup after the Shah left. He did hint that an Army mutiny could not be ruled out, but he did not elaborate on this. He said the Army supported any legal government and intended to safeguard the constitution. It had been subject to provocations recently in Tabriz, Shiraz and elsewhere. He warned demonstrators not to 'provoke' the Army, whose only purpose was to maintain order.

He was asked about rivalries in the armed forces, and replied that while rebels would be crushed according to military regulation, 'unity and understanding between the armed forces and the members of society could avert any foreign-inspired plot'. He said he was a soldier, and could not express himself in political language; but you got bad people in every organization, and anyone in the Army found guilty of wrongdoing would be punished. He went on to say that no patriotic Iranian could wish to see a confrontation between the Army and the people after His Majesty left. If this happened, neither the Army nor the nation would survive. This sounded a rather uncertain note, particularly when linked to his promise that there would be no coup. I just never knew whether Gharabaghi had enough starch in him if we needed to pull a military takeover. But I liked his declaration of allegiance to the Iranian constitution and to the legal government of Prime Minister Bakhtiar. He said that no one could guarantee that revolts would not occur in an army. 'But one thing we can say is that we will strongly crush any such attempts.'

All in all, I considered his article very beneficial. Just having his picture on the front page was a big plus for our cause. Also welcome were the main headlines: 'Shah to Address the Press Before His Departure'. We were pleased at this 'trailer' for his appeal to the nation. The paper reported the 38-1 Senate vote for Mr Bakhtiar, and said that today would bring the vote of the Majlis, and we would know if we had a government.

The Tudeh party was still appealing for an armed struggle, according to an article datelined Paris. We had long suspected a connection between Khomeini in Paris and the Tudeh party in Iran. We had heard several rumours of direct telephone connections from the Ayatollah to Moscow and to Libya, but we had no way of confirming them, although his well-known personal hatred of the Shah made it likely that he would use any resource that would further his immediate cause, regardless of ideology. We knew that Radio Moscow was coming on heavy, condemning the Bakhtiar government. The main object had been to create unrest and to drive a wedge between Iran and the United States.

About mid-morning, Gharabaghi's office said the Group were all together and would like to have us join them. On arrival, I decided to head off any lamentations about the Shah's departure with a practical review of the planning situation. I said I was delighted to see them give planning such a high priority. I congratulated General Gharabaghi on his statement, and said it showed real strength. I pointed to the front-page articles on the press conference and on the Bakhtiar vote.

The Group had no eyes for silver linings however. They drew my attention to the headlines in the middle of the front page: 'Khomeini Set on New Government'. He had said that the birth of an Islamic government was imminent, and declared: 'I would neither have the powers of the Shah nor would I be Prime Minister. I would be content with directing the nation.' Even the suggestion that Khomeini could come back to Iran, let alone run the country, really got the Group uptight. They then pointed to the article immediately below: 'American Living in Kerman Murdered'. I said I was aware of that situation but hoped it was an isolated case. I was still worried about our colonel who had not shown up that morning. I hoped this was not the start of a new trend, because these trends could spread like a bushfire.

The topic on everybody's mind was summed up in one big headline: 'The Shah Will Leave Today'. Some of them still refused to believe it, particularly Rabii, Badraie and Gharabaghi. I think Toufanian was too much of a realist to doubt it, while Admiral Habiballahi stoically accepted it as a precondition of reducing tension.

I told them that though I did not have a firm time, he would certainly be leaving today, probably about noon. We should review all possibilities to be sure we knew where we stood. Had they all set up procedures to keep a constant check on their forces? We needed to know immediately how the men reacted when the Shah left. Yes, they had all put their forces on Red Alert, and had carried out extensive checks that morning through their subordinate commanders. There had not been any murmurings in the ranks, nor were there any rumours of mass desertion. In fact the state of the armed forces seemed to be better than normal. This was a standard military reaction when they were on alert; the challenge of problems raised the level of cohesion.

Of almost equal urgency was the question of Khomeini's return. This was something to which they were still not reconciled. They seemed to think he might be persuaded to disappear like a djinn, or be eliminated in transit, or even on arrival. They were incapable of thinking straight on this issue.

It emerged that the Group had met with Bakhtiar the evening before and talked late into the night. The Prime Minister had also met separately with the Regency Council last night, so that Gharabaghi had had two audiences with him. The Group had gone over their contingency plans with him, and this served to strengthen the bond between the two sides. Mr Bakhtiar must now realize how the Army could help him to control the country, break the strikes, and get things back to normal. The Group were sure they would be ready on a twenty-four-hour basis to protect the power, fuel, communications and anything else. At last we were heading down the right track.

Then we heard helicopters overhead. Knowing that the Shah was going from Niavaran Palace to Mehrabad Airport by helicopter, and the route was almost directly over the headquarters, we immediately went out on the balcony. Sure enough, it was the Shah and his escort. There were six helicopters, and they were headed for Mehrabad. I am sure every one of us must have doubled his rate of heartbeat.

General Rabii told us the aircraft and crew were ready; he himself had test-hopped the plane earlier that morning. It was in good order, and all was set. Then General Gharabaghi turned to me and asked in an emotional way what my recommendations were on the departure of the Shah. I said I thought that he himself should proceed to Mehrabad Airport and represent the military leaders there. I would stay in his office with the rest of the Group and we could keep rigorous watch on all activities.

This was the first real test, since every one of them had repeatedly expressed his desire to leave with the Shah. Which way would they jump? Would they tell me to go fly my kite, and all skip the country, or would they follow my lead?

I continued impassively with my recommendations, particularly about keeping strict vigilance on the military forces, but my pulse-rate was climbing by the minute. It was almost beyond my comprehension that they would not all insist on going to the airport to bid the Shah farewell. Knowing how emotional they could be, and how rapidly they could change their minds, I would not have been surprised if they were to bid *me* farewell and leave the country with their master. So when General Gharabaghi addressed me and said he agreed with me, and the others supported him, it was a great relief.

Helicopters were constantly available within the compound to provide fast transportation, because it was now almost impossible to travel by automobile during the day. General Gharabaghi got his hat and gloves and left the office. I could almost hear the heartbeats of his colleagues, and they had my sympathy because I fully understood the depth of their feelings. I also understood the uncertainty and fear which they must be undergoing. All maintained their composure, but I'm sure they would have felt better if they could have openly wept.

We turned on the television in Gharabaghi's office, and as we waited and watched, they reminisced about the halcyon days under the Shah, and indulged in Monday-morning-quarterbacking about where the Shah had gone wrong. They felt he had lost his will and determination. He had not used the powers which he had at hand. It was the first time I had heard them talk like this.

The closer it came to takeoff time, the more emotional things got, not only in the office, but on the television screen and in the streets. Preparations had been made to keep the masses out of Mehrabad Airport by positioning the Imperial Guard – the elite of the uniformed men – around the airport. Only a very few people were permitted inside. With the level of anti-Shah sentiment on the streets, the potential for an explosion was too high to leave anything to chance.

The official farewell party was headed by Prime Minister Bakhtiar and two or three members of his Cabinet. We saw Gharabaghi on the screen, so we knew he had arrived. As the time of departure approached the Shah himself became very emotional. He must have been wondering if he was ever going to return. I doubt he himself really admitted defeat; but many other people must have thought that once he lifted off the ground, he had given up the Peacock Throne.

The spectrum of emotions in the office ran from sobbing – one of the senior officers laid his head on my shoulder and cried – to telling jokes. These were just variegated symptoms of fear and frustration. Admiral Habiballahi seemed almost frivolous, though I knew he loved the Shah. As the plane took off, he said in his quiet way: 'When rape is inevitable, relax and enjoy it.'

Tremendous crowds had collected in the streets throughout the city, and when the Shah lifted off, it was as if a big starting gun had been fired. Everybody seemed to respond at once. We went out on the balcony. Horns were honking, demonstrations erupting, and the whole city was alive with jubilation. The event was an indescribable, spontaneous paean of joy, and it went on for two or three hours, increasing in noise and tempo. We began to get reports that the crowds were pulling down all monuments to the Shah and his family. In front of the telecommunications building, on Tehran's Sepah Square, there was a huge and beautiful equestrian statue of Reza Shah, the Shah's father. The mobs took ropes and toppled it off its pedestal. During the afternoon we received word that five or six such statues – major landmarks which had stood for several decades – had been destroyed. They were killing the Shah – symbolically.

Before leaving, the Shah had given his statement to the press, and it would be helpful to the military. He said he was taking a holiday, which he badly needed after months of living in a state of near-siege. He had waited until the government of Mr Bakhtiar was fully installed. He appealed to the nation's sense of patriotism to pull the country out of its economic morass. He hoped the new government would be able to repair the damage of the past, and to lay the foundations of the future. To achieve this there must be a period of cooperation and patriotism in its highest sense. The economy must start again, and the people must renew their lives and prepare a better plan for the future.

About half an hour after his departure we heard General Gharabaghi's helicopter returning to the compound. He had a very grave, ashen look, as was to be expected. The first thing he said was that he was extremely proud of the Imperial Guard. They had ringed the airport and done their job well, and proved they were disciplined troops. He expressed his own great sorrow, and said the Shah and Shahbanou had openly wept.

I wondered how to handle the situation. Should I attempt some shock treatment to take their thoughts off the departure, or should I ride along and show the compassion I shared with them? I decided to let them vent their feelings. There was no question now that they had dedicated themselves to support the country and Bakhtiar. True, they were still discussing the idea of a military takeover that night – they had in fact established a time, 2.30 am the next morning, to seize power – but it was not too difficult to dissuade them by asking a couple of practical questions about the planning. What was wrong with the Prime Minister? Who was to be the new ruler of their country?

They speculated on Khomeini's next move, and this led to a very tense discussion. They were convinced that he would be coming back immediately. What was to keep him out? Why wouldn't he just come back now? The discussion worked up to a state which caused me to get a bit harsh. I said we were now ready to test our ability to support Mr Bakhtiar, and had sufficient plans to do so. This was greeted with a surprising outburst from both Gharabaghi and Rabii. Their response was, Yes, General, the Shah told us to trust you, to listen to you, and to obey you.

That word 'obey' was a new one. It shook me. I questioned it at once, but all of them confirmed it. This was a bit sobering, because I was certain that our government did not want me to go that far. I

had been cautioned on several occasions about getting too assertive. On the other had, Washington was certainly pushing me to
get things done, and done right, and on schedule. I felt I was in a
rather unenviable position. It put a completely different light on
the situation to know that if I gave an opinion, it would very
probably be acted on. One particular cause of concern was the
possibility that this information might leak out. The Russian press
were already making allegations along these lines. If anybody got
hold of that word 'obey', it would create enormous problems for
the US in Iran.

We lapsed into small-talk. I was not going to leave until I was
confident that they had rejected any precipitate action that night. I
also wanted to feel more certain that they were not going to leave
the country after all.

General Toufanian broke the ice. He said he had given serious
thought to leaving ahead of the Shah, or even with the Shah,
because this was his last chance; government officials had picked
up his passport. He would not say who these officials were, though
it seemed very unusual that such a senior military man should be
without a passport. He added that he was on a list to be tried for
corruption, but he believed he had made the right choice. He
would put his full weight behind the effort to make the
present government a success. Thus encouraged, I asked them
all point-blank: 'Are we through with the foolish thoughts of
military action tonight? Do you fully realize we do not have the
planning to the point where we could achieve success? We
only have certain elements of it which could be executed at
this time.'

They assured me that there would be nothing of that nature.
Several times General Gharabaghi told me that he had meant what
he said in his speech. He realized we were not ready, and
furthermore it was not necessary at this time. Mr Bakhtiar was still
in charge, and we should support him. We should push on with
plans for handling the crowds which would be on the streets on the
19th.

It was now late in the evening (I had spent about seven and a
half hours with them). My confidence had revived, the crowds had
diminished, and the military forces were stable to the point where I
thought I could get back to the Embassy, so it seemed like a good
time to make a move. I felt I must make a report to Washington on

that night of all nights. We said goodnight and went over to our office.

On arrival we were told that our missing colonel had been found hanged in his home. Our first thought was foul play, because it was only that morning that the press had carried the story of the American in Kerman. But the investigators said there did not appear to be foul play. We questioned this verdict at length, but they insisted there was no sign of it. General Gast ordered a complete investigation by experts to determine whether it was murder or suicide.

On arrival at the Embassy, we discussed the day's activities with Ambassador Sullivan, who had remained there all day. He gave no indication of his own feelings about the Shah's departure. Although it had been an exhausting day for General Gast and myself, it had gone better than either of us had expected.

While waiting to make my report, I scanned the UPI press reports on the teleprinter. They gave good coverage of Gharabaghi's speech, and a lengthy description of the new 'love campaign' of candy, flowers and kisses. Commenting on Gharabaghi's statement that there would not be a coup, the UPI said it came after the Shah and General Huyser had held extensive talks with leading Iranian figures to persuade them to throw their weight behind the Bakhtiar government. It said I had stayed in Iran for more discussions long after my scheduled departure date.

At about 10.30 pm I crossed the darkened compound to report to Secretary Brown. It was a crisp night and extra quiet; maybe the masses were worn out with their celebrations, but there was a different feeling in the air.

Once again, Dr Brzezinski had joined Secretary Brown and General Jones. I started by telling them that if things held up for the next twenty-four or forty-eight hours, I felt I had achieved success in my mission, which was to unite the military, to keep their leaders in-country and to swing them behind Mr Bakhtiar. So far so good. But how long would it last? Things had a habit of coming apart at the seams overnight. I told them I didn't feel my mission would be complete until I got some positive actions from the Bakhtiar government. We had made the plans; I now felt obliged to get some of them implemented. The departure of the

Shah ended Phase One – namely, those things the President had charged me to do; now I was ready to take responsibility for Phase Two. They did not register an objection to this statement.

I gave them a full picture of the day's extraordinary events. Secretary Brown asked about the solidarity of the Group, and my response was to report General Toufanian's speech, to which all of them had given unqualified assent. This was my cue to report on the Shah's instructions that the Group should 'obey' me. I said this put me in rather a hot seat. With Dr Brzezinski on the line, I was hoping that Washington would now give me more latitude in the implementation of Phase Two. But my statement was greeted by a resounding silence and zero acknowledgement.

The Secretary asked me about the likelihood of a coup, and I explained that the Group had got as far as fixing the time for it, but I now had absolute confidence that it was not going to take place that night. The Group were ready to give Prime Minister Bakhtiar a chance. But their apprehension about Khomeini's return was almost uncontrollable.

I reported that we had not yet had any success in arranging a meeting between the military and religious leaders. The military had tried, that same day, but without success. I thought it was essential to have contact so as to establish ground-rules for the demonstration two days hence. I reminded the Secretary that it would be directed by Khomeini and said it was my opinion – and that of the Shah, the Iranian military leaders and the US Ambassador – that Washington should make direct contact with Khomeini. Harold Brown said there were doubts in Washington whether this would be the proper thing to do. I acknowledged that there might be a good reason for this, but said that I would welcome some clue as to what the objection was, because we needed to give some explanation to Tehran. Again, I got no answer. The Secretary then asked about the morale in the military, and I was able to tell him of our latest reports; that the Air Force and the Navy were extremely healthy, but the Army, being larger and less educated, was not quite as good, particularly at the lower levels. However, I still judged it as satisfactory. The fraternization might make inroads among the very young troops, but the older ones were treating it as nothing more than a game. It was especially noteworthy that although the Shah had departed the military forces remained stable.

Dr Brzezinski now weighed in, urging me to be sure the coup d'etat option remained open. He pointed out the value of planning quite openly for this option: we could scare the opposition into supporting Bakhtiar by warning that the alternative was the Army. He said this might even make the Ayatollah think twice about coming back.

I explained that we were doing exactly what he suggested, the only difference being that the first priority would be to implement our plans under Prime Minister Bakhtiar. I began to wonder if this rather crucial issue had really been thrashed out in Washington. It should have been, for I had discussed it often enough with the Secretary of Defence.

I was hoping to be told that I was on the right track, and finally it was acknowledged that the planning was the same for both objectives, so I was cleared to proceed as I had been going. Harold Brown had got the message all right. I told them things were at a critical stage, as we were getting to the point where we could execute some of the plans. We had already started on the propaganda, with leaflets on the streets and General Gharabaghi's public statements. But if we were going to take action on any of the plans which required tanks and vehicles, then we would need a new source of diesel fuel and motor gasoline. True, oil production was up and there was an increase at the Abadan refinery, and an ampler flow of gasoline into Tehran; but we failed to obtain a larger allocation for the military. Secretary Brown said the Department of Defence would charter a vessel. This was good news, because when Harold Brown said he was going to do something, he did it. I could always count on him.

. I reviewed the outlook for the demonstration on the 19th. The instructions from the mosques were to keep it peaceful; but I could not predict the behaviour of third parties. The military had established their own ground-rules along the lines we had suggested, to confine the troops to key installations, but make it crystal clear that any misbehaviour would be handled severely. In other words, there would be no half-measures, like rubber bullets or firing overhead. Mr Bakhtiar had told the people he was going to maintain order, and was prepared to use the military to do it.

Secretary Brown asked me about Mr Bakhtiar's standing with the public now that the Shah had gone and his government had survived for the best part of a day. I felt it was much too early to say; the people in the streets were mainly opposition supporters, simply overjoyed at the Shah's departure, and there had certainly not been any indications of support for Bakhtiar. His survival depended on two things. One was a delay in Khomeini's return; the other was the progress he could make on implementing the plans. Mr Bakhtiar had said he needed a month or two to get these things done. If Khomeini came back immediately, there would be absolute chaos. Khomeini would probably be killed, and if so, it would certainly lead to civil war, because all factions would pitch in, and the opposition was well enough armed to make it a war.

Secretary Brown again expressed his confidence in my activities. Dr Brzezinski also thanked me, and asked me to keep up the good work. With that we parted for the night.

As I was leaving, the teletype operator handed me some messages. One was an article from the German periodical *Sudkurier*, datelined 15 January. It was entitled 'The Fever Curve of Iran as Closely Read in Stuttgart'. The sub-headline read: 'The area of US EUCOM responsibility includes the Middle East: General Huyser's mission in Tehran', by Hans Willauer. The article is worth quoting because it contains a good description of our Stuttgart command centre, and of my own functions in Europe at that time, and helps to explain why the Soviet propaganda machine reacted so strongly to my arrival in Tehran. Willauer wrote:

> In times of political crisis in Europe, in the Middle East, in North Africa, or in countries on the Persian Gulf, the US Headquarters in Stuttgart is the central agency where all reports are received. From here the messages are transmitted to Washington.
>
> The command centre in Stuttgart is constantly informed of the whereabouts of the US President, Vice-President, certain Secretaries and Commanders. Immediate contact can be established just by pushing two buttons, and within seconds a Washington switchboard answers and works the calls.
>
> Stuttgart headquarters reports directly to Washington. It is not a NATO command. Since the US Commander-in-Chief, General Haig, is also the Supreme NATO Commander, his deputy for all practical purposes acts as commander of the US Forces in Europe. Assigned to his command are the five Army divisions and the Air Force wings stationed in Ger-

many, Great Britain and Spain, as well as the 6th Fleet
operating in the Mediterranean and the US ships in the
Persian Gulf.

And this is the reason why the Deputy Commander-in-
Chief four-star General of the Air Force Robert E. Huyser,
was sent to Iran a week ago. General Huyser's official mission
is designed to assess the effects which local events could have
on the US installation in Iran. Several thousand US military
advisers are working there, and the US has established
several listening posts with electronic equipment capable of
penetrating deep into Russia.

It is not surprising, therefore, that Moscow has been
vigorously objecting to General Huyser's presence in Persia.

It was on about this date that I experienced a real surprise: H. Ross
Perot walked into our office at the MAAG. I had known this great
patriotic American for years. He came to seek our help to get Paul
Chiapparone and Bill Gaylord released from prison. Everything I had
believed about Ross was confirmed: his absolute loyalty and fearless
courage when it came to seeing that justice was done. My second
thought was what a priceless treasure he would be for some Iranian
elements.

I believed Ross that his men were innocent, and we wanted to help,
but our efforts with the Iranian military were futile. We did learn that
his men would soon be moved to Gsar Prison, where living conditions
would improve by an order of magnitude. I cautioned Ross not to give
the Iranians money unless he had his men firmly in his hands. He told
us he had Bull Simons in Tehran. I laughed—not at Ross, but at
knowing that if he got his men out of the prison, the Iranians were
defeated. Also, I assured him that if the present government failed,
there would be a prison break, and we would back his efforts all the
way (complete details of this are in Ken Follett's *On Wings of Eagles*).

2

Waiting for Khomeini

When I woke next morning, my first thought was of the military. Had they kept their discipline during the night? I was sure that if they had not, I would know as soon as I went down to breakfast. I hoped that they had stood firm and that the dawn had ushered in a new regime: a Regency Council representing the Shah, and a Bakhtiar government vested with a vote of confidence.

At breakfast I asked the Ambassador how things had gone. He said there had been no local activity overnight. The Shah had arrived satisfactorily at Aswan and been warmly received by President Sadat. He said we must now take the initiative. Could I get the military to meet with the religious leaders? I told him this would be a high priority for the day ahead. If we could get them working together, there was a far greater chance of smoking out the other destructive elements.

In addition to the Tudeh party, I was convinced that there was a whole stratum of troublemakers consisting of plain hoodlums and youngsters seeking excitement. More than fifty per cent of Iran's 34 million people were under sixteen years old: not one of them was in school (the schools were closed); they were free to do what they wanted on the streets, and could lay their hands on weapons; so they obviously had an unlimited capacity to make trouble. A third source of violence came from within the Khomeini forces themselves, who were by no means all sweetness and light. We

knew from both Iranian and US sources that some of his people
had been training with Gadhafi in Libya. A fourth faction to
contend with was the PLO. Weapons were coming in through their
channels, and they undoubtedly had their representatives in the
country, but we had very little hard information about their
activities, except that we suspected they were working under cover
of the National Front and Khomeini militants.

The morning papers were waiting for me in the office, and the
headlines were guaranteed to infuriate the generals. The *Tehran
Journal* carried the ultimate question, 'Final Farewell?', over a
picture of a very depressed Shah and Empress as they prepared to
leave. The story told of the emotion-charged airport ceremony.

A front-page article declared that the authorities would enforce
the law strictly, and that offenders were going to be punished.
Security forces would continue to guard military and other public
installations, and any attempts to attack them would be crushed.

Also on the front page was the story of Colonel Arthur W.
Heinhott, under the heading 'Suicide or Murder?'. It said his death
would be thoroughly investigated.

The back page carried the final vote by the overall parliament:
149 for Bakhtiar, 43 against and 33 abstentions. This was a
splendid start for the new government, though everything would
depend on the next few days. Khomeini was trying to undermine
the Regency Council by calling it illegal and urging its members to
resign.

The Group of Five were far more cheerful than I had expected.
They were distressed at the Shah's departure but cheered at his
warm reception in Egypt by President Sadat. I commended them
for keeping their cool, for not leaving their great country, for
refraining from any premature action, and for holding their forces
together. I said our first task must be to do some planning for
Friday, the 19th. We must establish contact with the religious
leaders. They seemed ready for a degree of cooperation, at least to
the extent of keeping the demonstration peaceful. But there were
outside factions who would try to stir up trouble. If we had an
agreement with the religious leaders, it would be easier to identify
the troublemakers, and we might be able to isolate them.

General Gharabaghi said he would get someone working on the

contacts and trying to make an appointment. That being settled, I opened a discussion on Khomeini. We had to accept that barring a miracle he was certain to return; our job was to get him delayed until Mr Bakhtiar had restored some economic stability and thus generated real public support. The Group accepted this.

I thought we could now start developing annexes for some of the plans. We should have a Public Affairs annexe to the psychological warfare plan, so that we could systematically publicize speeches like those just given by General Gharabaghi and Mr Bakhtiar. We also needed a Finance annexe for the military, as they no longer had the revenue they used to derive from oil. Our calculations showed that there was a reserve of about $10 billion, and at the current rate of expenditure this would only last about two months. If we couldn't get the oil flowing, or some other source of revenue, we could soon be out of business.

I reported Secretary Brown's promise to provide a tanker, so we had to do some intensive planning to get the oil into the military system when it reached port. I suggested that Gharabaghi should ask Bakhtiar to ensure that the tanker was safely unloaded. He agreed to do so.

General Toufanian reported that food supplies were running low. The military had learned that no less than 8,000 trucks were now held up at the Turkish border. We must try to break this bottleneck. I said we now had the customs plan, and what we had to do was implement it. Could not the military get Mr Bakhtiar's permission to take charge of the customs? They all agreed this was the thing to do.

I asked if they felt they had good reports on the morale and status of their forces, and all of them seemed to think they had. The Air Force and the Navy felt they were ninety per cent plus effective. General Badraie said the Army had suffered some desertions from the younger ranks since the hearts-and-flowers campaign, but nothing of a serious nature. In general, morale was extremely high. I believed this from my own experience. Even though the Shah was gone, I often heard the soldiers shouting *'Javid Shah'*.

We had met for nearly four hours, and our most important decision had been the agreement to press for implementation of the customs plan. This could mean food cartons via Turkey, and grain through the southern ports. It would also make it easier to get the oil tanker unloaded, and could reduce the inflow of arms, ammunition, propaganda material and other elements.

I was anxious to get back to our office and have an update on Colonel Heinhott's death. There seemed to have been no violence and no sign of anyone else being involved. It appeared that he had stepped off a chair which was still there, and within leg's reach. The investigation was not complete, but at this point we could find nothing to indicate foul play. It was a tragic occurrence; but at least this one could not be blamed on the Iranians.

We went directly to the Embassy, and I had a chance to discuss with Bill Sullivan and his people their views on the reliability of the Iranian military. The Ambassador and some of his staff were still convinced that they were a paper tiger. I felt I was better qualified and had a broader base from which to evaluate their capability. I was updated on the contacts the Embassy was having with the religious and opposition leaders. They still insisted that the Bakhtiar government and the Regency Council had to go, and when Khomeini returned he would establish his own council. There would be an Islamic Republic, and that was the only way it could be.

Ambassador Sullivan and I did not always agree on too many issues, but we both understood the importance of keeping Khomeini out of Iran as long as possible; and we both felt that Washington should make direct contact with Khomeini.

After dinner I rang Harold Brown and gave him a detailed report of the day's activity. I said I hoped the military and religious leaders would meet tomorrow. I reported on the plan to take control of customs and said this would be a major step forward for the Bakhtiar government. As to Khomeini, the only real answer was to keep him out of the country.

Secretary Brown brought up the question of a military takeover. He wondered whether there were not risks in following the priorities I had established. He feared that during the time required to give Bakhtiar a fair chance, the military might deteriorate to the point where they would no longer be an effective force, let alone able to mount a coup. I could hardly deny this, especially as we were losing a degree of capability every day. But I was still convinced that we had the strength to implement all the plans we had developed. Certainly the situation could change very rapidly. During the Shah's departure I simply didn't know whether the military would hang together or not. But they had. So I told the Secretary that though there was no way I could guarantee success, the Army was in good heart for the present. The Group of Five were becoming more competent each day, and Gharabaghi was showing more leadership. The plans were taking shape; we were getting close to the point where we could pull a military takeover, and would be in a position to do so in about a week. The Group was psychologically prepared for this in the event the constitutional government started slipping, but they would prefer to work under Bakhtiar's leadership.

Secretary Brown pressed me about General Gharabaghi and I said I had been trying to transfer the decision-making process from myself and Toufanian to him. Each day he was shouldering more of the leadership role. The Secretary asked if I really thought the military could run the country. I had to say they would not be able to run it in a sophisticated way. They'd already had one chance and had failed miserably, although we should remember they were probably constrained by the Shah. All their training and experience had kept them at arm's length from anything political. But if they did take control, and got the country back to work, they could appoint qualified civilians to manage the government offices.

Secretary Brown wanted to know my estimate of the bloodshed to be expected in the event of a takeover. I said I thought it could be rather high, but repeated my earlier view that this should be kept in perspective. The sacrifice of a single human life comes into the hardest decision category, but just as in battle, you must weigh losses against gains. Some 10,000 deaths now could save a million lives later.

I again reminded the Secretary that we were approaching another crunch-point – 19 January – and I had asked the military to make intensive preparations. Our meeting tomorrow would be devoted principally to this problem.

As I returned to the residence I had a rather upbeat feeling for a change. Secretary Brown had been very complimentary, and we had done the groundwork for some genuine progress by the Bakhtiar government. Just the same, the real ordeal was to come. The days ahead looked to me like I was about to climb Mount Everest without oxygen. When I turned back the covers, my prayers to the good Lord were that the hopes of the day would become realities.

Thursday, 18 January 1979

I met very early with the Group of Six – General Moghaddam was present, a silent figure who never contributed, just listened. Whenever he attended I always wondered if the Group were contemplating some sort of drastic action. This proved to be true today. Their morning greetings were very subdued and their spirits low. They were convinced that the Bakhtiar government would fall tomorrow. The demonstration would be massive, perhaps two million, and once they got on the streets Khomeini would declare his own provisional government. The crowd's leaders would present a proclamation to Bakhtiar saying that his government and the Regency Council were illegal, and that the Khomeini government would take over. To the Group, the presentation of a proclamation had official status. It was very hard to dissuade them of this idea. They saw this as the moment of truth. They would have to step in and implement the military option. They believed the plans were now advanced enough for them to enjoy success, for the planning had been accelerated, with staffs working twenty-four hours a day.

They also talked about external threats; they said that there was an increased level of alert in Iraq, Turkey, Afghanistan and the Soviet Union. I told them that I didn't think this was abnormal when a neighbouring country was in a state of crisis; it didn't signify any aggressive intentions. I said I had been specifically told by our Secretary of Defence that the US would take care of all external threats.

I had to weigh in pretty heavily to concentrate their minds on the planning for the demonstration. This was going to be one of the biggest groups ever seen on the streets, and if things were not done properly the Bakhtiar government would be off to a very bad start.

General Gharabaghi was passed a note, and then announced that there was to be a National Security Council meeting. Mr

Bakhtiar was obviously getting his act together. I took the opportunity to sketch out a number of possible scenarios for the 19th – seven in number, as I recall. They ranged all the way from a purely peaceful assembly to a running battle triggered off by Tudeh infiltration. Significant military action could then be needed, and it should be coordinated and directed by Mr Bakhtiar. This seemed to stimulate their thinking and caused them to shift gear into a constructive mode. We discussed at length how to address each level of violence. I suggested they should pull all the troops off the street, confining them to areas absolutely essential for both military and civilian operations. If the people on the streets wanted to kill each other, let them kill each other; if they wanted to burn buildings, let them burn buildings. The important thing was to protect those facilities which were vital to the functioning of the government. That would be sufficient show of strength.

They told me they had now fixed an appointment with the religious leaders, and General Moghaddam would be the contact. He would meet them to go over the rules for the demonstration. He would inform them that the permits would be granted, but the government would be very severe if things got out of hand. I strongly suggested that they advise Mr Bakhtiar to announce the rules in the press, on the radio and on television, warning that the consequences of violation would be severe. I also recommended that General Gharabaghi publicly address his troops so that they would understand what was expected of them and why. This would help close ranks and keep them in the fold.

Then I practically ordered them to discuss the customs plan with the National Security Council. That had to be a winner, because it went to the heart of the masses, with its promises of more food and fewer guns. It was time for the Security Council meeting, so we broke up, agreeing to meet later in the afternoon.

During the meeting Admiral Habiballahi had given me a clear briefing on which ports would be suitable for offloading the fuel tanker, so on my return to the office I prepared a wire to the Secretary of Defence on the subject. There were two ports which could handle the tanker, both with the capability of reverse pumping, to enable us to offload the fuel. One was Abadan, which could take a ship with a 27-foot draught. The other was Bandar-e-Mashur (43 feet), so we felt we could accommodate anything that he came up with. But we still had a major problem with the

National Iranian Oil Company. They had established a rigid limit on the ration delivered to the military, which of course was what had created the problem in the first place. The Group believed it was due to Tudeh party influence. I had told them that if we could contact the religious leaders we might enlist their support on this issue.

I received a message that the Secretary of Defence and General Jones were worried about the foreign military sales programme. They wanted to send my old friend Eric von Marbod to work with the Ambassador and with General Gast's people and the Iranians, to develop new thinking on these sales. I discussed the subject by phone with Ambassador Sullivan, and talked to our MAAG people about it, and no one had any objections. But we in Tehran were living under no illusions about what could be done. In Washington I think they were. The fact was that, with the banking system in a state of complete chaos, there wasn't any money available, and the Iranians had enough urgent problems without trying to think months and years ahead. It was ridiculous even to raise the problem; but if that was the way Washington wanted it, we would oblige. It would be helpful to have Eric with us anyway, as he had worked in Iran earlier in the 1970s and was very familiar with their programmes.

We were starting to write an annexe on Finances, but none of us understood exactly what was going on in the banking system. They had started operating three days a week, but they were very picky and choosy about their customers. The US could not do business with them, nor could the Iranian military. There was reason to believe that the Tudeh party was working behind the scenes, because we had reports that the banks were making prompt payments to Russia but to no one else.

Late in the afternoon I met the Group of Five after their lengthy discussions – some four hours – with Mr Bakhtiar. They had clearly gone in a very constructive frame of mind. Mr Bakhtiar had completely accepted their recommendations on issuing permits for the demonstration. They all assumed that the crowd could be two to three million strong. They knew of the mosque's instructions to keep the demonstration peaceful, but were very much alert to the fact that other parties were trying to envenom the situation. It was agreed that all troops would be pulled off the streets, and confined to the key installations. If there was any move to deliver a proclamation, it would not be accepted. It would be treated as just a piece of paper. This was a major breakthrough on the mentality that had existed.

Mr Bakhtiar had also said he would make arrangements to bring the fuel into harbour, and would commandeer some place to store it. I tried to get them to explain how he intended to do this, but they did not seem to know. I would just have to rely on blind faith that he had some connections with NIOC, or could talk some of the religious leaders into allowing it. He was also aware of the need to get the food flow started. He would back them on their plans to open up the Turkish border and the southern ports. He wanted the trucks to roll and the ships to offload the grain.

Mr Bakhtiar had sent Seyed J. Tehrani, the Chairman of the Regency Council, to Paris to talk to Khomeini. Apparently Tehrani was the man who had saved Khomeini's life under the Shah, so they thought he should be able to establish a dialogue. Tehrani's main message was to warn Khomeini of the danger of a third party; his obsessive campaign against the government could open the way for the Communists to move in and take over. This could only be prevented by a degree of cooperation between Khomeini, the government and the military.

We worked well into the evening, going over all contingencies for the following day. Then General Gast and I went back to the residence and debriefed the Ambassador.

At the Embassy was Eric von Marbod, who had just arrived from Saudi Arabia. Bringing him up to speed on the situation occupied the entire evening for all of us. Conditions in Iran were far worse than he had realized. I advised him to stay at the Embassy the next day and get all the briefings he could.

It was nearly midnight when I established the secure phone link with Washington. I updated Secretary Brown on the day's events and then discussed tomorrow's demonstration. I predicted it would be peaceful at the start, but there could be uncontrolled violence later. Yesterday in western Iran a mob had taunted the troops, and there were some killed and wounded. When I told him about Mr Tehrani, he said he had seen reports that Tehrani had resigned from the Council and was going to defect to Khomeini. That version of events was totally new to me.

He then asked me for my opinion of Bakhtiar. I said he had showed a great deal of skill and courage. From what I knew of the people available to fill that position, he was probably the best candidate. I reported that Bakhtiar was going to help get us access to the port and storage facilities, and he promised to let me know before too long how and when the fuel would be available.

I informed Secretary Brown that Eric von Marbod had arrived, but warned him not to expect any miracles, because obviously someone in Washington had failed to understand the state of chaos in Iran. He then bluntly asked if there were any real leaders among the Iranian military. Supposing the situation did call for a coup, were any of them capable of doing the job right? He particularly wanted to know about Gharabaghi, since he knew I had strong reservations about him. I had to admit that when it came to that type of crunch, I just did not feel he could do the job. I believed that Khosrodad could. I thought Toufanian could, and Badraie, and I felt pretty sure of Rabii. I had reservations about Admiral Habiballahi in this context, as I was never quite sure whether he favoured a military takeover. I told him that my constant hope was that Gharabaghi would develop to the point where he could run the show. He was getting steadily stronger, and would hopefully gain the necessary confidence, but I could by no means guarantee it.

I concluded by saying that we now had a good dialogue between Mr Bakhtiar and the military. But I was apprehensive about tomorrow. I would join the Group about 6.30 am and would be there all day, perhaps till near curfew, so I might not be able to make a report in the evening.

Secretary Brown gratuitously gave me another pat on the back, and said his colleagues in Washington had great confidence in me. They would let me know when they thought we had progressed far enough for me to return. I appreciated his comments, without feeling by any means so successful. I sometimes wondered about these pats on the back. Did they really appreciate how volatile the situation was? I had certainly achieved a good deal. But for every two steps forward with the Group, it was at least one step back, and only unremitting pressure produced even that limited progress. I wondered if they were not really exaggerating what we had been able to achieve.

As I signed off, the secure telephone operator showed me an

article from the *New York Times* with a Washington dateline. It said the US administration had reacted calmly to the departure of the Shah, but privately officials were giving the Bakhtiar government no better than a fifty-fifty chance. Those odds sounded pretty good to me, and I would have been perfectly willing to accept them. If we had that good a chance, steady pressure could tip the balance. The article went on to say that, having encouraged the Shah to take a vacation as a boost to the Bakhtiar government, the administration was not surprised by his departure. This concerned me a bit, as I was never really able to gauge how much persuasion the US government had applied to the Shah. All reports agreed that there had been some, but to this day I still do not know how hard he was pushed.

President Carter was quoted as saying in a news conference that he hoped the United States would maintain good relations with Iran. Fair comment; but it made me wonder if the President really knew how much effort Khomeini was putting into his 'hate the US' campaign. President Carter had said that a change of leaders did not mean Iran would no longer exist as a significant power. It would certainly do so, and Washington hoped that when the changes were complete, Iran would be free of any outside domination by the Soviet Union, the US or anyone else, and would still be a factor for stability. I thought we should acknowledge that we were intervening in order to try to keep the train on the track; I didn't think we should be so timid, moralistic and pure about it.

The President said he did not expect the Bakhtiar government to survive indefinitely, but he did hope for long-term stability. I didn't like this statement either, because I thought we should put our unqualified weight behind Bakhtiar. He said he personally believed the Soviet Union wanted a stable Iran. He further dismissed the once widely held US view that Iran was crucial to the security of the region. I tried my best to make sense of these statements, but to no avail. If his object was to persuade the Soviet Union to lay off, I knew it was useless; they just could not be persuaded to do good by example. Nor could any person of sense deny that Iran was vital to the security of the region.

The article went on to quote US intelligence officials as seeing no signs of any Soviet military movement along the border. The Group would be reassured to know that our intelligence people were watching the situation closely. It also quoted me as having reported yesterday that the likelihood of a coup was slim. This made me wonder once again about security leaks. The main question was whether Mr Bakhtiar could secure political support from the opposition leaders who had disavowed him earlier, and from followers of Khomeini.

With this I clocked out for the day. There were only a very few hours remaining before the dawn of a very big day.

Friday, 19 January 1979

I arrived at the Supreme Commander's Staff headquarters at 6.30 am and went straight to our office. One of the first things delivered to me was Mr Bakhtiar's speech – a welcome sight. It was articulate, firm in tone, and made it clear that things had better be orderly in today's demonstration. He gave the ground-rules for the demonstration, saying that soldiers would be withdrawn to protect vital areas, but any transgressor would be dealt with severely. He said it was time the strikes were broken, and that as from the beginning of next month of the Muslim calendar (Sunday 21 January) anyone who did not work would not receive pay. (Strikers had up to then been getting their pay, so they were not too concerned about whether they worked or not.) The whole speech was upbeat and strong. It showed he had the courage and resolution to lead the nation.

I asked if General Gharabaghi had made his address to the troops. They said, No, there was nothing in the media.

By this time the crowds were gathering, and the streets were starting to get noisy. I had noticed on the way to the compound, shortly after six o'clock, that people on motorbikes were gassing up at the filling station. These motorcyclists were the ones who carried the messages and seemed to manipulate the crowds. I often wondered just where they came from. They certainly didn't look like characters from a religious group. They just looked like a motorcyle gang, and they always operated very effectively.

We went over to General Gharabaghi's office at 7.30 am. The Group were very nervous; and their anxieties grew as the noise and

the crowds increased. I was pleased with Mr Bakhtiar's speech,
and thanked General Gharabaghi for encouraging him to make it.
I asked him why he hadn't given his own speech, and it eventually
emerged that it was because there was a convention to the effect
that any speech given by the Chief of the Supreme Commander's
Staff must end with the words 'Long Live the Shah'. I think he was
right; this would not have been a good time for him to come out
publicly with those words. But even though in his mind it was
unthinkable for him to violate the convention, I believed that it
was time for some changes.

From the tension in the air I felt the Group regarded this as a
worse day than that of the Shah's departure. Three million would
assemble, a proclamation would be delivered, and Khomeini's
men would name a new governing council which would take over
instantly.

To focus their minds I asked where we stood on planning. Their
report was positive; we had made good progress. The psychological warfare group was ready to move ahead full blast. I said we
should now work on the Prime Minister to have him put over every
achievement of his government on television, with complete
immodesty, whether it was that great or not. Whoever had done it,
he should take the credit. The increase in oil production, the
reopening of the banks – there was real psychological mileage in
these achievements. As head of the government he would get
plenty of knocks, so he should pile up a credit account.

I thought the customs plan could now be implemented, and Mr
Bakhtiar was ready to support it. I wanted some visible action and
this appeared to be the best way to get it. There would be little
bloodshed, if any, in taking over customs, and the results would be
massively popular. But we needed to win the public relations
battle, because the opposition would do their best to get the credit.
It would show the government in a position of authority. It was a
good plan, thorough and workable. We had the people designated
by name to go north and south to implement it. The military
personnel were in position. I finally persuaded the Five to get the
Prime Minister's approval to go ahead with the plan today.

Switching to Secretary Brown's tanker, I said we should get
ready to offload the fuel for military use. Controlling customs
would help, but we also had to commandeer the facilities run by
the Iranian Oil Company. We were going to have to back-pump

the fuel from the tanker into the lines normally used to load tankers. We discovered in our planning that this procedure would work, and we could pump it into the storage area at Abadan. It seemed possible from preliminary reconnaissance that NIOC might cooperate. However, we would need to be careful because once the fuel was in the tanks, they might try to take control of it themselves. We would then have to seize it by force.

Reports were now coming in that the demonstration was gathering momentum. We could see that the streets around our compound were full. Everything seemed to be very orderly, with no more than the normal amount of noise, posters, and pictures of Khomeini. But the tension within the Group was building. I proposed that we take a break, and that Gharabaghi should try to see Mr Bakhtiar to get clearance for the customs plan, and tell him we were moving ahead with the fuel. He had promised his support in both areas, but we needed permission. I suggested we move the customs people into position today, and then implement the plan tomorrow.

I then asked whether General Moghaddam had succeeded in meeting the religious leaders. The answer was 'Yes', and he had explained to them the ground-rules for the demonstration, stressing that neither the government nor the military wanted trouble; we expected the demonstrators to police themselves. He also explained what we considered the real dangers – the third element. The religious leaders had not attached great importance to this, but they acknowledged the dangers. I asked if there were any arrangements for follow-up meetings, but there were not.

We were not getting very clear reports on the demonstration so I thought we ought to have a look for ourselves; we could use a helicopter and overfly the crowd. This was agreed. General Toufanian and General Rabii volunteered to take the helicopter and make their own estimate of the size and temper of the crowd.

That left me with Admiral Habiballahi and General Badraie. I interrogated Badraie quite heavily on the morale and status of his forces. He said he had been out among his troops, and they were much better than the press had been reporting. He was struck by their neatness of dress, pride in their units, smartness in drill, the spotless state of their equipment, and their discipline and courtesy. He admitted there were some within the ranks whose loyalties were questionable, and a few who were Communist-influenced, but he seemed to think he had a good idea who they were. He confirmed that there were desertions, but far less than the media claimed.

Admiral Habiballahi gave the Navy an almost flawless report, and I think at that time he was probably right. They were not infected by mixing with the public, and they were comparatively sophisticated. Much of the oil that was being produced at the time was a result of the Navy's efforts. We hoped to expand their involvement by using them to break the strike.

Toufanian and Rabii were in really good spirits when they returned. They said the crowds were nowhere near as big as was being broadcast. They had marked on a map the areas where the marchers were assembled, and as we knew the width and length of the streets we were able to estimate the approximate size of the demonstration. We reckoned somewhere between 300,000 and 500,000 – not two to three million, as claimed by the broadcasts. This was good news. Clearly they had not enjoyed the success in getting the people out that had been prophesied, even with Khomeini's personal appeal for a bumper turnout. It had received saturation advance coverage in the newspapers, on tapes in the mosques, on tapes in the streets, on loudspeakers and bullhorns. Against that background, the event was nowhere near the overwhelming success Khomeini had hoped for.

Then Gharabaghi came back with more good news. Mr Bakhtiar had fully agreed to our implementing the customs plan. We immediately went to work reviewing it one more time, and Gharabaghi started issuing the orders for executing it. This was really heart-warming, because it was the first real, positive step forward by the government, and would be recognized as such by the whole nation.

It was good to watch the wheels in motion, with Gharabaghi masterminding the action. Badraie was busy getting the word out to his people, because it was his generals and his troops who would be taking over the customs. Habiballahi was involved with the ports, and was galvanizing his own men. Rabii was telling his people to provide whatever airlift was required.

This left Toufanian and me to ourselves, so I took the opportunity to talk to him about Eric von Marbod, whom Toufanian knew very well. I said he had come to look into the Foreign Military Sales (FMS) programme. Of course, Toufanian immediately retorted that this was a ridiculous time for such an assignment. The military had no money, nor did they know what weapons they would need in the future. I agreed, but suggested it might be as well to come up with some sort of position. If we did get the customs operating, and the other progress we were hoping for, we would need a follow-up plan to fill the gaps in equipment which had developed over the last three months.

I asked if he had had any dialogue with the new Minister of War, General Shafaqat. He said No, and showed a bit of animosity. I encouraged him to try to make contact, as we would have to work with him and we needed his full confidence. Was it not better to swallow pride for the good of the country? Shafaqat might be the link we needed, particularly since he had been appointed person- ally by Mr Bakhtiar. I mentioned that I hadn't observed any dealings between Gharabaghi and the new War Minister, and there might be some bad blood there too. I would talk to Ghara- baghi about it. Toufanian agreed to see von Marbod about the FMS programme.

By mid-afternoon most of the demonstration had reached Shahyad Square without incident, and they seemed to be dispers- ing much earlier than we had expected. It was obvious that there was not going to be any proclamation, nor would there be any challenge to the government or to the military. This too was almost unbelievable, and a tremendous relief to the Group.

It seemed like a good time to wrap up the day. I think all of us were feeling a little better than we had ever felt before as a group. We had made real progress. There had been far less trouble in the streets than anticipated, and we had something to look forward to with the plans that we had put in train. Still, I cautioned them to be careful how we handled the day's public relations aspects. We had to be sure we did not miss any opportunities, since this was almost as important as the events themselves. We must plug the message that the Prime Minister was calling the shots. This would help to swing some of the public to our side of the street.

As I left for the Embassy, the crowd almost ebbed to the level of normal traffic. On arrival, I gave Ambassador Sullivan a detailed debriefing and told him I finally had an upbeat feeling. He agreed. We both felt good about what had happened. I went over early to set up the secure communications and we got straight through to Secretary Brown.

After reporting somewhat bullishly on the day's activities, I mentioned the article which gave Bakhtiar a fifty-fifty chance of survival. I said these odds were quite encouraging, but it would be a lot more helpful if the American press could convey some impression of US Official confidence in Bakhtiar. The military would calm down a lot at every level if powerful friends were saying that Prime Minister Bakhtiar was going to make a success of it. In this battle for Iranian hearts and minds, the American press played a critical role.

I told Secretary Brown that I felt the Iranian people were getting fed up with having no work, no production, and a completely abnormal life. They were tired of turmoil and were hungry to improve their conditions. If Mr Bakhtiar could show any positive movement on the economic front, we would have our foot in the door of success. What we needed was time. The action we had programmed for tomorrow was a good first step; but I did not know how tough it would be to get the next step going. The Secretary asked if I still thought Mr Bakhtiar was the man for the job. I said I was even more sure of it than before. His speech yesterday and his recent behaviour had shown he had the character to do what was needed. Most of his problems arose from his still not having a completely established government to support him. The demonstrators and strikers were doing all they could to keep his deputy ministers out of office, using physical force. He badly needed to get them operating as a government.

Secretary Brown then asked me to tell the Group of Five, and through them Mr Bakhtiar, that the US government was concerned lest the regime swing to the left. He added, somewhat enigmatically, that Washington was not wanting to coerce Bakhtiar into a coalition with his enemies, but some coordination between the religious groups and the government would be a good thing. Next, he revealed that new instructions would be coming to me, and to Ambassador Sullivan, probably tomorrow. The President was working on them himself, and as soon as they were ready they would be dispatched. He did not anticipate any major changes, and they would be consistent with my earlier instructions, but updated.

He asked about my personal security. Apparently the President had suggested, and he agreed, that they should put an aircraft in Mehrabad Airport at my disposal in case of emergency. I had previously said that I didn't think this was necessary, because I had my own aircraft in Europe on alert.

Another reason why I felt tolerably safe was that General Rabii had promised me, right in front of all the other military leaders, that should things get too hot he would have his Air Force fly me out. I had absolute confidence that he could and would do this. At all events, Secretary Brown agreed there was no need to detach a special US aircraft for the purpose. He again thanked me for my efforts, assured me that I had been following my instructions, and said I should not be concerned about forthcoming changes.

This closed one of my better days in Iran. I went to sleep feeling more optimistic than I had at any time.

Saturday, 20 January 1979

I had breakfast early, as I wanted to meet with the Group as soon as I could. Among the newsclips from the day before, the *New York Times* had an article entitled 'Iran's Military Waits Silently'. It reported that the Iranian Army, a creation of the Pahlavi dynasty, had reacted more calmly than anticipated to the departure of Shah Mohammed Reza Pahlavi. Senior commanders, it said, appeared to have accepted what many of them had said only six weeks ago that they would never accept: orders from a civilian government. For the moment they were grudgingly giving Prime Minister Bakhtiar the benefit of the doubt. But the potential for a coup remained. At least, that was the view of Western analysts and most opposition politicians, especially if the Ayatollah Khomeini looked like supplanting Dr Bakhtiar with an Islamic Republic.

The article quoted one well-connected American as predicting fireworks next week if Bakhtiar was still unable to get people back to work. The military were not going to wait long without results; if Khomeini came back with the avowed aim of extirpating the Shah and the constitution, the Army would not stand for it. I hoped this reporter was right, because that was certainly the way we were planning. He went on to say that Iranian officers were giving a number of reasons why the Army had not taken over the country. Among the most important were:

1) A feeling among top commanders that a new military government might have no more success than that of General Azhari, whose failure one general called 'an extremely chastising experience'.

2) Loyalty to the Shah. Even in his absence they wanted to observe his wishes; and he had told his generals before leaving that he opposed a coup, because it would lead to further bloodshed.

3) The generals feared that the draftees, who make up half the Army, might not cooperate.

4) The danger that an unsuccessful coup might unleash economic and political chaos, and this would be exploited by the Soviet Union, which most generals considered the real enemy.

5) American pressure on behalf of Mr Bakhtiar. The intensity of this pressure could hardly be overstated, even though most of it had been conducted covertly. General Robert E. Huyser had been there for two weeks, meeting regularly with old friends in the military to drive home the message that a coup would command neither moral nor physical support in Washington. [The reporter was a little off-key there, because I certainly did not tell them that. What I had said was that a coup badly planned or prematurely executed would not get American support.]

The article said this theme had been echoed by the 175-member US Military Advisory Group and the 400-member Technical Assistance Group. Though the Iranian generals knew there was little the US could do to prevent a coup, they were inclined to listen to General Huyser and others because of the long American involvement in training their armed forces. But the question, one Iranian said, was: 'How long can we afford to keep listening?'

There followed the names of three people who would be involved in any coup: General Gharabaghi, General Rabii and General Badraie. The author said that Badraie controlled the troops, but would do exactly what the Shah told him. I was not so sure of that. I thought he would be quite capable of pulling a coup if he felt it was the right thing to do.

An article in the *Washington Post* was headed 'US Optimistic on Iranian Negotiations'. It said that talks were going on between all the parties, and the Carter administration believed they could lead to stabilization and a new national consensus. This was supposedly from a US official, but it was all news to me.

After breakfast I went to the Supreme Commander's Staff compound and asked to see General Gharabaghi right away, without waiting for the Group. Gharabaghi told me to come right over, and my first question was: How is the customs plan progressing? He told me that they had called it off.

I nearly went into a state of shock. I was not sure I could even believe what I had heard. I said: 'You dispatched the generals to implement it, and then you called it off?' His reply was that the opposition had relaxed their control on customs. They were allowing the trucks to cross the Turkish border so the generals did not consider it necessary to proceed with the plans.

I was furious, and not very polite. This was a body-blow for me, and I demanded an investigation to determine if there had been a leak. How did the opposition reach its decision to relax control? Was it coincidental? General Gharabaghi elected not to answer this. I asked him if the cancellation had been cleared with Mr Bakhtiar and again he declined to answer. I don't know the answer to this day, but I have never believed that Bakhtiar cleared it. Getting the food in was only one of the purposes of the customs plan. Just as important was to stop the flow of guns and ammunition. Perhaps more important than either was to show the nation that Mr Bakhtiar had the capability to govern. Yet it had been called off.

I was so incensed that I did not linger with Gharabaghi. I told him I would be back for our meeting around mid-morning. He knew that I had no intention of fooling with him much longer.

Back at my office, I was just starting to review the national papers when Major Ray Burnette announced that General Toufanian and General Rabii would like to see me. This was highly unusual because they had never before been to our office, and the two of them amounted to a delegation. When they came in they both looked physically shaken. The first thing they said was that

General Gharabaghi had turned in his resignation. It flashed through my mind that maybe this was a good thing; he never seemed to have the backbone to do what was needed. But what had happened? They explained that Prime Minister Bakhtiar had put out a press release the night before, declaring that he was going to do the best he could to make the government succeed, but that if he should fail, the country would be turned over to the military. They said this was what had caused Gharabaghi to submit his papers. They were really worried about it, and said it must not happen. It would be disastrous, just as they were getting unity. I must go straight to Gharabaghi and get him to withdraw his resignation.

I said maybe the three of us should talk it over, but they said No, they had already talked to Admiral Habiballahi and General Badraie, and all of them agreed. They had even talked to General Khosrodad. They were unanimous that I must go and persuade Gharabaghi to withdraw his resignation. I suggested that either one of them would make a good Chief of the Supreme Commander's Staff, but to my surprise they both rejected this thought.

I agreed to talk to Gharabaghi and the three of us went straight to his office, walking right in without ceremony. I asked him whether he had in fact resigned. He said not officially, but he had just telephoned one of the leaders of parliament to notify him of his intention.He had already told Mr Bakhtiar and two other parliamentary leaders. He just could not face the prospect of a military takeover, or the responsibility of leading it.

I came back hard and insisted that as military people, that was just the type of action we should expect to be called on to take. Did he want to keep clear of any role in government, as I had suspected for a long time? Or was he suffering a Persian pique because he had not been consulted by Mr Bakhtiar before the press release? Either motive would be enough to trigger off an emotional person like Gharabaghi. It might even be a combination of the two – the first the real reason, the second the excuse.

I laid into him, and told him that I thought it was completely irresponsible to resign. It was disloyal to the Shah, disloyal to his country, and I was not too sure that God would look favourably on it. He owed it to his nation to do the best he could to help it to survive. With the others chiming in persuasively, I told him that all the top brass wanted him to lead them, and to represent them with the Prime Minister. But I was not sure we had made any impression on him. He was very tight-jawed and did not seem to be responding. Moreover, I was having a bit of a wrestling match with myself, because I was not convinced that it would not be a good thing if he did resign.

Mr Bakhtiar's statement had been very wise. He was establishing the bottom line, and giving clear notice to Khomeini that if he did not change his tune, the Army might have no alternative but to move in. I doubt if Gharabaghi understood the pressures under which Mr Bakhtiar had to make some of his decisions.

I decided I must immediately discuss the position with Ambassador Sullivan. I was still in two minds about the whole thing. Clearly it could cause a serious dislocation just when it seemed we were making progress. At the same time there was no question in my mind that if we did have to pull a military takeover, Gharabaghi was not the man to head it. So if the bottom line was reached, we were anyway going to have to put somebody else in charge. Either way I felt really deflated.

At the Embassy I explained to Ambassador Sullivan that the customs plan had been cancelled. He was as mystified as I was; but it did not seem to shock him as it did me. He acted as though he almost expected it. This was probably due to his lack of confidence in the military. Working with them daily, I had much greater faith in them than he did. Then I reported Gharabaghi's resignation, giving both sides of the coin. We came to the conclusion that on balance the best thing would be for Gharabaghi to stay on, so the Ambassador called Mr Bakhtiar's office and made an appointment to discuss the situation with him. To my knowledge this would be the first time the Ambassador had visited Mr Bakhtiar since my arrival in Iran.

When he left for the meeting I took the opportunity to review the message traffic. A message had arrived from Secretary Brown giving my new guidance. It said that the basic guidance remained unchanged; we would continue to support the Bakhtiar government and urge the military to do so on a united basis. But it went on to say that the success of the Bakhtiar regime required dialogue with the other non-Communist factions. Bakhtiar needed additional suport, not least from the religious groups, and therefore talks with these groups could be helpful. There was no question of transforming the government into a coalition with Khomeini, but it needed a wider base and more support than it had at present.

Clearly a key criterion in these manoeuvres was the regime's attitude to the great powers. My object should be to try to prevent either a slide away from the West or a fragmentation of the military. Our basic goal was a stable Iran, which would genuinely cooperate with the West. Since that was the route I had all along been pursuing, I was not absolutely certain why the new guidance was necessary. Possibly Ambassador Sullivan had been recommending a coalition government with Khomeini. Washington clearly rejected this option. In their view there should be dialogue with Khomeini but nothing more intimate.

Another item which astonished me was an outgoing message from the Embassy to the State Department evaluating the Iranian military. It said they were just a paper tiger, they had no capability and they were ready to disintegrate. There were massive desertions, and the moment things started to get rough they would all go over to the religious side. If Khomeini came back, practically the whole lot would defect.

This evaluation had been made without the detailed information at my disposal which included daily reports on status and morale from all the military leaders, as well as advice from General Gast and his staff. I had found that when called on to do anything, the military responded well. Even with the Shah's departure they had maintained their structure, discipline and deportment. I believed the dedication was there. The media was talking of 2,000 to 3,000 desertions each day, but this was rubbish. A more realistic figure was probably 100 to 200, out of some 450,000. This left us with far more than we could even need, and therefore a high level of quality. As history has often shown, with prudent planning it does not take a great many troops to seize control of a country. The plans we had drawn up were very precise, and did not require us to take on the masses. The strategy was to defend the key installations; against such dispositions the masses could not hope to dislodge them. We had no intention of trying to dominate each city and thoroughfare; that would have taken a large number of troops and entailed a heavy loss of life. This way was both easier and more effective.

I thought it best to make my call to the Secretary of Defence without delay. I wanted to tell him what was going on before there were any leaks, and before they could get blind-sided. Secretary Brown was away so I talked to Under-Secretary Charles Duncan and the Chairman. I explained in detail about the Bakhtiar press release and its effect on General Gharabaghi. When Mr Duncan asked what the other military leaders thought of it, I told him they were very upset, and wanted us to try to stop General Gharabaghi from resigning. Considering that two of them – Rabii and Toufanian – would have done the job superbly, I had to take their support for Gharabaghi seriously. Charlie Duncan asked me who would be the best person to take the job if Gharabaghi did resign. I told him that I wasn't ready to answer that question yet. I said I would call them back as soon as I got word from Ambassador Sullivan.

When the Ambassador came back it was obvious from his expression that he had been successful. Mr Bakhtiar had agreed that it was right to have General Gharabaghi withdraw his papers. He himself had already done much to persuade Gharabaghi not to resign.

The phone rang, and it was Mr Duncan and General Jones anxiously awaiting the outcome. I told them of the Ambassador's success and we ended our conversation. But within half an hour General Jones was on the line again, telling me of Secretary Brown's movements the following day. I took the opportunity to say that I had read the Embassy evaluation of the Iranian military, sent to the State Department, and totally disagreed with it. I told him why at some length, with reference to their smartness, their orderly behaviour during the demonstrations, and the relatively small number of desertions. Bad morale in an army is almost impossible to conceal, since the men themselves will not cooperate in doing so. But things could go sour if Khomeini were to return right now. I expressed concern about the lack of sophistication among the military leadership and the uncertainty I had about Gharabaghi if political intervention were needed. Much the best way was to keep all decisions directed by Mr Bakhtiar. With that we signed off.

Several other significant developments had been taking place. First, Mr Bakhtiar released some 160 political prisoners that day, which I viewed with mixed emotions. Like the Shah he was trying to steer the nation on to a more liberal and popular course. That was fine in principle, but many of these prisoners were real troublemakers, and I wasn't sure we wanted to see them on the streets again just now.

Second, the Ayatollah Shariat-Madari announced a change in the customs procedure, on the grounds that there was a serious lack of supplies in the markets. This was certainly true of essential goods, such as baby food, and the Ayatollah had a good case for calling for the immediate release of perishable and essential goods for the people. He was one of the more moderate ayatollahs, and had friends in the military. But it made me wonder once more whether the opposition had known in advance about the military's plans to crack down on the customs agency.

Third, the Minister of Health and Welfare, Manouchehr Razmara, told the press that his department was bankrupt. He said that its annual budget, 100 million rials, had been variously mis-spent, wasted and embezzled to the point where he was going to have to borrow simply in order to make routine payments. The doctors and pharmacists had not been paid for eight months. That should hardly have startled him, as the government had not collected any of its bills since last September.

Dr Razmara blamed the whole situation on the corruption of previous ministers. He took a swipe at America by saying that the computer centre had consumed $100 billion over the past two years and was still a long way from being operational, in spite of being manned by 200 highly paid Americans. But most of his accusations were aimed at his predecessors and their luxurious life-style: their helicopters, boats and pornographic taste in office decorations. Doctors were getting away with charging private citizens a bonus for treatment, which upset the system because treatment was supposed to be free.

The truth was that this corruption was happening in all sectors, owing to the collapse of the economy. The remedy was to increase oil production to the point where there would be enough to export. In making our plan to take over the industry, we had calculated that the level of production required to satisfy the needs of the country and to begin exporting was about two million barrels a day. So far production had been less than one million barrels. Unless this changed, the economy was on course for disaster.

It had been reported that the Holy City of Qom had been under total Islamic rule since Friday. We knew for sure that the military had been in full control until Thursday. Our report said that half a million people had defied martial law on Friday, and the soldiers had withdrawn and handed over to the Ayatollah Shariat-Madari. This was not too disastrous or fatal to our planning, as there was nothing in Qom that the government needed, and therefore no necessity for punitive action. We could save that for more essential elements. But things were heating up. We had reached the point where there were now demonstrations every day; the only variable was their size. When Khomeini called a special day, as on the 19th, they were pretty noisy. Even on the other days they ran into thousands, and were always noisy. Every night there was chanting, punctuated by automatic weapons fire.

I spent the evening with Eric von Marbod. He and I had been friends for many years, and had worked on some high-priority and important missions together. In the days when Jim Schlesinger was Secretary of Defence, the US got interested in increasing the capability of the military in Cambodia. Schlesinger commissioned Eric and me to work with Ambassador Dean on building up the Cambodian Air Force. Eric was a good man if you wanted something done, done quickly and done right. He had no use for restraints or bureaucratic processes, and cut through red tape right to the heart of the problem. He was an extremely brilliant man.

Our next project had been during the evacuation of Saigon. He went in with two or three people to try to get out as much American equipment as possible before the country fell. I remember one of his last calls to me after getting another planeload out; in the background I could hear the guns firing and the bombs bursting. When I told him to pack up and leave, he said, No, they were just about to get another planeload going. He never wasted a minute.

I was pleased to see Eric now, and to have the opportunity to discuss with him all aspects of our grim situation. I had to explain that there was no organized element in Iran with whom he could do business on an FMS programme. The military had no money, and were so involved in day-to-day problems that they had no time to think ahead. General Toufanian was reluctant to make commitments. I didn't think he would want to sign any memorandum of understanding for the future. But Eric was well known to him, and something might just be done if General Gharabaghi could be brought in to speed things along.

In any case I thought Eric's visit a good idea, if only to have him back a first-hand report of how things really were. Washington still did not seem to have grasped how little control the government had of anything apart from the military installations.

Sunday, 21 January 1979

I had breakfast with the Ambassador and Eric. None of us could see any grounds for optimism, and it was not easy to come up with any game plan for the next stage. Eric had an appointment with General Toufanian. I was due to meet the Group at 8.30 am and went straight to our office; I decided to play the Iranian game myself, and waited for General Gharabaghi to call for me. I had come down very hard on him the day before about his resignation, so I felt it was up to him to make the first move.

Word came through almost at once that he would like to see me immediately. General Badraie and General Rabii had already arrived by helicopter, since they had some way to travel and traffic was bad. Admiral Habiballahi's headquarters were nearby, so he came by car, as did General Toufanian.

When I entered, the Group were gathered around General Rabii, who was holding a newspaper and looked very shaken. He shook the paper at me and I asked what on earth was wrong. He showed me the headlines, which proclaimed in large print: 'Imam Khomeini Arrives Friday'. This was the *Tehran Journal*. It said that the exiled spiritual leader would be back on Friday, and planned to celebrate weekly prayers in a Tehran mosque.

All the Group were visibly upset, and as usual Rabii was the most emotional. He always expressed himself more articulately than the others, except for Toufanian; the difference was that Toufanian had absolute control of himself, and only used his emotions for effect. Gharabaghi was very composed, though occasionally he would flare up a little, as he did this morning. The massive Badraie was calm, collected and almost stone-faced. Habiballahi was in absolute control of himself all the time. But all of them had a look of defeat and hopelessness.

The article went on to say that all the signs in Paris were that the Ayatollah was preparing to leave. He himself had not specifed a date, but had announced: 'I will join you very soon and, with God's help, will be in your service in a matter of days.' It appeared that Mr Yazdi, one of his principal assistants, had named the day. The article pointed out that this spelt trouble for Prime Minister Bakhtiar. An associate of Mr Bakhtiar had said that he was ready to be friends with Khomeini, but that Khomeini did not have a high opinion of the Bakhtiar government. If some accommodation could not be reached between the two, or at least between Khomeini and the Army, there would be a new eruption of violence.

Mr Yazdi also warned that there would be an early appointment of a five-man revolutionary council to replace the Regency Council. There was no word of any meeting of the Ayatollah with Mr Tehrani, head of the Regency Council, who had gone to Paris on Thursday. But it was reported that former US Attorney General Ramsey Clark was going to Paris to try to see Khomeini.

As may be imagined, this had a real impact on me. Here was a problem which needed immediate attention, and the adrenalin started to flow. The Group all argued that if Khomeini returned on Friday – five days away – it was all over; the moment he set foot on Iranian soil, that was the end of the Shah's regime, and the lives of all associated therewith. The armed forces would disintegrate.

I met this chorus head-on in very sharp terms, which I found was the only way to get their attention, although it was not my nature. I said I had been through all this just the day before with their leader. If they didn't pull themselves together and operate as a team, I might as well leave. I said that I too had high-priority work to do, and we in the United States had defence problems of our own. I was glad if I could help them; but if I was not being any help, then I would go straight back to my job at headquarters in Stuttgart.

The first one to challenge me was General Rabii. In very emotional terms he said that if the United States was backing them so strongly why couldn't I do something about keeping Khomeini away? Rabii had a way of making me feel a bit as if we were shirking our duties, and he was very adroit at it. I always had to grab hold of myself and think before I came back at him. But now I calmly told him that, as he knew full well, this was not within the principles of the United States administration. If the military were so keen to eliminate Khomeini why didn't they pay someone to do it themselves? There was no response, so I said that that was enough about that, and why didn't we get on with our business?

I turned to Gharabaghi, and said that while I thought he owed me an explanation as to why he tried to resign, I also wanted to express my appreciation that he had been man enough to change his mind. He was very frank, and went through his conversations with Mr Bakhtiar. His version was much the same as Ambassador Sullivan's, so I knew he was telling me the truth. He said his complaint to Bakhtiar was that he, as the Chief of the Supreme Commander's Staff, had not been told in advance what the Prime Minister was doing. The PM had made public statements without coordinating them with the military first. Several of his announcements had a direct impact on the military, but they had not received any warning. Again, Bakhtiar had replaced a provisional governor in the south with a military man without consulting Gharabaghi.

I could see that Gharabaghi had a real reason for feeling offended. But his reaction had been excessive. I felt sure that what had really triggered off his resignation was the fear of having to lead a military coup. But on balance, the episode was not wholly disastrous, because at least it cleared the air between the two men and started up a more regular dialogue.

I asked about the readiness of the plans. They said it was a good moment to review them because they had a National Security Council meeting that night. Mr Bakhtiar had asked them to report on two things: the status of their forces and the status of their plans. They were getting a thorough feedback from all installations about morale, discipline and numbers of deserters. They were rather upbeat about the plans, and I had a feeling that we were at last at the stage where the basics were all in position, and we were now down to refinements. They seemed rather pleased about what they were going to be able to report to Mr Bakhtiar. I reminded them that it was useless to have plans if they were not implemented when the time was right. I further told them that I still could not understand the cancellation of the customs plan. They did not offer any explanation.

I reminded them that we were going to have to settle down and think rationally about Khomeini's return. They would have to adjust their ideas and maybe accept the fact that, if he wanted to return as a religious leader, it was probably quite legal. I pushed them for more coordination with the religious leaders so that at least both sides would understand each other, and the opposition would know that the Army meant business. They claimed there was a continuing dialogue with the religious factions, but it sounded a bit vague. It was next to impossible to get them to talk about, think about, or do any planning about the return of Khomeini, although if the *Tehran Journal* was right, we were going to have to act pretty quickly. We would need to come up with plans based on those for the previous crisis, when we kept the troops off the streets but maintained a higher state of alert, so that we had them under tight control.

One encouraging sign was that most of the ministers had got into their offices today, which had never happened under this government. There were more people at work than ever. Some of the opposition strike leaders had been encouraging people to go back to work on a limited basis, and strictly for internal purposes. The banks were still only doing domestic business, with rare exceptions; the refineries were producing more for internal use, but nowhere near enough for the nation, let alone export.

I made a strong recommendation that they approach the Prime Minister at the Security Council to have a pro-government demonstration. They seemed reluctant for fear of failure. We pointed out that if they got six people in the street, it would be more visible support than had been exhibited so far. I thought it would work because I thought there were millions that would support the constitutional government. They finally agreed to discuss it with the Security Council.

We had an important success in our efforts to pay the troops in cash. The government, having no control of the banks, had so far been unable to do this. Previously payment had been made by depositing to accounts by means of a computer programme, which was hardly conducive to morale now, with the banks not functioning. We decided to beat the system by having money printed outside the country, bringing it in by aircraft and paying the troops in cash. This procedure was just coming into effect, and was naturally well received.

We discussed the fuel situation, because we still had extensive shortages in the military. The official reports were saying that the

Tehran refinery was producing 200,000 barrels a day. At Abadan there was progress on getting rid of the heavy oils; they had already loaded one tanker, and had another one lined up. Getting rid of that heavy oil was a godsend, because it would dramatically increase the Abadan capability from 160,000 barrels a day to 240,000. The Khuzestan oilfields were producing about 475,000 barrels a day. But this still totalled only about fifty per cent of the country's winter requirements.

The Group had dealings with the National Iranian Oil Company because the Navy was helping to run the oilfields; but they still did not have enough leverage to get their allocation increased. They were nettled by press reports that a French firm was making a strong bid to run the oilfields. This suggested an opportunist French link-up with the Ayatollah Khomeini.

I could get no further action out of them on customs, as they seemed to think they had done all that was necessary. They were not ready to move on the oil either, because they thought that with the rise in production, this problem was solving itself. That was all very well; but they didn't have *control*, and oil was critical to both the economy and defence. The blunt fact was that the NIOC were not sympathetic to the Bakhtiar government, and they were determining what was produced and how it was distributed. Unless the Group took control, the opposition could pull the plug at any moment.

Back at the Embassy I reviewed the message traffic and the news for the day. I got some mention in both the *New York Times* and the *Washington Post*, but the item that caught my attention was from *Pravda*. They said I was there to take drastic action, if necessary, to stop the revolutionary forces from taking over. This sort of talk could only increase the threat to my own safety, because everything they put out got pretty good play in the Iranian papers, and was piped in over the radio.

Reporting to Secretary Brown, I said I thought there had been one or two pluses out of yesterday's debacle. For one thing, there was now a better understanding between Prime Minister Bakhtiar and General Gharabaghi. The Secretary asked if I had any new thoughts about the cohesion of the military: was it really there? I repeated my reservations on Gharabaghi, but said I had a lot of confidence in Badraie, Rabii, and Toufanian. If necessary, any one of them could take over.

I reported on the morning session, when the Group had shown me the news of Khomeini's return, and demanded that the United States do something. I had the feeling that he agreed, and wished there were something he could do, but he gave me no encouragement. He said he would have another look at the situation. I again told him that Friday was too soon for Khomeini, and asked at least to be kept informed of his movements. Secretary Brown promised to increase vigilance on Khomeini's activities to ensure that we were not surprised when he did return.

He spoke of the US military forces in the area, and suggested that some of those in Europe might be put on alert. I advised him against this, arguing that the presence of our naval forces in the Indian Ocean and the F-15 visit to Saudi Arabia were enough for now. We had to keep things in balance, and reserve the next level of military action for any external threat. He was concerned about our intelligence sites in Iran. The press had reported that one was operating and one was closed. I told him that Ambassador Sullivan and I were watching this situation closely.

Secretary Brown then hit me with one that puzzled me for a while. He expressed concern that the Iranian military were proving a weak force, and less supportive of the government than we had hoped. That set me back a bit; but then it occurred to me that he had been reading the report submitted by Ambassador Sullivan after his meeting with Bakhtiar and Gharabaghi. It was not very complimentary to the armed forces in general, nor to the military leadership. I opposed this opinion in some detail. Plenty of things were wrong, but in working with the military daily, I found that corrective action was being taken on most occasions. They had taken stringent measures against troops who were causing problems or breaking the law. They had also come a long way towards keeping their troops informed; in fact, they had again broken precedent by establishing a military newspaper for this precise purpose. They were gaining strength in areas they had ignored in the past.

After we signed off, I got to thinking about Secretary Brown's offer to increase the US military presence in the area. Even though it was into the small hours, I decided to put my thoughts on paper and send him a message in the morning. The Secretary had said it was my boss, Al Haig, who had been pressuring to increase the US military in the area. Al had suggested that they send the aircraft carriers, introduce additional US forces and bring the European forces to a higher state of alert. I concluded that I should send a wire to Al Haig as well as Harold Brown, so that they would both have my thoughts.

In my message I gave two objections to these proposals. First, I thought that increasing the alert status was premature. We should wait until we had definite indications of a new external threat. True, unfriendly forces were hovering around the country like vultures, ready to dive, and the internal threat from the leftist elements was high. But we ought to save our blue chips until the external threat was perceptibly higher. Second, when it came to moving forward carriers and other forces, I thought we should bear in mind the request of Prime Minister Bakhtiar not to have too visible a US presence. It could certainly be counter-productive unless we were going to come through with real support. The opposition were playing him as a US puppet, and there was a great deal of anti-US feeling about. We should have been more forthcoming months before. *If we were going to move now, it should be all the way.* A limited increase in forces sounded a nice idea, but it was a day late and a dollar short.

I thought Washington should understand the true threat, which I headed: 'Now for the Real Cruncher'. I said the greatest potential for disaster would be the early return of Khomeini. While a large segment of the armed forces would remain loyal to the Shah, there were quite a number who were pro-Khomeini, and even a few Communists. The armed forces were convinced that the return of Khomeini meant the absolute finish of the Shah.

I took the liberty of outlining a number of scenarios. I started with the most desirable, but probably the most unlikely: that Khomeini would return in the role of a religious leader and not immediately try to pull the rug from under Bakhtiar. Even here, the reaction of the military could be somewhat unpredictable. But I would expect that they would stand firm and take no action.

The other end of the spectrum was that Khomeini would go straight for the jugular vein of the Bakhtiar government. In this situation the reaction of the military would depend to a large degree on Bakhtiar's response. If he ordered them to take action in his support, I believed they would obey. I thought that in doing so they would have considerable success in securing the vital elements of power, oil, communications, water and customs. There could be considerable bloodshed.

If Mr Bakhtiar did not use the military and just went down the tube, telling the military to take over, then the reaction could be different. General Gharabaghi would probably fold up at that point. The three Service chiefs would want to do their best to take over the country, and probably only a minority of senior officers would follow Gharabaghi's line. The real problem was that even if the military were successful in seizing control, what then? Did they have anyone sophisticated enough to act as head of the government and administer the country politically as well as economically?

Such were my thoughts. I particularly wanted Al Haig to have them, partly as a comment on his own opinions, and partly also because he worked very closely with the French, who seemed to be figuring more prominently in the equation.

I turned in for the night with the same hope and prayer that I had had every night: that tomorrow would be the magic day when we could really get the military and Bakhtiar marching forward in step. So far the improved conditions could not be attributed either to Bakhtiar or to the military. It was the opposition leaders who were ready to ease conditions, knowing that they had control and could change the situation to meet their needs. It was high time the Bakhtiar government showed it had some muscle.

Monday, 22 January 1979

At breakfast, reviewing yesterday's American newspapers, I was impressed by a couple of points in a *Washington Post* article. It said that while the religious leaders were pretty well aligned in opposition to the Shah, some of them thought that Khomeini was going too far. Their religion required them to monitor the actions of the state, but not to enter politics. I wondered if there wasn't some way we could put that thought to work. The article also said that to people in Paris who had met Khomeini, it was obvious that his fifteen years in Iraq and four months in France had left him completely out of touch with developments in Iran. Since he had been away, the changes had been tremendous.

Another message that caught my eye was the press wrap-up out of London. It quoted *Pravda* of 20 January:

> A military Ambassador, General Huyser, has been operating for several weeks now in Tehran, alongside US Ambassador Sullivan. This is a further instance of direct interference in events in Iran. The US press does not conceal that Huyser has been sent to instruct, and is instructing, Iranian generals in how to combat popular demonstrations. Political observers see some parallels between the way events are taking place now and the coup in Iran in 1953. At that time the Shah also left the country temporarily in order not to get in the way, and later returned.

This put my thought processes into overdrive, because the Shah was still in Egypt and had not departed as planned. I didn't know if he was just enjoying President Sadat's company or if he was loitering with intent to return to his country. I was certain that he was in contact with his generals, even though they denied it. I knew that General Rabii had been talking to his plane crew because he admitted it, although he said it was only about flight plans. I was confident that there was a direct line through to the Shah, who undoubtedly knew of Khomeini's plans to return, and may have thought he should be on hand in case things started getting out of control.

On arrival at the office, I picked up the *Tehran Journal*, which had very heartening headlines for a change. At the top of the front page was Bakhtiar's pronouncement: 'I am the most powerful of all Iranian Prime Ministers.' Just below, in bold print: 'I have no intention of resigning – Bakhtiar.' Under a picture of the Prime Minister at the microphone, shaking his finger, he was reported as repudiating rumours that he might be resigning: 'I am going to remain in the stronghold of the Constitution and protect it.' He called upon the people to break the strikes and get back to work, saying that a democracy needs calm and work: 'I am convinced that the majority of the people are tired of strikes and demonstrations, which represent very serious dangers for the country's economy.' He described the strikes as anti-democratic, and said they had caused more damage to the nation than all the thieves over the last fifteen years.

He gave the press a stiff lecture about the publication of 'poison messages'. He also said he would not tolerate any further press insults against the Army. He attacked people who claimed to be patriots but indulged in activities contrary to the best interests of the country, and declared: 'Under no circumstances will I abandon the responsibility of protecting the Constitution, and I will not allow this historic land to disintegrate.'

Bakhtiar said that the strikers had put forward two sets of demands. The economic ones had already been fulfilled, and he was now in the process of meeting the political ones. So what else did they want? He accused them of getting their orders from outside the country, and described these elements as 'traitors to the land'. He went on to say that he needed a strong central government, so as to cope with the country's enemies and safeguard Iran's survival. He wasn't worried about a foreign military invasion, because that would not be practical. But neighbouring countries would almost certainly want to cash in if there was an explosion inside Iran.

Referring to one of the slogans chanted in a recent march – '*Bakhtiar Bi Ekhtiar*' (Bakhtiar without power) – he said this was a total fallacy. He was the 'most powerful among all Prime Ministers who had held office in Iran'. Another calumny going round was that there was a shortage of wheat in the country. 'The Iranian nation is hereby informed that sufficient wheat has been purchased and imported, and with the Army's help is being speedily unloaded and transported to various parts of the country by lorries. There is no cause for concern, and you may rest assured that this government, which has based its programme on complete honesty with the Iranian people, will itself inform the people if there is an emergency and seek their assistance. The Iranian nation is therefore asked to pay no heed to groundless rumours, and to have full confidence in the government's honesty.' In a final blast he declared: 'All poppycock about my resignation is utterly baseless. I shall never resign and let the country advance to an absolutely unknown destination.' He would stand by the Constitution.

All this was most helpful to me. I could see opportunities to get the Group working on several of the points he had raised.

There was a front-page account of yesterday's Communist demonstration, headlined 'Marxists Hold First Mass March'. The paper estimated the turn-out at around 5,000 students from left-wing organizations, centred mainly on the University. One of their slogans was 'Neither For God Nor Against God'. They declared that they were not going to exchange the tyranny of the Shah for an Islamic dictatorship. The march left a curiously ambiguous impression. In spite of the anti-religious slogans, some of them were carrying Khomeini pictures, which seemed very odd. This did not prevent them being heckled by religious groups and Khomeini people along the route, many of whom shouted that they were 'Savak agents'. Others yelled 'Communists are traitors', and 'Communism has no place among our people'. When they reached Shah Avenue, a mullah appeared with a loudspeaker and called on them not to shout religious slogans or to carry Khomeini's picture. Another Islamic group piped up with '*Hezb Faghat Hezb-O-Allah*'. (The only political party is the party of God.)

The paper carried a perceptive but depressing economic review. It appeared that all the operations of the National Iranian Copper Industries (NICI) had come to a halt, because of its inability to clear the material through customs. Worse, one of its foreign employees had been killed, and the foreign subcontractors had decided to evacuate their employees for safety. Out of 174 technicians, only 27 remained, and they were all scheduled to leave within the week. It was impossible to operate the copper industry, or almost any other, without foreign technicians and help. Now everybody was leaving for his own safety.

Today's meeting included General Moghaddam. After the formalities I drew their attention to Prime Minister Bakhtiar's speech, and applauded its strength and leadership; he had supported the military, and they should respond in like manner. I told General Gharabaghi that if I were in his shoes, I would go straight to the press and make a statement that the military totally agreed with Mr Bakhtiar. I would say that the troops were loyal, and they were going to give him every ounce of their support. Somewhat to my surprise he immediately agreed to do so. This was a real turnabout, because he had always had a blockage about press statements. I chalked it up as progress.

I referred to the Prime Minister's statement that wheat was being distributed by army lorries, and told them they should capitalize on the public relations aspect of this. It turned out to be a very sore point with General Toufanian. They were his trucks, and he had personally instituted the programme to get the wheat distributed; but Khomeini's people had brazenly slapped their own signs on the trucks and passed the word that the wheat came from Khomeini. This threw General Toufanian into a frenzy, as he had no idea how to cope with it. I told him that he must beat Khomeini's people at their own game.

General Gharabaghi then reported that Khomeini's return had been discussed at last night's meeting of the Security Council, and Mr Bakhtiar had agreed to organize a pro-government demonstration to coincide with Khomeini's arrival. I took exception to this; to have two factions on the streets on one day, at a time of extreme emotion, would cause nothing short of a civil uprising. I strongly suggested the demonstration be as soon as possible, but before Khomeini's return. We needed to show visible support for the established government.

Bakhtiar had said he was going to warn Khomeini that if he came back as a political leader, it would be unconstitutional. Khomeini had said he was coming back strictly as a religious leader and would only monitor the government; but this was far from convincing. General Rabii said he had suggested to Bakhtiar that if Khomeini approached Tehran by air, they should intercept his plane and divert it to the southern part of the country. Rabii thought this would make it much easier to control the crowds, and would give Khomeini less opportunity to take over the government offices. There seemed to have been considerable discussion about this, but no decision. I got some encouragement here, because at least they were discussing Khomeini's return instead of going off like a firecracker at the very mention of it. Mr Bakhtiar had managed to concentrate their minds.

I asked if they had made any progress on getting petroleum for the military. It seemed Mr Bakhtiar had told them that he had now made arrangements with the NIOC for the approaching US tanker to offload and that transport had been arranged for national distribution. They did not appear to know whether this was going to be by pipeline or truck.

In answer to General Gharabaghi I gave them a rundown on the highly delicate customs situation, as reported to me by our Embassy staff. I said I had been watching closely the activities of

Ayatollah Shariat-Madari, who had been asking customs workers to show more compassion about clearing foodstuffs. Their reply was that they had never refused to clear foodstuffs, or medicine, and had even been willing to work on Fridays, which was their day of rest and prayer, in order to bring essential goods to the people. They told Shariat-Madari that from the time they went on strike on 5 November, they had cleared into the country some 17 million kilograms of foodstuffs including butter, cheese, meat, eggs and milk powder. They admitted that some trucks had still not been unloaded, but this was because the cargo included arms, ammunition and teargas containers. They said their basic orders from Khomeini were to refuse to touch that type of goods; so they claimed that the government was to blame for the hold-up in unloading these ships and trucks.

When we made our plans for taking over customs, we discovered there were about 6,000 employees involved. There were twenty-six different customs posts around the country, six of them in Tehran. The point that I wanted to make was that the talk about arms, ammunition and teargas containers was probably true, but they weren't being stopped; they were going straight to the opposition forces. Also the claim of letting in foodstuffs was far from a true story. Many trucks and ships were still waiting for entry.

Another topic which I suggested they should take up with the Prime Minister was the infiltration of saboteurs. We had intelligence reports that there was a definite contact between the Palestinians, Libya, and Lebanon, and that they were training Iranian guerrillas who would soon be coming back into the country. According to our reports, up to 2,000 had already been trained. We were also informed that they were being provided with Russian arms and financed by Gadhafi. We had reliable information that Khomeini had been in direct contact with the PLO, and with elements in Libya, within the last three weeks, and we knew that several Iranian Marxists had turned up in Palestinian camps in Southern Lebanon.

I welcomed the fact that the Marxists had now appeared in the open. It certainly proved they existed, and were not a figment of the military imagination. We should be able to make some form of common cause with the religious leaders against this menace, whose aims were clearly in direct conflict with those of the Iranian people. They had been skilfully manipulating and orchestrating a lot of the religious elements' activities, and their real objectives ought to be exposed.

I asked if the Group knew why the Shah had prolonged his stay in Egypt, and they said they understood he intended to leave for Morocco today. He would then go straight on to the United States.

General Moghaddam had not said much during the entire four-hour meeting, so I asked him about his links with the religious elements. He said there was still contact over the demonstrations, which were now occurring each day, but I could get no further elaboration. Being the chief of Savak, he was a past-master at finessing you out of a direct answer.

I went back to our office, where I was handed a message from General Al Haig. He thanked me for the reports I had been sending him, and said that he was indeed pressuring to increase the US military presence in the area, but somebody had misinterpreted the basic premise under which those actions were to be taken. He said they would be essential if (a) Bakhtiar and the military together took drastic measures to prevent anarchy, or (b) the military moved in unilaterally. He said that in either case we would need improved readiness – carriers in the area, the F-15s in Saudi Arabia – which would give a clear message of intent to the USSR, our European allies and Iran's Middle East neighbours. It would make it clear to everyone that such actions by Bakhtiar or the military had full US support. But it would make no sense to build up the US military presence in any other context.

He went on to say that it did not appear that either of these premises was being contemplated, so it would not seem sensible for the US to take any military action now. He also said that judging from my report, it no longer looked as if unilateral action by the Iranian military was feasible at all. (Since I held precisely the opposite view, I did not know how he could draw this conclusion. Clearly I was going to have to send him a corrective message.) He shared my view that Khomeini's return would be the 'bottom of the slope'.

Finally, he took a sideswipe at the administration. 'Given my lack of information on the whole state of play,' he said, 'I suppose nothing could be more counter-productive than to stick my oar in at this juncture. I merely send this message so that you will be assured that I haven't taken leave of my senses just yet. Anything I can do from here to help, please let me know. Best wishes, Al.'

I went back to the Embassy and reported to Secretary Brown. Today's bulletin was slightly brighter than I had anticipated. I did have a couple of positive things to report, in Prime Minister Bakhtiar's speech and Gharabaghi's promise to back it up at a press conference tomorrow.

We had a lengthy discussion on Khomeini's return, and I said that I had at last got the Group to discuss it. Secretary Brown said there might be dangers in going too fast. We could trigger off military action before it was necessary, or stampede some of the military into leaving the country. I agreed that either of those things could happen. Mr Bakhtiar had done well to bring out the need to do some planning for the return of Khomeini, but we weren't there yet. It was going to take hours of steady application.

Ambassador Sullivan and I had sent, through the State route, a joint appraisal of the military and their ability to take over the civil government. It was rather more pessimistic than I readily agreed to, but it was a joint message and represented a compromise. I thought much more highly of their capability than Ambassador Sullivan, but we agreed completely on their lack of qualifications to fill the government jobs. We also agreed that if there was to be any military action, it should be taken under Prime Minister Bakhtiar's leadership if at all possible. I did not rule out the possibility that it might be necessary to do it on their own should Bakhtiar fail. Secretary Brown asked me point-blank if the military were capable of taking over the essential elements, and I gave him an unqualified Yes. My only reservation was how General Gharabaghi would react to such an order. Would he implement it, or would there have to be a change of leadership? Any way you looked at the situation, the military needed a central leader who could call on the allegiance they had given to the Shah.

I told Secretary Brown that we were ready to unload the fuel as soon as it could be brought to port. I also reported that we had a new Chief of Police, doubling as Governor of Tehran. These musical chairs were getting to be a habit. But the new man, General Rahimi, was a good stable character.

Winding up, Secretary Brown said they were very pleased with me in Washington, and of course coming from those circles, this sounded good. But I can't say I was satisfied with myself. Time was running out, and I had not persuaded the Group to take one major step towards the goal of breaking the strikers' hold.

The secure operator then handed me some message traffic. The first item was an intelligence clip which said that the President of the Regency Council, Mr Tehrani, who had gone to Paris to negotiate with Khomeini, had resigned. Another intelligence clip said that the Tudeh party had anounced its support of Khomeini.

The news cuttings included a useful *Washington Post* article datelined France, reporting on Khomeini's address to his followers in Iran, in which he said that driving the Shah from the country was only the beginning of the revolution. He would return on Friday and establish social justice and religious tolerance in the Islamic Republic. He certainly did not sound lke a man who intended to operate from the sidelines.

Another article contained good news. It was datelined Tehran, and obviously came from one of the newspaper's foreign service reporters. The headline read: 'Ayatollah's Backers Fear Early Return'. It said that Khomeini's key supporters had expressed shock, dismay and downright alarm at his decision to return on Friday, and had advised him otherwise. Their reason was that they had not made enough progress in cultivating the support of the military, and were fearful of a coup d'etat. They didn't believe they could get the military to swallow Khomeini's demand for the abolition of the monarchy; many officers considered that even his return would be treason.

The article reported that Khomeini's followers were casting a wide net. They had been having talks with retired colonels and generals who had been forced out by the Shah for holding dissenting views. They had also brought in Mr Bazargan, the seventy-three-year-old opposition leader widely tipped to head the Islamic Revolutionary Council.

Why was Khomeini ignoring all this weight of advice from his followers? The article explained that he was trusting in God. For the past five or six months he had been making decisions that logically made no sense, and which had been opposed by his advisers, but in an astonishing way they had proved to be right. This time his advisers thought he should wait until Bakhtiar and the Regency Council had resigned and the Islamic Council had been set up. By then the military would have been softened up and Khomeini could safely come back. But once again, he was unlikely to listen. I was sure that this account stemmed from the National Front, as it put in focus what Mr Bazargan had been advocating.

This article attached great importance to my mission, stating that my job was to convince my Iranian counterparts that moderation, not a coup d'etat, was needed to forestall a Communist takeover. This warning should be effective, because no coup could succeed without the backing, or at least assent, of one of the superpowers.

Tuesday, 23 January 1979

At breakfast I reviewed with Ambassador Sullivan the state of the military. Although I disagreed with him about the capability of the troops, I shared his apprehensions about the leaders, particularly Gharabaghi. I called to mind a dictum of General John D. Ryan, one of our previous Chiefs of the Air Force, who said that if a man turned in his retirement papers and then asked to withdraw them, you should not let him do so. His original intentions would persist below the surface, and such a man could not be depended on in a time of crisis. Well, Gharabaghi had certainly shown his intentions. The chances were that if he were faced with any major decision, he would again resign.

Traffic was heavier than ever that morning and the journey to the office strained my patience, not least because of my eagerness to get at the local papers. In the *Tehran Journal* the big headlines were 'Tehrani Quits Regency Council', but there was good cheer in the next column: 'Military Will Back Bakhtiar – Gharabaghi'. He had made a forceful statement placing the armed forces squarely behind the Prime Minister, and pledging that there was no question of a coup d'etat. He warned the public against deliberately provoking members of the armed forces. He said officers had urged their men to exercise restraint in these situations, but from now on such acts were not going to be tolerated. This was the second front-page splash by the Chief of the Supreme Commander's Staff, and it would do nothing but good.

There was more about Tehrani's resignation. Mr Yazdi, chief aide to Khomeini in Paris, revealed that even though he had resigned as President of the Regency Council, Khomeini would not receive him until he declared the Regency Council illegal. Tehrani was quoted as saying that he originally 'accepted the Presidency of the Regency Council for the protection of the national interest', but since his departure from Iran 'the Council was not formed and never took office'. In the meantime 'the domestic situation has changed, and out of respect for public opinion, I believe it necessary to resign'. This explanation became embroidered in true Persian fashion when it was reported that in a telephone conversation Tehrani had said he only resigned because of family problems in France, where he had lived for a long time. Later, to make things quite clear, he explained in a talk with Khomeini's people that he had changed his allegiance for reasons known only to himself.

I was intrigued to find in the *Tehran Journal* the headline 'Bradshaw Leads Steelers to Third Super Bowl Win'. Under a Miami dateline it said that Terry Bradshaw had fired four touch-down passes and shattered two Super Bowl passing records, leading the Pittsburgh Steelers to their third national football league championship in a 35-31 victory over the Dallas Cowboys. It was good to know that life went on in the United States, and unbelievable to see this type of news in a land under such strife.

At the Group meeting I expressed pleasure at General Gharabaghi's press conference, and said this was real progress. He had established himself as the true leader of the forces, and this would be recognized by all of them.It would help to unify them and give them courage. General Rabii agreed, but said he had some serious trouble at Khatami Air Base, near Isfahan, and to a lesser extent at Shiraz Air Base. Apparently the Homofars (aircraft maintenance technicians who have a special status) had marched on the base headquarters carrying arms. This had scared the civilian contract employees at both bases, and they were thinking of withdrawing. Rabii said he was dispatching senior officers to investigate, and asked if I would be interested in sending our Air Force section chief, Brigadier General Kertesz, to review the situation. These were two top priority bases, where the F-14s with the most sensitive equipment were located, so I agreed with him, and we immediately took the necessary action.

Still on air problems, I brought up the state of play at Mehrabad Airport, where according to our defence attaché, Colonel Tom Schaefer, Pan American reported that they had a near miss when making an approach. The controllers, of course, were on strike. The tower was manned by Air Force personnel, but it only controlled visual traffic in the local control zones. Aircraft flying under instrument conditions were on their own, so the only information they had was such advice as they could get out of the tower about other airplanes in the area. I was trying to encourage a procedure we used in my old days of flying, by which every airplane informed the tower when it came within the control zone. This is far from precise, but it is much safer than random work. The tower has to accept extra responsibility and coordinate with pilots on altitudes, to keep them separated and tell them when to start their descents into Visual Flight Rules conditions. General Rabii immediately agreed to have the system introduced.

We then discussed the striking pilots of Iranian Air, some of whom had said they were going to Paris to pick up Khomeini in an Iranian 707. We all took a very dim view of this, and I was glad to hear that it had come up at the National Security Council meeting, and Mr Bakhtiar had said he wasn't going to stand for it. Nonetheless, the striking pilots were polishing an airplane and getting it ready to go. I told them I had complete confidence that General Rabii would be able to prevent this from happening.

But what if Khomeini did get an aircraft? General Rabii favoured preventive tactics to stop him landing in Tehran. He suggested three ways: intercepting the aircraft and diverting it; trying to get a third country to intercept it en route and destroy it; or blocking the runway. I must admit that it was hard for me to get my whole heart into these stratagems, but it did seem sensible to discuss closing the runway, because this would show that the government had control of the airfield and would provide a public demonstration of its authority. It could also buy time – a few hours or a day or two; I didn't think they could keep the airport closed for much longer than that.

The press were saying that Khomeini's security had been doubled outside his home in Paris, following new death threats against him. The French were complaining that this was extremely expensive. I pressed the Generals to see if they had started any action against Khomeini's life, and there were a lot of sidelong glances, but I never did get a straight answer. They mentioned a group in Switzerland who were into this type of business, but I was unable to judge whether any links had been established.

My thoughts turned to the Shah, as I had heard he had delayed his onward journey from Morocco to the United States, and there had been some talk of him back-tracking. I asked the Group if they knew of his intentions. They had heard that he was still in Morocco, and couldn't rule out a return to Egypt. I asked if there was any thought of him coming back to Iran. There was no reply, so I said I thought it would be disastrous, and just as unsettling as Khomeini coming back. They did not particularly like that sentiment, but I think they were realistic enough to see that it was true. It would not help the Bakhtiar government one bit.

All our basic planning had been done, and we could, if only Mr Bakhtiar would give the order, implement any of the plans. I asked if they contemplated further action on the customs, and General Gharabaghi said No, the food was flowing satisfactorily, which was a gross overstatement. This was a time when I would have much preferred to be in the directive rather than in the recommending role. I had been cautioned many times by Washington against doing so; but had I been directing, I would have enacted the customs plan, because from now on I felt that the input of guns and ammunition was going to be decisive. We were receiving a flood of intelligence reports from their sources and our own, and from foreign sources, that guns and ammunition were streaming across the border.

General Toufanian said he was about to implement a plan to break the transport strike. He would use the government transport, together with military trucks and drivers, to meet the needs of the country. This particularly pleased me because it was a goal to our side, whereas all other relaxation measures had come from the opposition. But our aggregate score still wasn't good enough. We just weren't making enough progress to cope with Khomeini's return. All the omens were that it was going to be a disaster. When I pressed them hard on why Mr Bakhtiar would not implement the plans and break the strikes, their answer was that he only wanted to bring in the military as a last resort. Maybe I was wrong, but I thought we had been at that point for some days now.

Among a miscellany of items, it seemed that government people were now getting to their offices without hindrance. After a spate of resignations by Majlis deputies there had been a turn for the better over the weekend, and seventeen of them had made a firm statement saying they would continue to operate, come what may.

Further afield, depressing developments were taking place in Iran's overseas missions. Many of their diplomatic posts abroad were vacant. Some of the incumbents had just quit. The Bakhtiar government was recalling those who had been appointed strictly as Shah people, like Ambassador Zahedi in Washington. The Khomeini camp were taking immediate advantage of this by either sending their own people, or suborning the people on the spot and establishing a Khomeini embassy. There were so many clever moves on Khomeini's side that I continually wondered who was doing their planning for them, and I would still like to know the answer.

I again quizzed General Moghaddam about his contacts with the religious leaders. I was now particularly interested because one way of heading off Khomeini's return might be to let him know, through these channels, that he stood a good chance of being assassinated. Moghaddam said that they were having discussions, and though they were not at a very high level he thought they were significant. He was giving them the facts of life as he saw them, and warning them of the machinations of third parties and the treachery of Khomeini. He had made it clear that any attempt by Khomeini to take over the government would be illegal, and the armed forces would not stand for it.

I told them I had been pulsed again from Washington as to the security of sensitive equipment, especially the F-14s and the Phoenix missiles, and I wondered if there was anything more we could do to protect them. In our planning we had resurrected an old idea from the early sixties for moving equipment to the southernmost bases. The armed forces had gained a lot of capability in the south because of their new bases like Charbahar and Bandar-e Abbas; so it would make sense to move military elements in that direction. In a crisis, they could fight their way back north. In the ultimate event of a civil war, this option could save the day.

They seemed to be ahead of me. Rabii told me they had moved bombs, aircraft and supplies to these southern bases. He was a little reluctant to spell this out, probably because he and Toufanian were the only ones involved, and they had not told Gharabaghi all they had been doing. I believe they thought he would have objected. I myself strongly supported their actions.

I asked about the pro-government demonstration, and they

replied that it was approved and would be held on Thursday. This was really too quick to plan properly, but both General Gast and I encouraged them to press on.

These moves by Rabii and Toufanian helped to explain a message I received from Secretary Brown telling me that they had heard that General Djam, when Chief of the Supreme Commander's Staff, had drawn up plans to deal with a serious breakdown of law and order in Iran. The plans, which had the Shah's approval, envisaged withdrawing the armed forces and the central government to Khuzestan, at the head of the Persian Gulf. There they would control the oilfields and occupy a bridgehead from which to cooperate with Western nations. They would seek to work outwards and gradually reimpose control on the rest of the country. These sources further revealed that General Djam had recently asked the Shah if the plan still existed. The Shah supposedly replied that it no doubt did, but that no one had considered its current application. I had discussed it with the Shah on 11 January during my audience with him. For some reason he had it in his mind that I had helped to work on it, but I had not. He thought it was probably so out of date that it would be of no value.

Secretary Brown was now looking for a report on this plan. Did it still exist, and what was its status? I could have written a reply right then, but I preferred to check back with General Gharabaghi and the Group first, so I deferred action until after our next Group meeting.

I was anxious to get the report from Brigadier General Kertesz on the F-14s at the southern bases; so while waiting for it in the office, I decided to reply to General Haig's message of the day before. As things turned out, my response was to acquire international celebrity on 3 June 1980. On that day, Khomeini's government was holding trials on 'US Intervention in Iran', and Ramsey Clark went illegally to attend. The Iranians claimed they had retrieved my message from a computer, and submitted it as prime evidence of American 'crimes'. There were two versions of Ramsey Clark's comments – 'very distressing' and 'very disturbing' – and the Iranians made the most of it. (We have now learned they reconstructed many classified messages by piecing together shredded paper.) As best I can recall, the message quoted in the media is word for word the same as the original.

This is the text of my reply to General Haig with my personal comments in square parentheses. A and B refer to Haig's two hypotheses in his message (see p.177), namely (a) joint action by Bakhtiar and the military, and (b) a military coup.

Personal and eyes only for Gen. Haig from Gen. Huyser

1.   Received your reply 2251 20 Jan. 79 [date and time message was dispatched]. I fully understand now, and after last night's conversation with Washington I know your msg [message] was relayed to SecDef. [Secretary of Defence.]
2.   Ref. para 2 of your msg I will comment on both your A and B, for further clarity. As I see it here we are doing what you say in 2A. [This referred to the current plans to be executed under Mr Bakhtiar's leadership.] It is placed step by step at the rate we judge can be done without causing a complete uprising by the factions working against the Bakhtiar Gov. I would accelerate the pace, and have encouraged them to do so. It has taken considerable pressure to get them to move as fast as they have, but believe they will pick up speed in near future if they can hang together. The actions I am pressing are to break the strikes by use of military in customs, oil, and banking. We have made some progress in all three areas but a long way to go yet. Now for your 2B [military coup]. This option is not ruled out. The word 'Now' in your statement is what I want to elaborate on. The way I'm working the problem is essentially to do 2B but under the direction of Bakhtiar. [Have the military take over all the essential elements – oil, customs, power, water, banking and media – but under Bakhtiar's leadership. In other words, establish a government, not destroy it.] I have been encouraging him to take these steps. [This was through the military.] He has shown willingness to do so and that is the pace I would like to accelerate. If that fails, then my guidance to them is we must go to a straight military takeover. [Haig's 2B.] As you can see, the planning is the same for either option. We are working on these plans on a high priority 24-hour-per-day basis.
3.   Ref. your para 3. I would not say case B is no longer feasible. All things are done by degrees and I think they have

a fairly high capability to do the job. In fact we are planning
for that option if necessary. The point I wanted Washington
to understand is the military does not have the capability after
doing the initial job of picking up and running a sophisticated
government. Just isn't talent available as they have always
kept their military in a strictly military role. That does not
rule out success, as I don't know of many countries where
such action has occurred that the governmental functions
didn't go back to grass roots for a period. Then they grow
back to more sophistication.
4.   The point on Khomeini returning at this time is one of not
gaining sufficient stability [actions on implementing plans] to
cope with the emotional actions and reactions. I believe there
would be a big upheaval, then things would go to hell in a
hand basket. The bottom line would probably be your case B
but without Bakhtiar at the throttle. [This did not happen.]
Also I think there are several elements outside the Gov. that
want a complete civil war. One good way to trigger that is to
have Khomeini return and be assassinated. Emotion would
take over and I believe the result would be a civil war.
5.   Hope this helps some on the picture here. If Khomeini
does not come back this week and if Saturday's activities
don't get out of control, I'm going to ask to be released
Sunday.

Best wishes, Dutch.

I had the message typed, then signed it and asked the administrative personnel to dispatch it to Mons, Belgium.
   Brigadier General Kertesz returned and reported that all the
F-14s at Khatami Air Base were safe. He said there had been some
activity by the Homofars, and pointed out they were far better
educated and more serious than a lot of the other military people.
They had not been kept very busy lately because they did not have
enough fuel to fly their aircraft, so it was the age-old problem of
idle hands. He told me that the discipline and morale of the
majority of the troops at the air bases were good. He felt that they
were fully capable of performing their missions.
   I went to General Gharabaghi's office, as I wanted to discuss the
problem with him and General Rabii. According to Rabii the

trouble started with press stories about our plans to safeguard the F-14s and other sensitive gear. The Homofars thought we might try to take the equipment out of Iran. They considered that it belonged to them, as their country had bought and paid for it, and they felt fully capable of protecting it. Clearly it was important to their own defence, so they just weren't going to let it get away. Both Gharabaghi and Rabii recommended that we trust them to protect the equipment.

I returned to the Embassy, a hectic trip because of the demonstrators, including those coming out on the government side. There was one pro-government group around a stadium near the Embassy which was large enough to impede the traffic. But they jostled with other groups, and it was hard to tell who belonged to which faction; about the only way was by the posters they carried. Some of them looked us over very carefully, and we had a feeling that we could be yanked out of the car almost any moment. I was glad I had now started wearing a bulletproof vest.

At the Embassy gate there was an extra truckload of Iranian security guards. We stopped for identification, which took a little longer each day, and while we were waiting I saw out of the side window that one of the soldiers had his rifle pointed straight at my head. The muzzle looked to me like it was about two inches in diameter, and he had his finger on the trigger. Actually it was probably a 30-calibre, but it certainly looked formidable.

That night, in the course of rather disjointed conversations with Secretary Brown, I was asked about the unpleasantness at Khatami Air Base and the Grumman people. This had fed back very rapidly to the US, no doubt because Grumman had decided that afternoon to send their people home. I gave them a full report of what we had learned from Brigadier General Kertesz, and said it might be wise if we just accepted the risk on the sensitive gear. I suggested the incident reflected well on the Homofars, and showed a real sense of dedication to their country. If they were prepared to protect their equipment from Americans, I had some confidence they would give it even better protection against unfriendlies!

I reported that there was little progress in our preparations for the return of Khomeini. Most of the Group's discussions centred on how to prevent him from arriving in Tehran, by blocking the runway, etc. Yet again, I was queried on the loyalty and stability of the forces. It seemed that my friends in Washington had been reading the press and were starting to believe it. I told them we had not lost our capability, and had plenty of elements who would support Mr Bakhtiar. I also passed on General Kertesz's observations on the overall state of morale. In any case, it would not take all 400,000 troops to straighten things out. I thought that with about 20,000 real crack troops we could do almost anything we wanted. I wondered sometimes whether the people back in Washington realized what you could do with 20,000 troops. We had that many in the Imperial Guard, and I knew they were first-line. The Russians had needed a much smaller force than that when they went into Ethiopia.

They wanted to know if I thought someone in the military was privately keeping the Shah informed, and I told them I had discussed this extensively but couldn't be sure. I thought the contact was through Rabii, but didn't know whether it was direct. The Group had told me that the Shah was worried that he might be *persona non grata* in the US. I had told them that was absolute hogwash; the US had invited him, and he would be welcome in our country.

Then they asked what I thought would happen should the Shah return to Iran. I said the only chance of stability was for both Khomeini and the Shah to stay away. Mr Bakhtiar had a lot of steel in him, and could survive a lot of punishment. My only concern was that he was not taking advantage of his military capability to break the strikes and bring the country under control. I complained that statements from the US were still having an adverse impact. The Iranians tended to believe them as though they were right out of the Koran.

On my way back to the residence, an Iranian guard in civilian clothes appeared out of nowhere and asked me in broken English if I was getting ready to go home. He was armed, and I really didn't know whether he was friend or foe. I just gave a very straight No, and wished him good-night. That was all; but those steps to the residence door seemed very long, and gave me another rather tense moment.

Wednesday, 24 January 1979

In the morning news traffic, a Russian report claimed that events
in Iran had driven to distraction those sections of the Washington
apparatus connected with the Middle East and Persian Gulf. It said
the anti-American feeling among the Iranians had reached such a
pitch that Washington could not expect to maintain its intelligence
installations much longer, and we were hurriedly searching for a
nearby site to relocate this intricate equipment. It went on:

> At the same time as American General Robert Huyser is
> 'settling' matters in Iran itself, the US State Department is
> inviting the Crown Prince and First Deputy Prime Minister of
> Saudi Arabia, Fahd, to Washington, where, according to the
> local press, it is proposed to hold 'very important talks'. But
> according to information which has become known in Amer-
> ican press circles, the electronic espionage equipment is being
> prepared for installation on Turkish territory.

The report said that Turkish officials had objected to any new
military installation on their soil, but it was possible that we would
put it on one of our own bases there. It attacked Washington's
elaborate complex of intelligence installations, warships in the
Persian Gulf and military planes in Saudi Arabia, and warned that
they constituted a serious threat to the peoples of the region and
the cause of national liberation.

I sometimes wished that I really had the authority with which the
Soviets credited me in their press release. No doubt they really
thought I wielded such power; for when they themselves move into
a country to protect their interests, they make no bones about
calling the shots. Indeed, in retrospect many Americans probably
think that we should have been considerably more forceful in Iran.

I left the Embassy for the SCS compound shortly after 7 am, and
the traffic was already grim. Every day it was not only heavier but
also more chaotic. Traffic has never been orderly in Tehran, but
now the police were almost completely ineffective; civilians on the
street had to help direct it. Our security people logged the morning
trip as a 'very high sweat' event. The big iron gates on the SCS
compound were a welcome sight.

At the office, the *Tehran Journal* and the *Kayhan* on my desk both carried disturbing headlines. The *Journal* said: 'Khomeini Council Next Week Says Bazargan'. The *Kayhan* announced: 'Bakhtiar Has No Option – Bazargan'.

Mehdi Bazargan, who was chief of the liberation movement in Iran, Khomeini's top representative and the man expected to be his Prime Minister, had held a large press conference. He said that despite Khomeini's widespread support, he would have liked the Ayatollah to delay his return until a provisional revolutionary government could be established, possibly even under Bakhtiar. Bazargan said he had known Bakhtiar for thirty-four years and had always found him to be reasonable, logical and patriotic.

But, he said, it wasn't going to happen that way. Khomeini would return on Friday, on his own personal decision, and that was final. Bazargan was concerned about the instability of the Bakhtiar government. He said it might collapse from its own inner weakness, and if this were to happen, the Army would not tolerate any action against the constitution, and its response could lead to a bloodbath. He referred to General Gharabaghi's 'unprecedented' broadcast to the military to ignore the religious leaders and mobilize all their support behind Bakhtiar, head of the 'legal and constitutional government'.

He argued that the only thing Bakhtiar could rely on was the Army. It could not save him, because the strikes would continue and government employees would not go to work. So Bakhtiar must step down. This was the best way to keep the Army from intervening. Bloodshed otherwise looked inevitable, because Khomeini's supporters were determined to give him a tumultuous welcome. Khomeini would name his Revolutionary Islamic Council on Friday or soon afterwards. Bazargan contended that Bakhtiar would anyway have to step down after that announcement, because his government would then be illegal.

Of course, the official Bakhtiar position was diametrically opposite to this view. He considered that Khomeini was coming back as a religious leader. If Khomeini announced a council, this could be ignored unless he took overt action to install that council in the government offices. That would amount to an attempted coup d'etat, and would call for very swift and direct action. Clearly Bazargan and Bakhtiar were on a collision course.

The *Tehran Journal* front page carried a large picture showing really crack troops on the march. They were dressed in combat fatigues and carrying weapons. Under the caption, 'Royal Immortals Still On Guard', the story read:

> If Ayatollah Khomeini thinks he is simply going to walk into Iran and take over the reins of power like slipping on his religious cloak, then he has not reckoned with the Immortal Brigade of the Imperial Guard. At least that was the impression they did their best to give foreign newsmen on a snow-swept morning at the Lavizan Military Compound yesterday morning.
>   Their catch-phrase, drilled into them through months and years of the toughest training in the country, is 'Javid Shah' or 'Long Live the Shah'. It echoed continuously around the barracks yesterday as 1,500 of Iran's crack force were put through their paces for the benefit of the foreign press. It is all one could expect from the men trained to lay down their lives at an instant to save the Shah. For them the Shah is just on a holiday, and anyone who thinks otherwise is in for a fight.

This demonstration of military capability was part of our plan to show the strength and determination of the force. We had other demonstrations planned which would be larger and more public. In the days ahead the military would be in the streets, and in the air over Tehran, to display the power that under-pinned the Bakhtiar government. The people had to recognize that the armed forces had the power to defeat the opposition and break the strikes. Oh how I prayed to God that Prime Minister Bakhtiar would recognize the value of this asset. If our Ambassador or someone high on the US political side would only encourage him to do so.

Another front-page item in the *Khayan* showed a picture of Ramsey Clark, and quoted him as saying: 'Khomeini has 99% backing'. He claimed that during his eight-day visit to Iran, 'anyone could see' that ninety-nine per cent of the people were behind the Ayatollah. This report was filed after Clark had spent an hour and a half with Khomeini at his home in Neauphle-le-Chateau. He said the Ayatollah had warned him of immediate dangers ahead for Iran.

Clark attacked the CIA. He hoped that they and the American advisers would not interfere with the outcome of the national revolution. Washington was violating its own principles of freedom and self-determination by supporting Bakhtiar, who was appointed by the Shah, and had no following or political base. He said that if the Khomeini movement won, he had the highest hopes that it would introduce social justice. (I wonder what he thinks today?)

In Gharabaghi's office I was not surprised to see this article prominently displayed in the middle of the table. But I had not expected the great pride expressed by the Group over the picture of the troops. Their enthusiasm was exhilarating, because it was such a change for them to pick on the good news first. I even felt good when Gharabaghi skipped the Khomeini headlines and addressed the Ramsey Clark statements. He said that Clark and Senator Church were being extremely counter-productive. Clark carried the authority of an official because he had previously been one, and in Iran people retain an official prestige even after they have left office.

Among other things the Group were worried about the impact that these statements would have on Iranian students in America and on their own dependents there. There were many other officers at all levels whose wives had gone there for safety reasons. In the last few days these men had ceased to be able to communicate by telephone with their dependents, so their only source of information would be the media. The telephone system still operated effectively, but there was now a lot of deliberate interference on long-distance calls. Unless they were talking to Paris, they were liable to be cut off, and it was pretty clear that people were listening.

We were not sure just what means the opposition were using to monitor, but they seemed able to control almost everything they wanted. I fully sympathized with General Gharabaghi about the damage Clark and Church were doing, and promised to bring the matter to Secretary Brown's attention. Gharabaghi said he would be grateful if we could get somebody high up in the United States to make a very positive statement to the media repudiating these negative American voices.

I told the Group I wanted to get busy on preparing for the upcoming demonstration. I said I was delighted with the press coverage of the troops, and of the pro-government demonstrations. I hoped those demonstrations which we had planned for today would be larger; and we needed to get cracking on the one scheduled for tomorrow to make sure that it really hit pay dirt. We had to be certain there were no pictures of the Shah. One or two had shown up yesterday, and we thought the opposition must have inserted them, because we had issued firm instructions to the contrary.

We decided it would be better not to have an all-day parade, but to run from 10.30 am until noon, since we had no idea how many people we could muster. We could use the afternoon for a show of military force in the streets. We would deploy troops to show the people that they were well dressed, well disciplined and ready to support the government. It would be a repeat of yesterday's parade at Lavizan. It would help to offset the masterly public affairs programme of the opposition, who were seeing to it that everybody knew who was really controlling the economy. They said they were controlling it for the people, and could cut it off at any moment, and they were absolutely right. The only way to change that fact was to introduce military control, and make it work.

I asked if there were any new developments at Khatami or Shiraz. General Rabii said he thought things were well under control, but to make certain he had sent two C-130-loads of special forces to Khatami. He wanted to make clear to the troops there that he meant business. The F-14s and Phoenix missiles, he said, were quite safe.

On customs, I got little sympathy from them, and they were not interested in taking further action. The tanker-load of fuel which Secretary Brown had provided was anchored just offshore, as we had not succeeded in getting it into port, nor did we have any guarantee of being able to offload it. We might yet have to use force.

We discussed what technicians we would need to enhance oil production. We had some expertise in the Iranian Navy, but the bottom line was that to do it right, we were going to need foreign help. The key parts of all the systems had been operated by foreigners, because these sytems had grown far more rapidly than the manpower base in the country. Now the foreigners were departing rapidly. Today, the Japanese had ordered all 4,000 of their people out.

We noted that Prime Minister Bakhtiar was going to submit two special bills today. One was designed to dissolve Savak, and the other proposed to set up special courts to try former politicians and businessmen accused of corruption and misuse of power. Both, of course, were a bid by Bakhtiar to gain favour with the public. Savak was associated with the Shah. There would have to be a similar organization under anyone's rule, but it obviously would need to take a different name.

General Badraie announced that the Iranian peace-keeping force on the Golan Heights had returned to Iran. He said they were not familiar with what had been going on in the country, but they were very good troops, well trained, and well disciplined, and would be a great asset to our programme.

Oil production was up slightly to about 600,000 barrels, but this was still 300,000 barrels short even for our internal needs.

I thought the Group were now ready to address Khomeini's arrival with some degree of detachment. I mentioned the press report that the opposition had been trying to get live television coverage for the event. They had appointed a special committee for his reception, and had outlined the tactics to be pursued. One was that the marchers would behave in an orderly manner – possibly a response to their meetings with General Moghaddam. Another one was that the welcome ceremony should be as simple as possible; there should be no elaborate rituals such as the setting up of victory arches. Welcome activities should only be organized with the knowledge and approval of the committee.

The Group had already figured out where Khomeini was going to make his policy speech; it was to be at the Behest-e-Zahra Cemetery. I said I could see no reason why they should not ask the opposition what route he intended to use. We could then determine where the government would have to protect him, and where he would be turned over to his own people. I had heard that he could not come back by Iranian Air, and would be arriving by Air France. This being so, I felt confident that he could not slip in on us, as we could easily find out when an Air France aircraft was approaching.

General Rabii and the Prime Minister had discussed the idea of closing Mehrabad Airport, by blocking the runway with tanks. The Group debated what would happen if he were diverted. It would no doubt cause a fairly heavy ripple through the opposition, but we didn't think the situation would get out of control.

An alternative was to let him come in, on the basis that he was returning as a religious leader. All of us felt that this was a ridiculous scenario. We thought it much more likely that he would immediately attempt to form his own government. Since Mr Bakhtiar had already spelt out that this would be unconstitutional, things could get very messy and a little bloody. To my surprise General Gharabaghi declared himself ready to deal with this in a very firm fashion. If necessary he would arrest 1,500 to 3,000 people to keep in order, which was quite consistent with Mr Bakhtiar's guidance. It was clear to me that Mr Bakhtiar was just like tea – the hotter the water, the more his strength came out. It was encouraging at least that the military was of one mind in following his lead.

To delay Khomeini's arrival by even twenty-four hours at that point represented a welcome opportunity, and precious time for action. We felt the best solution was simply to announce that the airport was closed, rather than actually keep the runways blocked. We would have a stand-by capability to block it if necessary. This would allow us to keep supplies coming in, and the evacuation of our people could continue; we were starting to put pressure on all Americans to leave Iran.

In a final round-up of the pro-government demonstrations planned for the next day, we were glad to note the extensive press coverage of the gatherings at the stadium, even though these were only dry runs. With a civilian demonstration in the morning and a military display in the afternoon, we stood to get an even better press.

Back at the office I prepared a formal answer to Secretary Brown's message on 'the General Djam plan' to regroup the armed forces in the south. I said that if anything was being done to resuscitate it, they were withholding it from me. But undoubtedly, as General Rabii had said, some equipment was being moved south. In the same message I decided to include General Gharabaghi's plea for prominent US citizens to reply to people like Ramsey Clark and Senator Church. I got the message prepared for dispatch and then left for the Embassy.

Later, at the normal time, I got through to Washington, and Secretary Brown's first remark startled me. He said we should let Bakhtiar and the military know that we were behind them, and I should work hard to ensure that the military were united in their support for Mr Bakhtiar! I wondered what he thought I had been doing for the last three weeks. He capped this by saying it was important to keep Khomeini out of the country. He added that in a showdown, it would be up to Bakhtiar and the military to decide what to do; and whatever they did we would support them. I was not to discourage them from having a military takeover.

Again, I was mystified, because it sounded as if he was playing back what I had been telling him ever since I arrived. But it was music to my ears to hear him so anxious to keep Khomeini out of the country, and I wondered if Washington was at last working on such plans. The suspense of waiting for Khomeini was very unsettling. It was not easy to keep the military psychologically tuned up so that if the situation turned sour, they could take over, but if it stayed healthy they could switch their full weight behind Mr Bakhtiar.

The Secretary again asked about the sensitive equipment, and I told him what had been done at Khatami Air Base with the special forces. I suggested that any more pressure could be counter-productive, because the Homofars were getting distinctly possessive.

General Jones wanted to know if it would be helpful to have the Shah send word to the Group urging them to support Bakhtiar. I told him that I thought this would be a bad mistake, as I had tried to eradicate the Shah from their minds. In any case, they were already solid for Bakhtiar.

Secretary Brown had received my wire, so I asked how he felt about General Gharabaghi's request for public US support. He said he would take it under consideration; but how could I balance this with my view that we must be careful not to make Mr Bakhtiar look like a puppet of the United States? It was a good question. Of course, what I was looking for was objective appraisals of Bakhtiar's success by respected Americans. He was entitled to this sort of recognition and wasn't getting it.

I ended by thanking Secretary Brown for providing the fuel tanker, and regretting that at the moment there was no prospect of offloading it. I explained that even if there was, we didn't want to offload it until we were sure we would have control of the fuel. He understood, and agreed that it was worth the cost to keep the tanker in the area.

Later, reviewing the evening news traffic, I noted that the Khomeini reception committee had persuaded the Iranian postal employees to end their strike. They planned to clear the backlog in the mail, which had been accumulating for over a month on top of mail from a strike they had staged last November. The evacuation of all foreigners was proceeding rapidly, and there were now only a small number left. The British had flown out about a hundred US citizens, eighty British and some Dutchmen, Australians and New Zealanders.

Before turning in, I gave the papers a final glance. I got a chuckle out of the *Kayhan*'s back page column entitled 'The Town Talk'. It said: 'Town Talk used to be a social column in the balmy days when we could afford everything, caviar, cocktails, $70,000 Mercedes plus $1 billion which we just threw at the Persian Gulf as a surcharge. Most of these have disappeared, including the column's lovely ladies who now seem to be somewhere in sunny California. The moods and *mores* have changed, and so will Town Talk's copy.'

One article in *Kayhan* gave a good portrayal of Tehran traffic:

It's a paradoxical situation. There's not enough petrol. All are said to be on strike. Yet the streets are choked with cars. The worst jam was on Monday, when a mile an hour was the order of the day in downtown Tehran. The traffic lights were either off because of power cuts, or tampered with, or, as is the custom these days, simply ignored.

The paper said that not only the streets were chaotic; the whole economy was just as bad. The grand bazaars were deserted and completely closed. The banks were open every other day, but still primarily for domestic business. All the other regular stores were bolted and shuttered except for the florists and dried fruit shops. The reason the florists were open was to sell wreaths for the fallen victims at Behest-e-Zahra – today the world's most famous cemetery. Dried fruits were always in demand, particularly water-melon seeds. These are said to be the best antidote to broken nerves – Iran's new endemic disease. There were many casualties, I reflected, in this terrible war of nerves.

Thursday, 25 January 1979

Once again I made an early start. I was anxious to get an outbrief on last night's National Security Council meeting, and hear about Wednesday's dry run for today's demonstration. When General Gast and I reached the office the Group was already assembled and requesting our presence. This was extremely early for them. We hustled on over, and received a warm and enthusiastic greeting. General Gharabaghi was in good form, and anxious to give a report on last night's meeting. He said Mr Bakhtiar had been very firm and definite. He had asked about our plans, and Gharabaghi had told him they were near enough complete to be considered executable.

About Khomeini's return they had made two key decisions. One was to declare a military red alert; this would bring all troops on to the top line, and they would be prepared for whatever might occur. The other was to put some starch into the martial law. The government had it in theory, but they had been lax about enforcing it in practice. Now they were going to put a stop to that. Mehrabad Airport was to be put off limits. Only those who were required to operate it and protect Khomeini would be allowed in. There would be no crowds. All airfields in Iran would be closed to commercial traffic for three days.

They agreed that if Khomeini arrived by Air France while the airfield was closed, he would be diverted to Kish Island. It would be explained to him that this had been done for his own protection. They realized that if something happened to him they would have a civil war on their hands, so they would keep him in protective custody at Kish Island indefinitely, at least until they had a clearer idea of how things were going to develop. Should this plan not work as programmed, or should the people get out of control, or should Mr Bazargan attempt to form his own government, they would take over, seizing the power, oil, customs, banks and all essential elements of the country.

Gharabaghi said they had debriefed Mr Bakhtiar on General Moghaddam's meeting with the religious leaders. In essence, Moghaddam had told them what was planned for the arrival of Khomeini and explained the ground-rules. He made it clear that they meant business, and fully intended to enforce martial law. Mr Bakhtiar had told them he thought they should break off contacts with the religious leaders for the time being. All his efforts at a dialogue had been futile. Every time he had tried to reason with them, it was just like a broken record: all they ever wanted to talk about was his resignation. What was more, these religious elements, with their strong media contacts, were rushing out to the press and quoting the discussions out of context. So it was agreed between the military, Mr Bakhtiar and the whole National Security Council that all their contacts with religious groups would cease forthwith.

Mr Bakhtiar was very pleased with the publicity given to his own and General Gharabaghi's articles. No one could now doubt that the military and the Prime Minister were completely in step. Just the same, the National Security Council had decided to cancel today's military parade, on the grounds that it could backfire. It was felt to be going a little too far on the day before Khomeini's scheduled return, and might cause violence. I did not agree, but the decision had been made.

General Rabii, reporting on the situation at Khatami Air Base, said they had found some Homofars who were clearly agents of the opposition, but the special forces had the situation well in hand. The suspects would be evacuated, and tried by the Army. This was a bit of a gamble, because a punitive verdict could cause the whole Homofar force to rebel. But they felt it was a remote risk, and now was the time to grasp the nettle.

Another disturbing symptom had been a pro-Khomeini demonstration in Tehran by some Air Force people, including officers. General Rabii said they had all been apprehended, and steps would be taken to cut off such capers right now. It seemed sad that all these troubles were surfacing in the Air Force; that was one place we had least expected unrest because of its high educational level and its close association with the United States.

A messenger brought in a note saying that most probably the Ayatollah Khomeini would not now return until Sunday. This brought a ripple of relief. But it did not take us long to recognize that two days were going to do very little for us. We must still plan for Friday, and we must stay ahead of the planning. Also, the change created an alarming possibility. If the crowds had not been told of the postponement would they assemble and, cheated of Khomeini, become uncontrollable?

General Gharabaghi made a call to Mr Bakhtiar to discuss these developments. Mr Bakhtiar reiterated that they had already determined to have strict martial law, and that was how they were going to handle it, whatever developed. It was encouraging to see a new intimacy between these two men.

As best we could tell, the pro-government demonstration had assembled rapidly and we were getting a far better turnout than anyone had anticipated. It was now in full swing, and press reports were estimating numbers between 100,000 and 600,000. It was all very orderly. There had been a bit of rock-throwing by the opposition, but that was short-lived. We sent a helicopter to get our own estimate, which ran out somewhere in the middle – between 300,000 and 350,000 people. This was a tremendous show for the Bakhtiar government; and particularly significant in Tehran, the scene of so many pro-Khomeini processions. To get this number of volunteers on to the street at such short notice was very heart-warming. I had always wondered just how many really supported Khomeini and how many the constitutional government. There were 34 million people in Iran, and the most we had seen demonstrating for Khomeini was about 3 million.

The opposition, for whatever reason, had made us an intriguing offer. They told us beforehand that they had additional people in town whom they had brought in for their own demonstrations, and for a price we could use them in ours. Naturally this was turned down! We only wanted genuine supporters, so that we would know how many they were.

We were interrupted by another call from Mr Bakhtiar, who said he would announce martial law enforcement at 2 pm today. He would tell the opposition that they could have marches and demonstrations, but these would have to be approved by the government. He wanted us to do all we could to monitor Khomeini's movements in Paris, including his expected time of departure.

Well satisfied with our demonstration, I went back to the Embassy. I felt it was very important that I should debrief Ambassador Sullivan on the National Security Council meeting, and on our plan for the reception of Khomeini. Knowing that he and his people had very good contacts with the opposition forces, it was a good chance to pass them the word, both on the successful demonstrations and on the plans to block the airfield. Either of these developments might make Khomeini think twice about an early return to Tehran.

When we had completed our discussion, Ambassador Sullivan suggested that I attempt to call Secretary Brown, even though it would be four or five hours earlier than usual. The Ambassador thought I should get it over with and then spend a relaxed evening watching a movie about general Douglas MacArthur. So I got straight through to Secretary Brown and General Jones, gave them an extensive debrief, and passed on the Iranian request that the United States monitor Khomeini as closely as possible. Secretary Brown assured me that this would be done. With regard to Khomeini's return, I said we had taken a careful look at the military, and had high confidence in the Air Force, Navy and infantry. But we did have reservations about the artillery. They were rather different from the others, as most of them had been trained by the Soviets. This may seem strange, but the Soviets manufactured very good artillery, and the Shah had not let his political sympathies deprive his army of the equipment it needed.

There had lately been a most helpful article by Senator Henry 'Scoop' Jackson in the newspapers, and I asked if we could have some more like that. Secretary Brown said he would try to arrange for some.

In closing, I told him there was no way I could be optimistic about the future, but I would throw in the big 'if' again: there was hope for Bakhtiar, if there was any way to keep both the Shah and Khomeini out of the country. The military were solidly behind him now, and they seemed to be in lock step. But we needed time to consolidate, and above all we needed some action. I paid my respects and signed off.

After a fine dinner, we watched the movie on General MacArthur, and had a running critique from the political side of the house on how military people should conduct their business!

Friday, 26 January 1979

When I awoke, my mind was heavy with apprehension. I had a nervous stomach. As I shaved and showered, all types of thoughts were running through my head. How were we going to cope with the day? Was this the final act, the end of the line? At breakfast the Ambassador confirmed that Khomeini had decided not to return today; he now planned to come on Sunday. I felt like giving a shout of glee; the two-day reprieve seemed like an eternity. But I knew we really needed at least another month.

Reviewing the message file, I noted that the Soviets had picked up the tempo of their attack on America and myself in particular. A French newspaper editorial assessed the new virulent tone of the Soviet media: 'Until today, Moscow was content to accuse the US of blocking Khomeini's return. Now Bakhtiar himself is named. According to *Pravda*, he follows the orders of US General Robert Huyser, now in Tehran.' It went on to say: 'Since the Russians clearly have no intention of starting a nuclear war over Iran, and since the US doesn't either, is Moscow gambling that the situation is ripe enough so that the Bear can raise his big voice without much risk?'

I felt sure this *Pravda* article would find its way into the Tehran media, and that would cause many problems. The opposition were already saying that I was in complete control of the military. Should anything happen, there was no question in my mind that the opposition and Moscow would fix the blame on me. The most accurate record of my daily activities had always come from Tass, *Pravda* and Radio Moscow. Every day they reported correctly on my whereabouts and who I had seen. Neither the American nor the Iranian press had so clear a track on my activities. This caused me considerable concern. I knew that somewhere within the SCS compound there must be an informant, because the Soviet media frequently got the exact time of day when I met with the Group. They also knew when General Moghaddam was there. They even knew when I had a short solo session with General Gharabaghi. As I have said, I now believe that the information came from Major General Fardust, who was in an adjoining room to General Gharabaghi's office.

It seemed to me that Washington should decide whether to pull me out in advance of any major development, such as the collapse of the Bakhtiar government or a military showdown, so that I could not be accused of masterminding it. I was anyway getting frustrated, because I thought the US should 'fish or cut bait'. If I had been calling the shots in Washington, the first thing I would have done would be to put Ambassador Sullivan and myself on the same course. I would also have given both of us a more assertive and directive role. I would have given the constitutional government of Iran whatever support was necessary to ensure its survival.

As we drove out of the Embassy the change in atmosphere hit us like a blast of hot air the moment we reached the gates. Traffic was so jammed that it did not appear that we could even get into the street. Consequently we went out of the gate, made almost a 180-degree turn and ploughed up the sidewalk, which was about ten feet wide. We took our entire convoy right up it until we had bypassed most of the traffic jam at that corner. This caused a lot of anger – not surprisingly, because we were just forcing our way through the pedestrians, bumping into some of them, so that I felt sure they would round on us sooner or later. I assume they all thought this was the day Khomeini was returning.

However, we managed to get through in one piece. At the office I started reviewing the news, and one of the first articles that caught my attention was by a retired General, Nassami. He was a man with whom General Djam had stayed when he was in Tehran, so I was amazed to see that this article was strongly pro-Khomeini. This made me wonder about Djam. One could never be certain who would be the next to swing over to the Ayatollah.

Our own public relations programme had got some printed matter on to the streets the day before. More was due out today. It was superbly produced under the guidance of Admiral Frank Collins, who had an instinct for what was needed. It appeared to me that this programme had great possibilities, because it was patently obvious now that there was a silent majority who wanted to support Bakhtiar and stay friendly to the West.

General Gharabaghi asked me in right away, before the others had arrived. Bakhtiar was holding another National Security Council meeting that evening, and they needed to have definite revised plans for Sunday. When the others came, we all agreed that we should stay close to what we had previously planned for

Friday. But we looked at a range of options. We considered bargaining peacefully to delay Khomeini still further. We thought Mr Bakhtiar might volunteer to go to Paris to talk with the Ayatollah. Conversely, and more problematically, we could go ahead and extend the closure of the airport till Sunday, even if this meant a confrontation there with the Khomeini supporters. We decided to present both options to the Prime Minister at this evening's meeting.

Again, we could let Khomeini come in unhampered, and cope with the situation when he arrived. The military would maintain control at Mehrabad Airport and from there to Shahyad Square, and then hand him over to his followers and withdraw to key government installations. If the crowd became unruly on the remainder of his route, they would be at each other's mercy, and we would just have to accept the outcome as a 'happening'.

A fourth alternative was to leave the airport open until Khomeini took off from Paris and then close it, diverting the plane in mid-air. We now thought this one of the less desirable options, owing to the risk of a showdown with the mob at the airport. Once he left Paris, and the people knew about it in Tehran, they would converge in large numbers to greet him and could become uncontrollable.

As we talked, a crowd of up to 20,000 had gathered in the streets and moved towards the airport in expectation of Khomeini's arrival. Knowing that this might happen, we had kept the military in position at the airport. We had full confidence in our airport protection plan, and this would provide a good test.

Admiral Habiballahi thought that if we were going to block the airport indefinitely, the Ayatollah would find some other means of arrival, either by sea or by land. This did not appear very feasible to me, and after a lengthy discussion most of us felt it was unlikely.

The press was keeping close track of Khomeini. Even though we figured he could outmanoeuvre them for an hour or two at a time, he could not keep it up for much longer. We were actually depending on the press as our prime intelligence source on his movements, and we knew it would be reliable.

We next reviewed some of our contingency planning. At last we had agreement with the National Iranian Oil Company to offload the tanker. The plan now was to pump the fuel into storage tanks which could be protected by the military.

General Toufanian said he had been meeting with Eric von Marbod. He recognized that we might have some internal problems in the US as a result of stoppages in the foreign military sales programmes to Iran, but even if the Bakhtiar government settled down, the country had suffered such a loss of economic blood that these programmes would have to be adjusted as the situation developed. This being so, it made no sense for the United States to draw up a memorandum of understanding for the future. I had to agree. The military had no money of its own, or access to national funds, while the government had quite enough on its hands without having to peer into the future. It had barely any present programmes, let alone future ones, and Toufanian thought we were completely out of our minds if we imagined we could come up with a document which anyone could sign.

Nonetheless Eric's orders from Washington were quite specific: he had to consummate a memorandum of understanding. He had done a superb job of reviewing the plans and identifying those projects which could safely be cut so as to reduce costs. But I was afraid we would never get a signature on any such memorandum.

Word came through that there was a demonstration going on at the University, with up to 2,000 people involved, and that they had got out of hand. The troops had tried to bring them back into control, and fired over their heads. This had no impact, so they lowered their rifle-barrels and fired into the crowd. There were an estimated fifteen to twenty fatalities. We felt sure this would have repercussions.

We had been at it for about five hours, and they seemed confident that they knew what they wanted to talk about with Mr Bakhtiar and the National Security Council. We had noted an increase in the numbers of desertions, and in the amount of fraternization. We also noted some new threats against the military by the opposition, which concerned me. It showed there were elements in the opposition forces who preferred violence to the Khomeini tactic of love and flowers, and this could spark off the explosion we were trying to avoid.

Back at the Embassy, Ambassador Sullivan brought to my attention an article in the *New York Times* that morning which he considered a breach of security. It read: 'US Encouraged by Firm

Stand of Iranian Premier on Khomeini'. Overall, it could have a beneficial effect in Iran, but Ambassador Sullivan objected strongly to a section revealing the procedures in Washington by which the President was meeting regularly with Secretary Vance, Mr Brzezinski and Secretary Brown. It said that a key role was being played by General Robert Huyser, who had been in Iran since the Shah decided to leave. General Huyser had been working closely with the Iranian military, urging them to support the Bakhtiar government. His daily reports to the White House, regarded as critical to the American understanding of the situation, were transmitted by secure means, and the information was treated as classified at the highest level, because if it were to leak out it could be fatal to what we were trying to do. I told the Ambassador that I would draw this to Secretary Brown's attention.

Knowing that Washington must be very anxious about the course of events, I got straight through to Secretary Brown, even though it was four hours earlier than usual. I brought up the *New York Times* article, pointing out that any leak of plans would bring an immediate counter-action from the opposition, who were very adroit at this kind of psychological warfare. Secretary Brown assured me that all correspondence and conversations concerning my reports were given very limited distribution and treated with the utmost security. I said that nevertheless it looked as if there must be a leak.

Then I discussed the pros and cons of staying in Iran. I made no request to leave, then or any time later, and I told the Secretary that as far as I was concerned the decision was entirely up to Washington. He said they would give this full consideration; meanwhile he thought it was time to do what the President had been proposing, namely to position an aircraft at Mehrabad Airport to take me out in an emergency. I suggested that it be a C-130, and preferably one with the same camouflage as the Iranian C-130s. It could be parked among them, and would not draw any attention. I assured him that I felt comfortable with the arrangements for getting me out of the city to Mehrabad Airport under almost any conditions. General Rabii was ready to have a helicopter lift me either from the Embassy compound or from the SCS compound direct to the airport. I had absolute confidence that this transport would be available.

Secretary Brown inevitably brought up the matter of foreign

military sales. I told him that Eric had been very busy and had gathered all the information. But as for a memorandum of understanding, that looked completely out of the question. Secretary Brown said he understood the difficulties, but he hoped I appreciated the problems they were having with Congress on these programmes.

He spoke of complaints in the international media that Washington, having sold F-14s to Iran, was now trying to repossess them. He suggested that there should be a fly-over demonstration to show that the F-14s were still in Iran. I agreed, especially as it would also demonstrate the military strength behind Mr Bakhtiar.

On my way back to the residence, the night air was menacing with the noise of weapons being fired. My state of mind was not the best. Things were looking grimmer than at any time since my arrival in Tehran.

Saturday, 27 January 1979

Among the press items from the US for the day before was a barbed question at the State Department briefing. The questioner referred to a report that a high official of the administration was thrilled by Bakhtiar's strong stand, and then asked whether the killings in the student demonstration were part of that strong stand. The administration was in fact exercising plenty of restraint – if anything too much to achieve their objectives. Tom Reston, the State's spokesman, regretted the casualties and loss of life, and said our desire was that the Iranian people get back to peaceful conditions. But he repeated our view that the Iranians could not be dictated to from outside. The questioner then asked: 'In that connection, is General Huyser still there?' Of course, the innuendo was that I was the one who was doing the dictating.

This would only add fuel to what *Pravda* and the opposition were saying. The heat generated around my presence was already getting to be uncomfortable. 'Death to Huyser', in Farsi, was becoming a popular graffito. The soldiers saw it every time they entered or left the compound, and obviously it had to have some

impact on them. I had also been elevated to the status of appearing
on placards carried by marchers, complete with picture, sharing
that honour with President Carter.

At the office, General Gharabaghi asked me to come right over
to talk about the National Security Council meeting. The Group
were assembled much earlier than usual. Apparently the religious
leaders had submitted requests last night to conduct demonstrations today. They let General Rahimi, the military governor of
Tehran, handle this; but Mr Bakhtiar insisted that the proceedings
should be peaceful, and that they did not go towards the airport
beyond Shahyad Square.

The Group had carefully reviewed yesterday's incident at the
University, and were satisfied that the military had conducted
themselves properly. When they first confronted the crowd, they
tried to restore order without using weapons. This, of course, got
them nowhere. Then they fired over the heads of the crowds, but
the demonstrators were used to this and did not expect any further
action. So, far from dispersing, they made an overt armed attack
on some of the troops, who lowered the muzzles of their guns
below head level. The troops were very discriminating about it,
and only fired at people who were armed and openly attacking
them. It was hard to fault them.

The Army believed they had located a couple of caches of arms,
one of them underneath a hospital. The National Security Council
had discussed how to handle this, and it was agreed to find civilian
employees at the hospital, who would check whether it was true. If
weapons were found, they could send in troops to get them. I gave
them every encouragement.

General Gharabaghi said they had received indications of a
change in the French government's attitude to Khomeini and
Bakhtiar. They seemed to be getting more sympathetic towards
the Prime Minister. Air France had cancelled all their flights to
Iran, and would not be bringing Khomeini back. So we now had to
find out who was going to Paris airport to pick up Khomeini and
bring him out tomorrow.

Mr Bazargan had contacted General Gharabaghi and wanted to
have a meeting with him to find out whether the Army was really
solid for Bakhtiar. He also thought they should have a talk about
Khomeini's return. As this sounded constructive, Gharabaghi said
he would meet him, but it would have to be in Bakhtiar's office.

Bazargan didn't go for this. Some of us pushed hard for a meeting either in Bazargan's office or Gharabaghi's, but the General stood very firm. It must be Bakhtiar's.

I asked if Bakhtiar was still feeling hostile to the religious people, and Gharabaghi told me that things seemed to have thawed a bit at a meeting yesterday with Ayatollah Beheshti. Beheshti had changed his tune about the Bakhtiar government being illegal. This development coincided with some splits emerging in the opposition, and the hiving off of several factions into their own little committees.

Gharabaghi said that no decisions were made on the handling of Khomeini's return next day, but Bakhtiar would go on the radio tonight to tell the people to stay away from the airport, and to explain what had happened in the fracas at the University. He wanted to give his side of the picture. He would tell the public that when necessary, the military would protect themselves and the laws of the land.

The National Security Council would be meeting again today and would make a firm decision on how to handle things. By then they hoped to know whether the Ayatollah would be coming back tomorrow. The cancellation of the Air France flights suggested that he would not. If so, they could open the airport. On the other hand, there was something to be said for leaving it closed; though this could cause a confrontation, some sort of bloodshed was probably unavoidable, and it might be better to have it with Khomeini out of the country. They would discuss these alternatives with Mr Bakhtiar tonight, and Gharabaghi said he would support him either way. He was sure the Army could control the airport and access to it.

We were interrupted by a top-priority phone call to General Gharabaghi. A reliable source had intercepted a phone call from Paris to a woman in Tehran, who said that enough arms had now been delivered in Iran for the arrival of Khomeini to proceed. She said that as soon as they knew of his departure time from Paris, they would distribute the weapons. Knowing as we did all about the gun-running and stockpiling in the mosques, this merely confirmed our worst fears. General Gharabaghi said he hoped to get back to me after the National Security Council meeting, and I bade them farewell.

In the office I was told by the Executive Officer, Major Ray

Burnette, that he had received two telephone calls over the military circuits threatening my life. He had received such threats before, but never over the military circuits – only the civil network in our office. This incident really got the attention of my body-guards. They were always closely attuned to all reports and activities, but to know there was access to our communication systems was a new dimension. I left all aspects of security in their hands; I wasn't indifferent, but I had more than I could handle without that extra burden, and I knew I could trust them. From time to time they would make a major change in their methods, and I simply assumed they had received new threat information.

By this time we were getting reports on the day's Khomeini demonstration. The radio and television news were counting it at a million plus. We knew it was very large, because we had watched it pass the compound. Our own estimate, based on the area of streets filled, was around 300,000. They adhered to what they had been told by General Rahimi, proceeding to Shahyad Square and no further. There was a small group of about 200 Bakhtiar supporters; it was good to see a little of our side on the streets even though the group was small.

I told my security people to dispatch an advance car to check our routes. After twenty minutes they called back and gave us a route to the Embassy, which we took without incident. I debriefed Ambassador Sullivan on the government's strategy for tomorrow, and brought his attention to the threats on my life.

I waited till midnight for a report from General Gharabaghi, but in vain. So I made my briefing to Washington without it. Secretary Brown asked if Mr Bakhtiar had enforced his 'No Work, No Pay' decision. I told him it was a little early to say, because the first pay-day subsequent to that order would not be until next week. Mr Bakhtiar was still insisting that he would enforce it to the limit, which was music to my ears.

Secretary Brown was all in favour of speeding up the evacuation of Americans. I made a hard sell for permission to start a draw-down of the military, and much to my surprise he agreed, and gave me unqualified authority to start reducing the MAAG. I asked him to institute all procedures possible to monitor the arrangements for flying Khomeini to Iran. Secretary Brown said they were doing that, and would continue to do it.

I repeated my apprehensions about the return of Khomeini. I explained that I had been reporting incremental progress day by day, but this was modest against the background of the almost total economic paralysis. The next few days would be very touch-and-go for Mr Bakhtiar.

On the control of the airport, Secretary Brown became very precise and said this was a decision for the Iranians. I could by all means advise them, but I was not to force a decision on them.

Secretary Brown then read me two cables. The first was from Paris, saying that the French were beginning to tilt towards Bakhtiar. Along with the cancellation of the Air France flights, this made sense, but I said it all seemed too good to be true. The other message had been sent by Mr Bakhtiar to Khomeini in an attempt to delay his arrival for three weeks. This, he said, would enable him to stabilize the situation and create a more favourable atmosphere for Khomeini's reception. Bakhtiar said he was ready to go to Paris and discuss these points in person. Khomeini had replied that he would be willing to talk, but Bakhtiar must resign first.

Before signing off, Secretary Brown said he would be most anxious to hear my report the next day.

Sunday, 28 January 1979

At breakfast I read a *New York Times* article on the scale-down of arms sales to Iran. It told of Eric von Marbod's mission to work out a plan for continuing American sales, and said that both Ambassador Sullivan and General Huyser were deeply involved in the discussions. Disturbingly, it alleged that the administration's immediate concern was that owing to the critical state of the economy, the Iranian government might not be able to pay for any new hardware or logistic support. This could mean, according to officials, that as early as next month the administration might be forced to cancel several arms sales, including a $1.6 billion deal for four guided-missile destroyers, and over $2 billion worth of fighter airplanes. The failure of Iran to meet payments on existing military contracts could also result in the rapid withdrawal of American technicians and logistics support, and this could cripple the Iranian armed forces. The withdrawal was already well under way but had nothing to do with the payments; it was strictly for self-protection.

Ford Rowan of the NBC News had covered the same ground. He quoted Prime Minister Bakhtiar as saying that he would cancel some of the contracts because Iran could not be the policemen of the Persian Gulf. General Robert Huyser had been talking with Iranian officials about contracts to be postponed or cancelled outright. A decision was expected soon.

The part that bothered me about these items was the implication that we would only support the Iranians if money was available, which of course it was not. I would now have to reassure the Group that we were ready to operate on good faith. But I held little hope that we would achieve what Washington wanted, namely a comprehensive memorandum of understanding signed by both parties on programmes for the future. In addition to the practical obstacles, there could also be some danger in signing such an agreement – the paper could be used in evidence should the Bakhtiar government fail. The military leaders were taking great care not to sign documents which could incriminate them. The fear of imprisonment or death was constantly there, and did much to explain their vacillation in face of problems. For them, many of these decisions were a matter of life and death.

I had a wire from General Al Haig, saying that because of the possible involvement of military elements under his command, he would like me to keep him abreast of my message traffic.

An article from *Pravda* castigated American interference, and said that without any question the decision to prevent the return of the Ayatollah last Thursday was taken on American advice, transmitted by General Huyser. The United States was in the business of activating subversive war against Muslim movements in the region, because of its strategic importance to Washington. This charge would reach the Iranian people through one means or another, and could only increase the threat level on me from both the religious element and the Tudeh party. This growing threat was cramping my movements at a time when it was becoming more and more urgent that I should move around to get results.

At the office my copy of the *Tehran Journal* boldly stated: 'Bakhtiar to Meet Khomeini in Paris'. It said that Bakhtiar would leave for Paris within forty-eight hours. It looked as if something had transpired during the night.

In the *Kayhan*, two-inch black letters proclaimed: 'Break Through', and 'Bakhtiar Wins Khomeini Audience'. The Prime Minister had announced that 'as a patriotic Iranian who considers himself a small member of the glorious movement, and as a person who believes in the leadership of the Ayatollah, I have decided to go to Paris within 48 hours to have the pleasure of meeting him and to seek advice on the future of the country.' He said that the Ayatollah had every right to return, 'but under the present alarming conditions that we have here, there are irresponsible elements in all ranks of society', so Khomeini's return after fourteen years in exile must be arranged carefully. There were technical difficulties at Mehrabad Airport which must be removed before it could be reopened to commercial traffic. Bakhtiar didn't say how long that would take. He said he hoped to negotiate with Khomeini in Paris on several subjects, including the method of his return, and he also wanted to make it clear that he was in absolute control of the government and the Army. He was very specific about this: 'The legal government knows its responsibilities, and the government has full control over the Army.'

He predicted that the strike and demonstrations would subside. He accused his opponents of using mosques, schools and hospitals to store weapons, as well he might. As to demonstrations, he had no objection to peaceful gatherings if they were held with permission, but unauthorized gatherings by irresponsible people could not be allowed. Mr Bakhtiar's letter to the Ayatollah was published, and is worth quoting in full.

To Your Respected Excellency Ayatollah Sayeed Ruhollah Khomeini. After extending my greetings and respects to the sacred prominent religious leader on whom God has bestowed the knowledge to fight for truth, I hereby ask your permission to bring a few points to your attention. I hope by dint of God's assistance, I shall succeed in explaining that which, as a fighting Iranian Muslim, I am obliged to explain, lest I should come to shame for failure to tell the truth.

1. Your Excellency is fully aware that the programmes of

the present government, from the details to the major points, are the same points that have been called for by yourself and those martyrs and crusaders who have fought for freedom during the past period of suppression. As soon as I undertook the post of Prime Minister, I started implementing these points, relying on God's assistance, and with willingness and honesty. There is no doubt that if I am given a reasonable period of time, I will implement these points in detail to preserve the legitimate rights of the Muslim people of Iran, relying on my 25-year political fight to preserve the independence and territorial integrity of Iran, and respecting the martyrs who have lost their lives for freedom. To this end, I need God's help as well as Your Excellency's assistance and the prayers of all the friendly people of this country.

2. Although to meet such a prominent religious leader as yourself is an opportunity that I, like most Iranian people who are for freedom and the independence of Iran, wish for, in my opinion, and because of the various intrigues and disturbances which are prevailing between pro and anti groups, your return would result in further disturbances which would prevent the government from continuing its programme, which has been approved by all the devout, freedom-seeking people of Iran. Therefore, I beg you to accept a delay in your return to Iran.

3. If, on your arrival, you announce the formation of a political organization which is not reconciled with the constitution, you will definitely face the government with a difficult and dangerous situation. Therefore I would not undertake the responsibility for what may happen as a result of this.

4. With due regard for the present situation and your benevolent ideas for the prosperity of the Iranian people, I hope you will allow that any change in the country's system must take place through peaceful means, and according to democratic principles which have been accepted universally; or after a quarter of a century of domination of selfishness, absolute brutality and general corruption, we will be faced with an even deeper and greater catastrophe. If that happens, all I have done will be useless. Your Excellency, only God knows who is the friend and who is the enemy, because only

God is aware of what is happening in their minds. With such a belief, I hope that my sincerity and devotion to freedom will be revealed to you, and that I can be successful in proving that such a demand is merely to prevent those incidents which, if they happen, will only cause deep grief and sorrow. The amount of sorrow that may appear to us may make all the crusaders who have fought for freedom mourn for a long time, and will also hurt the spirit of those martyrs who have lost their lives for freedom.

Sincerely,
Shahpur Bakhtiar.

Under the heading 'Khomeini Agrees to Receive Premier', the *Tehran Journal* said that the Ayatollah had been scheduled to leave Paris on Saturday night, but Air France had told him Tehran airport was still closed. The report became cloudy at this point. It said that Khomeini would be meeting Bakhtiar, but also that he would be leaving France tonight to arrive in Tehran on Monday morning. It was not clear how he could do both. Nor was it clear how he could arrive in Tehran if the airport were still closed. It seemed more probable that Khomeini planned to leave on Monday night or Tuesday night. The Group thought that his personal staff, having heard about the security problems at our end, were not too unhappy that they had the excuse of the airport being closed.

The other front-page article covered yesterday's demonstration. A picture showed marchers carrying a big placard in English: 'No Imperialism (USA)', and a banner: 'No Communism (USSR)'. The headline proclaimed 'Millions Call for the Return of Khomeini', an outrageous exaggeration.

The back page of the *Tehran Journal* showed some attempt at balance. Under a panoramic view of Saturday's demonstration for Khomeini was a picture, admittedly much smaller, of our Thursday demonstration in support of Bakhtiar. Its caption read: 'Supporting the Constitution – a section of the vast crowd which took part in Thursday's march in support of the present Iranian Constitution'. The article correctly reported the number of marchers as nearly 300,000 and added that such groups had demonstrated all over Iran.

The Group, six strong today, looked a little haggard. They had been in session with Mr Bakhtiar until well after midnight, discussing the 'what-ifs' of Khomeini's return. They had decided to keep the airport closed for at least two more days. They also discussed Mr Bakhtiar's proposed visit to Khomeini. We were all pleased about this effort to get direct contact, hopefully with a view to delaying Khomeini's return for at least a month.

They told me of a nasty incident with the Homofars yesterday at the Isfahan helicopter training school. About 4,000 Homofars were going to work when the base commander got word that there were some troublemakers among them, and refused to admit any of them to the facility. On the way back to town they engaged some Army troops and had a real scrap. There were no casualties, but each side had taken captives. The present situation was kind of a stand-off, and it would have to be settled this morning. It had been badly handled, in the Group's opinion, by the post commander. They would send some higher-ranking people to sort it out.

We were interrupted by an urgent telephone call which informed General Gharabaghi that Khomeini had refused to see Mr Bakhtiar unless he resigned first. This information came from representatives in Paris and not Khomeini, but we decided we should come up with a position to put to Mr Bakhtiar. We agreed that the military would not tolerate his resignation; so far from that, he should firmly consign the Ayatollah to a religious role, and make every effort to delay his return as long as possible. The Premier should be flown to Paris by the Iranian military, leaving on Monday morning. This would give time for the terms of reference to be resolved between himself and Khomeini. We relayed these conditions to Mr Bakhtiar's office immediately.

With the Prime Minister due to be out of the country, we discussed the possibility of the Shah returning. He was still in Morocco. The Group told me that his children had joined him, so it looked as if he planned to stay there for a while. The rumours had it that he planned to return to Egypt, but the Group did not believe he would risk coming back to Iran.

Reviewing the arrangements for the airport, they said Mr Bakhtiar had agreed to keep it closed for two more days. The military wanted it to be closed to all commercial traffic as long as Khomeini threatened to return. We discussed this in some detail, because we were trying to help foreign nationals, including US personnel, to get out of the country. Equally, some of our essential supplies had to come in by air. The military were unimpressed by this, and said the airport must be kept closed indefinitely.

We agreed that Khomeini's ultimatum was so intolerable, and Bakhtiar's attitude so reasonable, that the Prime Minister should go on the radio and television that evening, or the next morning, to explain the situation to the people. We also thought he should issue a personal message to the troops, in keeping with the new procedure we had set up to keep them informed, and it struck us that it might be a good idea to find a retired general to make a similar statement. This could have a very definite impact, particularly on younger members of the armed services. We also worked up papers for local commanders to explain the situation to their troops.

We heard that several people had headed for the airport, under the impression that Khomeini was coming, and were dispersed at Shahyad Square. On their way back to town, near the University, there was some gunfire and several casualties were reported. We didn't know how serious this was, but at least things were far better today than they had been on either Friday or Saturday.

General Rabii objected to the pressures applied by the US to protect the sensitive weaponry. He understood our concern, but his people were doing the job adequately. He asked us to try to keep it out of the American press. It was a real irritant to the Homofars, who were well aware that the equipment had been paid for by Iran, and suspected that we planned to withdraw it from the country. I told him I had reported this to the Secretary of Defence and would now do so again.

General Gharabaghi welcomed a US warning that Soviet intervention in Iran could well trigger off an American response. This was most helpful, and fortified the Group's confidence in Washington's support. They called to my attention the report of a news conference in which President Jimmy Carter had said he had decided to send emergency fuel supplies to Iran. What caused them concern was his disclosure of the location and route of the tanker. We had it going up the river when the National Iranian Oil Company changed their minds and we had to reverse course. Now it was again anchored twelve miles offshore. The Group immediately blamed the President's announcement for this setback. I thought that was unfair, because I didn't believe that NIOC could react that quickly.

We reviewed the oil production, which was improving slowly and was now up to 660,000 barrels per day. It looked as if there would be enough to meet the needs of Tehran and surrounding suburbs, but it would still leave shortages in other parts of the country. The NIOC had asked the public in the cities to reduce consumption so that they could distribute more to the remote regions.

There was a new chill in the opposition's attitude to the military. This could have been due to the crackdown on the disorders at the University, or to the clashes at Khatami Air Base, where special forces had been sent to keep order. False rumours were now going round that 165 airmen had been arrested and were to be executed by firing squad. Though denied by Mr Bakhtiar, these stories may have done damage.

We learned that in yesterday's affray eight soldiers had been wounded, three of them seriously, when an unidentified gunman opened fire on them. This man was said to have been wearing a military uniform and using a Russian automatic rifle. To inflame things further, the opposition chose to exhibit in Shahyad Square the bodies of seven of the people who were killed on Friday at the University. Many opposition demonstrators had warned that if Khomeini did not arrive, the machineguns would come out. This was further confirmation of our view that they were getting their weapons distributed, and we could be heading for a fire-fight.

The Group mentioned media reports that the military had been meeting with Khomeini's people. The implication of these stories, put out by the opposition, was that the military were acting independently of the Bakhtiar government. It was quite an astute piece of public wedge-driving.

I asked them again, with due finesse, if they had had any contact with the Shah. General Gharabaghi immediately replied that there was nothing direct, but they had heard that he planned to stay in Morocco, and that he was very tired, very silent and very sad. He was having difficulty in sleeping, and suffered periods of profound depression. They said one of the reasons they expected him to stay in Morocco was that the royal children and the Shah's mother-in-law had joined him at Marrakesh, and this could hardly have happened unless His Majesty intended to stay a while.

General Gharabaghi told me that Mr Bakhtiar had been in touch with Hassan Nazih, an Iranian lawyer friend of his who lived in

Paris, and who was also a friend of Khomeini. He had passed on to Mr Yazdi the Prime Minister's message suggesting that Khomeini should delay his return for the sake of his personal safety; but Yazdi had told him it was too late. The Ayatollah had made up his mind, and nothing would change it.

Within three hours of getting this reply Mr Bakhtiar had closed the country's airports, and Khomeini suddenly had no means of getting home. As the lawyer put it, this was the latest act played out in a stark drama on the Iranian stage: the Ayatollah in one corner, the Army in the other, and the tottering Bakhtiar regime caught in the middle. Mr Bakhtiar had given the impression that the airports had been closed by the Army, but the Ayatollah blamed Bakhtiar and branded him as a traitor – language he had not used about anyone except the Shah.

The lawyer considered that Bakhtiar should resign and let Khomeini return. He said that after extensive talks with Khomeini he had reached two conclusions. One was that the Ayatollah would not settle for any form of government which did not abolish the monarchy, and the other was that he genuinely did not want any government position for himself. The first point confirmed what the Shah had told me about Khomeini's deep personal hatred of the Pahlavi dynasty. I was much less convinced by his disavowal of political ambitions.

Back at our office, I complied with General Haig's request that he be included in all message traffic. I prepared a message telling him that we would certainly do this, but he should understand that nearly all my dealings with Washington were by secure phone.I knew he would understand the reason for this, as we had discussed it many times. I told him that the outlook was far from bright, but I did believe we had gained some ground. By way of progress I cited the impressive parade of the Imperial Guard, our orderly 300,000-strong demonstration on Thursday, and the restrained behaviour of the opposition demonstrations. I pointed out that when Mr Bakhtiar announced the enforcement of martial law, the opposition started requesting permission for demonstrations, and when it was granted they conducted themselves responsibly. The problems at the University had been caused by the Tudeh, and were handled promptly and severely. Nobody could say that they had not been warned.

Again, closing the airports had shown resolve. There had been signs of splintering in the opposition. A few more people were back to work; and even though this was brought about by the Khomeini forces, nonetheless it had a stabilizing impact. The banks were open for limited business three days a week. The customs and transport services were at about half speed. The telephone and telegraph strike was called off, though the workers had been very slow to report back.

On the debit side of the ledger, there seemed to be a deadly effective Communist group, and the authorities did not have the expertise to cope with them. Neither police nor soldiers were trained or sophisticated enough to ferret them out and take them into custody. I explained how the Communists would infiltrate a group, fabricate a problem, and then just vanish into the crowd; we had no one smart enough to catch them. To make things worse, there were more underground-trained people about and arms were flooding into the country each day.

Finally, on Bakhtiar's readiness to go to Paris, I said we thought he had made a very reasonable offer. He had had to swallow a lot of pride, and Khomeini's reply was completely unreasonable. Bakhtiar would certainly not resign.

I went back to the Embassy and met Ambassador Sullivan, who told me he had learned that the opposition had little sympathy with the conditions Khomeini had placed on a meeting with Bakhtiar. They were disappointed that Bakhtiar would probably not be going to Paris. Sullivan was convinced that opposition figures such as Bazargan and Ayatollah Beheshti had been pushing Khomeini to moderate his demands. Many of them would have liked to see some negotiations. But we were stuck with a cantankerous, hard-headed, seventy-nine-year-old Ayatollah who seemed to be absolutely inflexible.

The Ambassador told me that some opposition leaders would have been quite content to keep the Shah, but in an honorary position, much like King Olaf of Norway. In that role he could have kept up some of the excellent programmes he had started. By no means everyone in the opposition wanted to plunge the country back two or three centuries under an unbridled Ayatollah Khomeini. It appeared to me that the situation was starting to take the shape we wanted, but unfortunately if Khomeini was to return in the next few days his arrival would very probably change the course of events. If only we had the additional thirty to sixty days.

That evening we had more than usual difficulty with the secure phone. I started by reporting on the Homofars, but Secretary Brown soon switched to his old theme: what did I really think about the military? Did I still believe they would measure up to a real crisis? I answered with an unqualifed affirmative. I said there were increasing problems every day, but they seemed manageable and were being addressed promptly and sensibly. I thought most of the unrest was due to inactivity, as with the Army aviation and the Air Force, who did not have enough fuel to fly. The ground forces were busy with law enforcement, and could train without fuel, and they had presented few problems.

Secretary Brown was very interested in Mr Bakhtiar's putative trip to Paris, and wanted to know how it might affect the situation. Would the military get uneasy if he stayed away too long, and take some precipitous action? Might the Shah think this was the moment to step in to keep things under control? I gave him a flat No on both points. I felt confident that the military would ride along, provided no one tried to overthrow the government; if that were to occur, I thought and hoped they would act. I had asked the Group about contact with the Shah, and all six of them denied they had any. I was sure they agreed that if the Shah were to return, the effect would be devastating, and if there was any contact with him, I suspected he would get the message.

Secretary Brown then spoke of the US forces in the area. The aircraft carrier *Constellation* had been in Singapore for some time as one of the military reinforcement elements. Now it needed to go back to Subic Bay for maintenance work, and he wanted to know if this would cause me any problems. I said No, because as far as anybody in Iran was aware, the carrier force had never got as far as the Indian Ocean, so I couldn't see how its removal could be interpreted as a signal to anyone. The Soviets might draw a different conclusion, but as far as I was concerned the carrier could be moved.

I closed with the latest instalment of the tanker saga. Once again we had it up the river, with high hopes of offloading the fuel where we could protect it; but just as had happened with other initiatives in that area, the plan had gone kaput. The tanker had now gone back down the river and was again anchored twelve miles offshore.

However, I pressed them to leave it there, because if the situation got really tense, I felt we would come up with some way of offloading it.

Monday, 29 January 1979

The next day broke to an onslaught in *Pravda* describing me as the 'Vice-Regent' and blaming me for all Iran's troubles. It was implied that I was helping to direct the sanguinary policing of the demonstrations.

At General Gharabaghi's office, the first thing we discussed was Mr Bakhtiar's plans. He had decided not to go to Paris, and he was equally firm that he would not resign. He had promised to open the airport, and even though he had not given a date, he implied that it would open today. He had also said that he would let the Ayatollah return, though he did not say when.

The Group had discussed with the Prime Minister the procedure to be followed when Khomeini did return. They agreed to keep the troops out of contact with the masses, and use them only to protect the essential installations, as well as Mr Bakhtiar and his government. They had decided to seek a high-level meeting with the opposition to clarify the ground rules. They particularly wanted to see Mr Bazargan, and had invited him to meet them today.

The Prime Minister would tell the armed forces that he was going to allow Khomeini to return. Hopefully the Ayatollah would be more reasonable once he was back in Iran; but, if he did not modify the views he was expressing in Paris, then they were in for a scrap. Bakhtiar was now convinced that the day-to-day delay could not go on forever. Khomeini must be allowed back, and now was as good a time as any. There were still a lot of unsettled questions about exactly how they would handle him, and how tolerant they should be of his antics. So Mr Bakhtiar had scheduled a meeting with the Regency Council for this evening to finalize plans, and he would then go over them with the military. He was also going to discuss them with Ambassador Sullivan. This pleased both General Gast and me very much.

The Group gave me an update on the Homofar situation in Isfahan. They said the problem now seemed to have been solved, as the Homofars had turned in their guns. But there had been a nasty incident involving an American employed by the Bell helicopter people. He had been riding in a taxi, and when the driver tried to collect the fare, an argument took place in which the driver drew a knife. The American pulled out a gun and shot him, and ran to a hotel where he barricaded himself into a room. This had all the earmarks of a major incident, and we would have to monitor progress closely. On our side, it would be up to the Ambassador to call the shots.

I told them that Washington had been getting more concerned each day about the safety and welfare of the remaining Americans in Iran. We had received a directive from the State Department to evacuate all remaining dependents. I told them we would also try to reduce the size of our MAAG. With the constant increase in the threat level, we would like their help in requisitioning a building where our people could be housed together for better protection. I thought we should consider a hotel in Tehran, principally for the remaining MAAG people. We were still hauling people out on Military Airlift Command planes, even though the airport was closed to commercials. This was a help, but inevitably the opposition wanted to know why American airplanes could move when others could not.

The anti-American fever had been growing rapidly in the last few days. In fact we had a preliminary report that one of our officers, Lieutenant Colonel Larry Davis, had been attacked last night. He was returning to his residence in the early evening when a man ran up to him, fired two shots at close range from a small-calibre pistol, and fled. Colonel Davis was wounded, but not seriously.

Gharabaghi suggested that I myself must be careful. He asked if I was aware that my picture was being carried in the streets and they were chanting 'Death to Huyser'. I said I was, but if they heard of any more threats I would be glad to know of them. If they thought I was attracting assassins to other Americans, I would, of course, consider leaving the country. They were very firm that they did not want me to do that.

General Toufanian brought up Eric von Marbod's mission, and we discussed in some detail the memorandum of understanding.

He said it might be very difficult for him to sign it, and if he did, he would have to backdate it to 1 January. He thought that anybody who did sign it would be jeopardizing himself in the event of the opposition taking over. I told him I recognized this, and we would try to persuade Washington to be as accommodating on the wording as possible, but I would appreciate his cooperation as we had to have a document.

We discussed the fuel tanker, and they thought there was a chance of getting it up the river for unloading tomorrow. I did not share their optimism.

While we were talking, a flight of F-14s roared overhead. I asked General Rabii: 'What are you up to?' He said: 'Fulfilling your request to show strength and make it clear that the equipment is still in-country.' I said: 'Fine. How many do you have airborne today?' He said: 'We will have more than a hundred sorties, which should show the public that we have the capability to fly, and the equipment is still here.' He had a real look of pride and achievement.

Suddenly we got a telephone message that the opposition was preparing to storm the Gendarmerie headquarters in Tehran. I advised that it should be considered an essential element of the government, and should be protected. The proper way, in my opinion, was to fire over the demonstrators' heads and use teargas. If that didn't work, the gun barrels must be lowered so there could be no question that the troops meant business. General Gharabaghi immediately got on the telephone to Mr Bakhtiar, and then rang for his executive officer. After giving him some very rapid-fire instructions in Farsi, he turned to me and said the situation would be handled precisely as we had discussed it.

The next phone call informed us that the demonstrators had seized a Gendarmerie chief, Major General Taqi Latifi. Soon after, we got a report that the troops were following our directions right to the letter. They had tried to stop the crowd without lowering their gun barrels, but to no avail. So they had picked out the leaders and shot them. We did not have an accurate report on the loss of life, but these tactics had certainly turned the crowd back.

We received a message that Khomeini had decided to delay his arrival in Tehran for two or three more days. Again we reviewed all contingencies for that fateful event. They seemed relaxed and rational, but I wondered how long this mood would survive Khomeini's return. I simply could not rule out a spontaneous breaking of ranks.

I returned post-haste to the Embassy, anxious to find out how Ambassador Sullivan's meeting had gone with Mr Bakhtiar. He told me that Mr Bakhtiar was obviously more worried than he had been at their last meeting, but did not have much else to report. We discussed the capability of the military again, and I still maintained that they had good discipline and organization. The Ambassador simply disagreed. He thought that the moment Khomeini arrived, the great majority of the armed forces would immediately capitulate.

We then discussed the possibility of the military taking action if it looked as if Mr Bakhtiar was going to fold. Here again, we disagreed. I was of the firm opinion that if Mr Bakhtiar gave an order for military to take over, they would obey. Ambassador Sullivan was convinced they would not.

That evening, as I made my way across the Embassy grounds to the Chancellory, the streets were noisier with gunfire and incantations than ever before. Emotions were building and we were slithering back to less peaceful times. The guards acted jumpy.

In Washington, Secretary Brown was not available, so my report was taken by Charlie Duncan and the Chairman. One of the biggest stories of the day was the incident with the taxi-driver in Isfahan. The American was still barricaded in the hotel and a good many Iranians were wanting to get their hands on him. Our consulate people were on hand, trying to sort it out.

I reported that the decision had been made to open the airfield, and this would probably happen tomorrow. I did not expect the Ayatollah for a couple of days, but if he found out the airport was going to open, he might want to get back immediately. Meanwhile, the Regency Council was meeting tonight to finalize decisions. They asked how I expected the crowds to behave. I said it depended to a large extent on Khomeini; he could keep them in control if he wanted. They then asked whether I thought we should stick with Mr Bakhtiar. I gave an unqualified Yes. In the last two or three days he had shown more strength than ever. He showed absolutely no sign of folding.

They were very glad to hear our plans to protect Americans in-country. I told them we were trying to evacuate all we could. It was just a matter of how fast the aircraft could shift them. We had taken out over 250 that day and 300 more were scheduled to leave tomorrow.

I was asked about my own personal security. I told them that thanks to *Pravda*, Radio Moscow and Tass giving me credit far beyond what I deserved, and the local press blaming me for much of the violence, my threat level was at quite a peak. However, I had very good protection, and was not concerned.

I asked them to relax their pressure for an arms sales memorandum of understanding. I stated that some people in Washington simply did not seem to understand how paralysed and helpless the Iranian government was, and how every ounce of energy was needed for the immediate battle. The day after tomorrow was like a century ahead. I again emphasized that the PLO/Communist activity was increasing, not only in Tehran but all over Iran, and that the flow of weapons from outside was becoming a flood. Some were coming in from Afghanistan, which could present a real problem.

On my way back to the residence, the shindy made me realize that, after a relatively tranquil couple of weeks, the level of general turbulence would probably be back to where it was when I arrived on 4 January – only now it could be worse, because they had the fuel for automobiles. Again, the night air was fouled by the smell of burning rubber.

Tuesday, 30 January 1979

Over breakfast I read a message from General Haig, who said they were following the drama minute by minute. He agreed with my general assessment, and went on to say: 'There are clearly matters over which you and I have no control, and about which I will talk to you upon your return.' I thought this was significant because he was obviously referring to the view we both held, prior to the trip, namely that it was a 'no win' situation. He had clearly concluded that all further efforts were now futile. He said he was standing by to offer maximum assistance for the next evacuation phase, which he expected to become somewhat hectic as the wolf got closer to the carcass. He told me to feel free to task him personally on any issue which I or the Ambassador might feel needed a shove, either directly or indirectly. It was good to know that he was in there rooting for me. He ended by saying: 'Keep your head down. We are all in admiration. Best wishes, Al Haig.'

The other message that caught my attention was another *Pravda* report, this time promoting me to 'Governor-General in Iran' and saying that I had successfully replaced the Shah. 'Thus General Huyser, together with the Bakhtiar government and the military bosses, bear responsibility for the daily bloodshed in Tehran and other Iranian cities.' They claimed that a sort of creeping military coup was being carried out as a result of crude and open US interference in Iranian internal affairs. But for this interference, the situation would long since have settled down.

At the State Department's press briefing one of the questions mentioned *Pravda*'s 'rather ungenerous comment' in calling me the Vice-Regent, and asked if our government had any comment. The spokesman said that if he were speaking in a private capacity he would call it 'baloney', but in his official capacity he would just say it was untrue. He added that he did not need any help from *Pravda*.

I left for the SCS compound, and as we arrived at the huge iron gates the driver became quite excited. There was a large red-painted message in Farsi on the compound wall, and he kept pointing at it. The guards showed their normal courtesy in passing us through, but they seemed very apprehensive and looked intently in the car. I asked what the excitement was about, and was told by the driver that the writing said: 'Death to Huyser'. That must have given him a nasty sensation, because he had been driving me every other day since my arrival, and we had developed a warm friendship. His apprehension may have risen many times in the last three weeks, but this time they must have pegged the scale.

When I read the Tehran newspapers I understood why things had been so noisy the previous night. Following the bloodshed at the Gendarmerie, the opposition had chosen to burn down the entire red light district of Tehran, as well as the Shams Brewery in South Tehran. These, of course, were symbolic religious acts to rid the city of evil. Tehran had a notorious red light district, and its torching was the worst arson incident since the big day of 5 November. The Shams Brewery, a complex which included a cinema, some liquor stores and several restaurants, was totally destroyed in what an eye-witness described as a 'spectacular blaze that sent huge piles of smoke boiling into the sky'. As the rioters stormed through the brothel areas they shouted: 'Purification by fire!' One prostitute watching her place of business go up in smoke lamented: 'First it was the 11 o'clock curfew, just at the time we started work, and now they burn us down. If this is the Islamic Republic, I prefer the Shah. At least he let us work.'

The headlines of *Kayhan* declared: 'Bakhtiar Unmoved'. The article referred to his refusal to resign, as demanded by Khomeini. There was a picture of General Latifi, the man the rioters had captured when they stormed the Gendarmerie. It showed him apparently unconscious in the hands of the mob. He was described as being in a coma, and was covered from head to toe with stab wounds, bruises and scratches. The report said that his ordeal began when his official blue Mercedes entered the Square and was set on by the mob. The driver pleaded for mercy, but his assailants kicked him viciously and left him nearly senseless by the burning car. They then turned their full fury on the General, shouting: 'Kill him, kill him.' Clawing hands reached to rip out his hair, gouge his eyes and scratch his face. He was already bleeding profusely when someone pulled out a dagger and stuck it into his side.

According to another article, the Shah held President Carter personally to blame for the collapse of his country. He also criticized his former aides who, out of misguided loyalty, had shielded him from reality and led him to misunderstand the true mood of the country. He said that President Carter had pledged undying brotherhood during his New Year's Eve toast at the Niavaran Palace in 1977, but ever since then Washington had constantly sniped at him. The reason he had failed to act decisively as the Iranian political crisis worsened was that he could not count on Washington's support.

Ultimately, the Shah said, Washington tried to force him to abdicate. When he refused to step down, the CIA was ordered to undermine him. He said he had been appalled by President Carter's whole attitude towards the Persian Gulf, and his doctrine that the United States no longer needed a policeman in the area.

He apparently complained to President Sadat that the Americans could not grasp the dimensions of the Russians' ambitions.

The Shah's failure to act has to this day been a mystery to me. It could have been his health, his dedication to the US, coupled with the human rights problems – who knows? But I have always regretted that he would not discuss the subject when I asked the question during our meeting on 11 January.

In General Bakhtiar's office I was delighted to see General Rabii looking rather pleased with himself. He was proud of what his Air Force had done the day before to show strength and cohesiveness. They had flown 120 sorties, including the display by the five F-14s over Tehran.

Gharabaghi told me that he had met Bazargan yesterday to compare notes on Khomeini's arrival. The meeting had gone very well. He had impressed on Bazargan that the military would continue to give their full support to Bakhtiar. He covered the principles of behaviour and rules of engagement for Khomeini's return, and found Mr Bazargan very receptive and keen to avoid a head-on collision on the streets.

Rumour now had it that the Ayatollah would not return until at least Thursday, 1 February, but it was certain that he would be back by the weekend. Bakhtiar had announced that the technical problems at the airport had been corrected, and explicitly stated that he would permit Khomeini to return. Khomeini had said he was coming as soon as he could get clearance. The Group's collective nerve did not seem to be standing up too well to the prospect, and their cohesiveness showed signs of splintering. Some favoured military action ahead of Khomeini's arrival. Others thought he should be assassinated on landing. General Gharabaghi and Admiral Habiballahi thought we should leave the decisions to the Prime Minister.

Gharabaghi told me that they wanted to finish the meeting before noon so that the chiefs of the military services could address their forces that day. The troops themselves were getting apprehensive, knowing that D-Day was now definitely this week. Other items on a busy day's agenda were meetings of the Regency Council and the National Security Council.

We ran through some policy points for those two meetings. Our basic principles were still to avoid direct military contact with the masses, to continue to take orders from the Prime Minister and to concentrate all security on those buildings and elements essential to the government. We agreed that a ground force parade through Tehran tomorrow would show strength, provided that Mr Bakhtiar agreed.

I told General Rabii that, as he had suggested, I had sent Brigadier General Kertesz down south to visit some of the bases, but he had steered clear of Khatami Air Base because of the sensitivity of the Homofars there. On the other air bases, General Kertesz would be submitting an evaluation which I would pass on to Rabii.

General Gharabaghi got rather emotional over the previous day's affair at the Gendarmerie headquarters. Having a general officer treated in that way must have brought home what could happen to any of them. He blustered, and tried to blame me for having ordered the troops to lower their guns and fire into the crowd. In fact, he shook his finger at me and said: 'You're to blame.The blood's on your hands.' This was more than I was ready to take, considering that he had personally given the orders, and it brought back my fears about how he might react in a real crisis. He became very excitable, and once again I had to raise my voice and get tough. My final question to him was, did the tactic achieve the objective? As always, this gave me an odd sensation: I felt like I was scolding children.

We discussed last night's epidemic of arson; but this did not seem to focus their thoughts as might have been expected. There was an alarming whiff of indecision about their demeanour, and there seemed no point in going on. We agreed to meet again after their two Council meetings, or at least to confer by phone.

I reflected upon the tidal breakthrough by the opposition in the last few days. Against the elemental power of this popular movement, we had made little headway. Yet even now, we were still afloat. One thing to our credit, which I don't believe Ambassador Sullivan ever appreciated, was that the soldiers were obeying orders to enfore martial law. They were prepared to shoot their brother-Iranians and fellow-Muslims. They had shown they would do what was necessary. This had obviously impressed and perhaps surprised the religious leaders who had embarked on a battle for the hearts and minds of the armed forces. They were coming on very strong, and lashing out at the 'illegal' government of Bakhtiar, and without question it must have made an impact on some of the military. But I felt that as long as the leadership held together, the troops would be steady on parade.

On the way back to the Embassy compound the midday traffic was extremely heavy. It was more than possible that I would be the next general to be dragged out of his car and thoroughly worked over. There were many glances through the window. Riding in our little Iranian Paykan, dressed in civilian clothes with an Iranian driver, they could hardly have known I was American; I believe that if they had ever been sure of it, my car would certainly have been turned over and torched.

I went directly to the Ambassador's office. Talking with him and his people I learned that the opposition were as apprehensive as anybody about Khomeini's return. They would have preferred delay as the safest thing for all concerned. Tensions were building by the minute, and I wasn't sure how far this could go on without some kind of internal explosion.

Ambassador Sullivan repeated his belief that it would be better to unplug the military from the Bakhtiar government, switch them off, and when Khomeini returned in triumph, just plug them into him. I could not agree with this. My choice was to stay firmly with Mr Bakhtiar, not only because that was my belief, but also because it was my instruction from Washington. I thought a military coup would be infinitely better than accepting a Khomeini government. I would maybe have been reconciled to some coalition between Khomeini and Mr Bakhtiar, provided our side's principles were not compromised, but even here the Ambassador preferred to go straight to a Khomeini government. I suggested that I should relay our two opposed views to Washington; this would give the administration a clear choice, supported by reasons and first-hand evidence. Mr Sullivan had no objection. In fact, he thought it was a good idea to give them a wider base to operate from.

After dinner I made contact at the normal time, and Secretary Brown was available for the conversation. The burning question was, of course, when Khomeini was coming. I told them it could be as early as Thursday, but might be Friday, so that Khomeini could take advantage of the Muslim day of rest and prayer. That way he was guaranteed to have access to the maximum number of supporters from the start. Also there was a little problem with Air

France, who had asked their government to guarantee the safety of the flight. To the French government this was an unheard-of request, and they were in no hurry to grant it.

I think Secretary Brown could feel the apprehension at my end, because he started harping back on the attitude of the military leadership. I had to admit they were increasingly nervy this morning. Later they were missing for several hours, and I could not locate them. They had had the two Council meetings and I had heard the choppers go over late in the evening, so I deduced that they had sat late.

I next covered the Gharabaghi/Bazargan meeting, and said I thought it was on the plus side of the ledger. At least the religious leaders and opposition knew what the ground-rules were, and that Bakhtiar and the military were determined to see them observed.

Secretary Brown wanted to know if I thought third parties could make trouble, and of course this was one of my abiding fears. They were the ones who had caused most of the latest bloodshed. I told them I wasn't sure precisely which the third party was – the PLO, local terrorists, Communists, or a combination of all of these. I thought it probably included plain hoodlums. Certainly it was growing in strength. There were a lot more arms circulating in the street, and a phenomenal amount of weapons fire went on at night.

When I reported our planned parade of ground forces there was a pause, and I got a feeling of apprehension on the other end of the line. Secretary Brown asked if I had considered the balance of risk and gain in such an operation. I had of course done so. I knew you had to take risks to get gains and the gains here could far outweigh the risks. We'd had violence, and we were ready for more if necessary, to show that we had the strength to cope. I then laid before them my views of the troops' capability, and carefully explained why Ambassador Sullivan disagreed with them. I also said that Bakhtiar's survival depended entirely on the military, because the economy was completely under the thumb of the opposition.

I reported on our evacuation programme. Over 300 had left yesterday and about 200 could go today. If all went as planned, we would have every Department of Defence dependent out by tomorrow night.

When I told the Secretary how I had had to get tough with the Group that day, he commented rather forcefully that my job was only to advise. The decisions were to be made by the Iranians. It was clear that Washington felt very strongly about this. I could understand the administration's sensitivity, with *Pravda* branding me as a Military Governor, and a Vice-Regent replacing the Shah, but in my heart I did not agree. I wanted action. Of course it was true that Washington would get the blame if anything went wrong, which could happen at any moment. Yet throughout this whole period I had always tried to stick to my advisory role. The problem was that the Group had been told by the Shah: 'Listen to him, trust him, and obey him, he is your general.'

I reported on General Kertesz's trip to the bases in the south. He had nothing but praise for the level of discipline, morale and military status. Some fraternization had occurred, but not enough to cause concern.

The burden of my report was that though my spirits were pretty near the bottom of the barrel, I thought Bakhtiar would hang in there as long as the military stood firm. They had the ability to do so. But my apprehensions about Gharabaghi were now stronger than ever since his comments on the Gendarmerie battle. I gave a complete and unbiased report on Bill Sullivan's and my views on who should be supported by the military, and added that I would appreciate guidance from Washington on my differences of opinion with the Ambassador. It would be well to know more precisely what type of government Washington really had their eye on at this time. He said that he would discuss the subject with the President, and I would be advised.

On my way back to the residence, the noise in the city was even louder than the night before. Automatic weapons were crackling in all directions, and the caterwauling was unbelievable considering it was after curfew. It just seemed that the emotions of the whole city were boiling over. Everything was building towards a terrifying climax.

Back in my room, I was not ready to go to bed even though I was absolutely exhausted; the adrenalin was flowing high with my apprehensions of what might happen in the next forty-eight hours. I decided to sit down and write a position report to my boss, General Al Haig, to bring him up to speed. He seemed anxious to know what was going on, and he was obviously not being informed from any other source. He had every right to know, if only because the forces most available to the area in case of any outside intervention were those under his command. He was also a key figure in the formulation of Western policies towards the USSR and the Warsaw Pact.

I told him the situation had changed completely in the last twenty-four hours. Prime Minister Bakhtiar had agreed to the return of Khomeini. The airports were now open, so there was nothing at this end to stop him. I hoped that the Ayatollah's enthusiasm might be dampened by the rising level of the security threat, of which he should have been kept informed, but we were not sure that his aides in Paris, particularly Mr Yazdi, were giving him a true picture. We were not even sure about the precise motivation and allegiance of some of those aides – whether they were genuine Khomeini clerics, or were aligned with the Communists or the PLO or were merely opportunists in pursuit of their own ambitions.

I explained to General Haig that these third parties were almost entirely responsible for the outbreak of violence in the last two or three days. Up till then it had been relatively peaceful and orderly. I was convinced the situation was being manipulated to a large extent from an external source, and I thought its headquarters were in Moscow.

I reckoned the Soviets had two objectives. One was to gain control of the country, and the other was to discredit the USA, using my name to do so. I mentioned this because I knew how closely Al Haig followed the reports of what Radio Moscow, *Pravda* and Tass had been saying. The anti-American campaign was now at full throttle. It was being well managed and methodically implemented, and was having an impact on both the opposition and our side of the camp.

About the Ayatollah's return, I repeated the views I had given to Washington, stressing that there were now enough weapons on each side for a sizeable civil war. If Khomeini were ready to be sensible, there could be an advantage in having him come back for negotiations, man-to-man. These would take account of the views of the more reasonable local religious leaders, as opposed to the truculence of the Paris aides. I pointed out that I had no illusions about Khomeini being sensible or even rational on the subject of control of the country.

Wednesday, 31 January 1979

Quite early the streets were in an uproar. The disorders had now
reached the point where it appeared that bloodshed would be
necessary so as to keep some semblance of order. For the
authorities, the occasional whiff of grapeshot seemed unavoidable,
while the opposition were having to resort to Persian tactics,
ranging from abuse to the mutilation of bodies, to get the attention
they wanted.

The Ambassador and I discussed how much longer I should stay.
His sources indicated that my presence, spotlighted by the Soviet
propaganda reproduced in the Iranian media, was now attracting
threats to other Americans. We debated whether my presence
would be a plus or a minus during the really critical period just
after Khomeini's return. I promised to give this considerable
thought. Having hundreds of thousands of people chanting 'Death'
at you really did bring a conclusive feeling of being unwanted.

The morning message traffic contained more trouble. It now
looked certain that Khomeini would return tomorrow, the 1st of
February. What was more, he had called on all Iranians to disobey
the government completely. This message had been delivered by
way of tapes transmitted into the country electronically and then
distributed over a very elaborate network. His agents played them
over public address systems and reproduced them in leaflets and
posters. It was psychological warfare executed with consummate
skill. This 'message to the nation' declared that the present
government was no different from the previous one; it had
embarked on mass killings in Tehran and the provinces (this was
quite untrue). 'Mohammed Reza's hatchet-men' had been let loose
on innocent people under the guise of the law, patriotism and
independence. The government was a conspiracy to promote the
interests of the colonialists in Iran.

Khomeini went on: 'You have forced the main traitor into
disgraceful escape. Keep up the struggle and push this abortion,
which is no more than a marginal entity, into the sea.' Addressing
the Army, he called on that 'noble class of military forces who have
not yet soiled their hands with the blood of young people, to refuse
to undergo the disgrace of obeying traitors . . . This is your nation.

You are the nation. Do not indulge in fratricide for the protection of foreign interest.' He urged the civil servants to disobey the government, which he called a usurper of the people's rights. Just possibly Khomeini might confine himself to the war of words; but if he came straight in and appointed members of a provisional government, this could not be tolerated, and our reaction must be very severe.

I asked if the Ambassador had any additional word on the affray with the taxi-driver in Isfahan. This turned out to be quite a story. After the fight, the American could have been in real trouble with some bystanders, but he was rescued by a friendly group of Iranians and hustled into the nearby Kaurash hotel. Someone summoned the US Consul, David McGaffey, one of those unsung State Department heroes who can always be relied on in an emergency. He showed real courage and dedication. There was a crowd outside the hotel, and they became very angry as he tried to get inside. However, it proved possible to keep them at bay until contact was made with the local Ayatollah, who was the city's Muslim leader. His name with Ayatollah Khademi, and he soon came to the scene with a couple of representatives. He said he would escort the two Americans to his home for safe haven until further notice. As they left, the crowd took advantage of the opportunity and roughed up both McGaffey and the Bell helicopter man. They were taken to the Ayatollah's home; but instead of being released, they were held hostage. It appeared that they would only be released if the authorities dropped charges against some Air Force cadets who had been arrested for taking part in a demonstration in Isfahan.

On the way to the office it seemed that half the population were in the streets reading newspapers. I could hardly wait to get to the compound to find out what it was all about. Inside the compound was a tank with its gun pointed right at the gates, and it clearly wasn't there for target practice.

In the office my copy of the *Tehran Journal* explained the excitement. 'Khomeini Due Tomorrow' it proclaimed, plastering the last word right across the page. Under a picture of the Ayatollah in his black ensemble was the caption: 'Be Calm and Patient Until I Join You'. The article said he would arrive at 9 am. The *Kayhan* rang out: '9 AM Tomorrow'; 'Green Light for Khomeini Flight'.

The announcement had been put out by the special welcoming committee. It went on to say that the Iranian government had approved the request by Air France for a special charter plane, carrying Khomeini and his entourage, to land at Mehrabad Airport. According to the article the Cabinet had decided last night to reopen the country's airports, so that now any plane carrying the Ayatollah was free to land at Mehrabad. No special approval would be needed, but any commercial flights into Iranian air space would need prior clearance with the Air Traffic Controller. Air France had confirmed that they had received approval for a chartered plane to land at Mehrabad, though there were still some technical difficulties to be worked out. It looked as though the dreaded day was here.

Just below the Khomeini headlines was an article headed: 'US Evacuation'. It told how the US Embassy had ordered all American dependents and non-essential government employees to leave as early as possible. All Department of Defence dependents were due out today.

Another article was based on a release by Mr Tom Ross, the Secretary of Defence's Chief of Public Affairs. Headed 'Iran to Slash US Arms Deal', it explained that owing to the government paralysis and lack of funds, the United States would be cutting off arms programmes. It said that Eric von Marbod and myself were discussing the details with officials. I had a feeling this article would create problems with the military.

Inside the *Tehran Journal* was the headline: 'US Must Share Blame for Bloodshed – Pravda'. Datelined Moscow, it read: '*Pravda* said yesterday that US General Robert E. Huyser must share responsibility with Iran's government and military command for the recent bloodshed in Tehran and other cities . . . The Communist Party newspaper claimed Huyser functioned as Vice-Regent, guiding a coup by military leaders receiving orders from the Shah.' *Pravda* said that: 'Huyser, who arrived in Tehran in early January, was assigned the role of Vice-Regent, and established effective relations with the Iranian command to assure it took orders from Washington . . . This really means that General Huyser bears the responsibility, together with the government and top military leaders, for the daily bloodshed in the streets of Tehran and other towns.'

I called Ambassador Sullivan and raised again the question of my continued usefulness in the country. He told me his people had reported a good deal of hostility to me among the crowds. They were stoking up strong emotional resentment, because it helped their cause to personalize the devil. Americans were being stopped on the streets and told to go home, or they would be shot. Any day now it could become counter-productive for me to stay, especially with Khomeini arriving at 9 am tomorrow. He said that the Embassy had been notified that either I must leave the country or action would be taken against American nationals throughout Iran.

I explained in print to Secretary Brown that in the last few days life had become very hot for me, and the resentment was rubbing off on all Americans. I brought his attention to both of today's papers, which made clear that I was now a walking target. This message was clear from posters, placards and graffiti all along the streets. My own instinct was to stay and continue my work, but the Ambassador judged that it could be counter-productive for the US and the Iranian government, and I did not feel I should disagree with the assessment of the senior US representative in Iran when he recommended that I should leave before Khomeini arrived. I was not concerned about my personal security – I was convinced we could handle that – but for the greater good. If the Secretary of Defence so ordered, I would have my aircraft pick me up at Mehrabad Airport on the 1st of February, at 6.30 am local time. I would handle the scheduling of the aircraft, and it would be done as covertly as possible.

I next prepared a wire back to my headquarters. It stated:

This is the pickup order. Request coordination and directives be handled by best means possible to maintain security until I am airborne and across the Iranian border. Do not use any special call signs or code for the aircraft. Have aircraft arrive Mehrabad Airfield, 1 February, 0630 hours. Repeat, 1 February, 0630 hours, local Iranian time. They are to taxi off the runway to the military side. They will not cut engines. I will board through the nose hatch and we will take off immediately. You are to confirm understanding by flash message to the American Embassy, Tehran, addressed to me. Thanks and best wishes.

I was then notified that the Group had assembled and were ready for me to join them in General Gharabaghi's office. I left the messages to be typed with instructions to bring them for my approval when complete. Then General Gast and I went directly to General Gharabaghi's office, knowing how emotions would be high on our arrival. As we entered the office, all were standing and all of them had a copy of the *Journal*. Their copies were in Farsi, but in identical format to the English version: the picture placement and the size of the headlines were the same. My friends were now face to face with reality.

Clearly this was the sternest trial we had faced, surpassing even the departure of the Shah. Before we could even take our places, they were drawing my attention to the *Pravda* article. I told them my feelings about it, and said that the Ambassador and I had decided it might be better for me to leave before Khomeini's arrival. This did not appeal to them at all. I am not sure what they expected of me, except perhaps a guiding hand in executing their plans through the rest of the day. We had a very lengthy discussion, but I never got them to agree that my departure was the best thing from their own point of view. Inevitably General Toufanian brought up the question of arms sales, protesting that it looked as if the only reason America was supporting Iran was for the money.

Reviewing our plans for Khomeini's arrival, we confirmed that he would be received at the airport by the military. The crowds would not be allowed into the airport. In fact they would not be allowed to go beyond Shahyad Square. He would be protected at the airport by the military, who would accept full responsibility for the security of his motorcade from the airport to Shahyad Square. At that point he would be turned over to 'his people', and they would be responsible for his security until such time as he had finished communing with the crowds, when the military would again take charge and deliver him to his quarters. These rules seemed to be still valid,and they had already been conveyed to Mr Bazargan by General Gharabaghi. We hoped there would be an opportunity to close the loop with the local religious leaders once more to ensure that all aspects had been covered. We wanted to do everything possible to ensure the minimum bloodshed, violence and confusion. These ground-rules would be presented to the Prime Minister for approval at a Security Council meeting that evening.

We then considered all the contingencies. If the affair went off peacefully, with no uprisings, no referendum, no proclamations or attempts to unseat the government, then no special action was called for.

The next option was violence created by either the religious groups or third-party elements. These we agreed must be dealt with on the spot, firmly and decisively.

The next level of escalation would be a call by the Ayatollah for the dissolution of the government and its replacement by his own provisional government. This too, we decided, must be handled firmly on the spot.

The scenario which concerned us most was an attempt, successful or otherwise, to assassinate the Ayatollah. We felt this would lead to complete chaos, and probably a civil war countrywide. In that case, we would be called on to engage all armed forces at a high level. We had the ammunition, the transport, the tanks – everything we needed except fuel. The night before, the tanker was up the channel as scheduled, but we got an ultimatum from the National Iran Oil Company saying they would unload the tanker, but the oil must go into the normal system, and an announcement would be made that it was a present from the Bakhtiar government to the people of Iran. Of course we could not accept this. We needed that petroleum ourselves if we were to cope with an operation of any magnitude.

We then considered the status and morale of the forces. Each head of service had checked that morning very thoroughly, down to and including unit level. They had a strong feeling of confidence, and when asked to give an estimate of the desertions we would suffer through the arrival of the Ayatollah, or if we should order action, they said not more than five to ten per cent. That would be 40,000 – a sizeable group but not too damaging to the cause. The assessment I received from my people was much the same.

I suspected that this was too optimistic an estimate, so I questioned them in depth, but they all stood by the figures. I reminded them of the opposition's latest tactics, including the unmerciful beating of General Latifi. There had also been an appalling incident in which a major had been disembowelled by tying one of his legs to one car and the other to another car, and slowly driving the cars apart. In one of the outlying cities an officer's wife had been stripped of her clothing by a mob and publicly raped.

These were Persian tactics which Westerners do not fully understand. They are repugnant, but in Iran they were unquestionably a good way to get the undivided attention of the Group. In America you could probably achieve the same results by death threats. But in Iran, death is not the worst thing that can happen to you. Worse than death would be for a woman to be publicly stripped of her clothing and raped, or for a man to suffer torture of the barbarous kind inflicted on the major.

In spite of these exemplary acts, the Group were still of the opinion that their forces, if given an order from the top, would respond unquestioningly. During the last three or four days, they had not been reluctant to shoot. Their behaviour during public demonstrations had been immaculate. I had to agree with this assessment in general. The big question, in my mind, following discussions with the Ambassador and his staff, was how many of them would join Khomeini once he arrived. Estimates in the Embassy were as high as seventy or eighty per cent. My own estimate was ten to fifteen per cent. The answer to this question would decide the outcome, because the only power that the Bakhtiar government had was that of the military. I thought he also had a great deal of latent power from civil circles, as had been proved by our successful pro-government demonstration; but it would not surface unless Bakhtiar decided to play his trump card, namely the armed forces. Even though I had a strong feeling that more than 25 million Iranians would stick with the constitutional government, they needed the reassurance of a strong leader – they all seemed to gravitate to power. Meanwhile it was going to get rough. We had all the makings of a holy war on our hands. There had been clashes between soldiers and civilians, fights between followers and enemies of the Shah, 'acts of popular justice', punitive expeditions against places of pleasure and entertainment, and arms sales in the streets. The cities were awash with weapons.

We next discussed today's parade of force. Here, everything was 'go'. The plan was to take as many troops as we could, probably about a division and a half, through the city. They would demonstrate to the people that the Army were sharply turned out, well disciplined and on top of their job. Troublemakers would be warned that they would have to be true martyrs to try conclusions with such a body of men.

We were interrupted by a message that one of our MAAG C-12 aircraft had just crashed on its way from Isfahan to Tehran. Preliminary reports said there were two survivors and five fatalities. There was no indication of the cause of the accident. In the current situation it was natural to suspect foul play.

The Group was deeply concerned about the exodus of foreign nationals from Iran. The country's technical expertise was almost entirely dependent on foreigners. They had heard that in addition to evacuating dependents we were also reducing our military mission and other professional elements. I explained that there was not much we could do about this, as we were responsible for the lives of Americans in foreign countries. When they were in jeopardy there was no alternative but to evacuate them. They didn't like this, which was hardly surprising because the impact on the country was devastating.

Our people brought me my message for dispatch to Washington, and I added the Group's reactions to my proposed departure – that they accepted it but didn't like it. I had explained that if I left, they would still have General Gast to work with them. They had every confidence in his ability, and he had been in on all my meetings. He had been a tremendous help to me and the Group. He was one of the best officers I had ever known, and I too had complete confidence in him.

We discussed the situation of the reopened Mehrabad Airport, and I told them we would not have the Military Airlift Command aircraft coming in tomorrow, because it would be asking for trouble on the day of Khomeini's return. The Iranian Air employees had said they were going back to work tomorow. Even so, Mr Bakhtiar had insisted that Iranian Air was not to fly Khomeini in.

Various items of intelligence came in. Mr Yazdi, chief spokesman for the Ayatollah, had said that he could not rule out a civil war on the Ayatollah's return. He claimed that many people were asking for weapons, and when the time was ripe he would release them. This was certainly no idle threat. I was told that General Latifi, who had been beaten up on Monday, had regained consciousness, and his condition was listed as critical but satisfactory. There was renewed turmoil in the city. They were firing on buses and cars, and burning garbage. Most of the shooting was in the streets; there were no reports of any buildings being set on fire such as had happened in the red light district.

A steady stream of vitriol was issuing from Soviet-based radio stations. They were getting more active every day, beaming their radio waves on to key areas of Iran and castigating the Americans. Their tone was shrill: 'Now that the Shah has gone, it is the turn of the Americans. US imperialism should be kicked out of the country and to hell.' The State Department had protested against this propaganda, but of course the Soviet media blasted right back. Again and again I was pilloried as the apostle of violence and the representative of the Shah and the United States.

The problem of the BBC was now getting even more intense, and we all considered that action was necessary. For some reason I could not persuade them to take jamming measures. This was a mistake, because I had been informed by the secure phone operators in the Embassy that the country did have the ability to block many of these broadcasts.

Having gone over everything very thoroughly, I went back to the Embassy, where I got a message from Secretary Brown agreeing to my departure plan. I also received confirmation from Stuttgart that the airplane was en route for Turkey, and would arrive at Mehrabad at 6.30 am. Another message told of more trouble at Khatami Air Base. As our people were leaving, the Homofars had pulled a customs inspection to ensure that none of their equipment was going with them.

The *New York Times* reported that protesters were carrying posters which said: 'Huyser is the ring-leader of the Iranian generals'. Another slogan was: 'Carter is Bakhtiar's real boss'. All the US media were reporting on the chants and posters demanding 'Death to Huyser' and 'Death to Carter'.

That night at dinner I expressed my gratitude to the Sullivans for the kindness they had shown me during my stay. We were all very apprehensive about the forthcoming day, each with different expectations but identical concerns.

As I crossed the dark grounds to make my final report, I was feeling more on edge than ever before. The tremendous emotional tide of hostility that was causing me to leave the country made me wonder about the Iranian guards in the compound. What were their real allegiances? I thought tonight would be a good night to make their mark if any of them were less than loyal. But my deepest feeling was one of distress at having to leave my friends at their time of greatest need.

I made my secure contact with the Secretary of Defence, and he immediately told me the President had changed his mind: I was to stay in Tehran until further notice. I 'rogered' and said I fully understood. I didn't argue. In fact I was pleased. Harold Brown said that in due course I would receive authority to leave, either by message or by a telephone call from himself, Charlie Duncan or Dave Jones. He explained that Secretary Vance, Dr Brzezinski, himself and the President were all concerned about the effect on the Iranian government if I left either just before, or just after, Khomeini's return. In addition to implying a lack of support for Bakhtiar it would remove a vital channel of communication with the Iranian armed forces, and thus reduce our chances of influencing them at a critical moment. However, when the time did come for me to leave, it might happen very rapidly. They were sending a C-130 to stand by at Mehrabad Airport for my exclusive use. It would be painted to blend in with the Iranian C-130s. So there was no need to bring in my aircraft to pick me up. He said the Chairman would work out the details.

I decided that probably the best thing would be to notify my headquarters to station a C-135 at Incirlik, Turkey. Then if I left in the C-130, I could change planes and take the C-135 from there to Stuttgart.

Secretary Brown asked if the Iranian military, being now resigned to my departure, would be upset by the latest switch of plans. On the evidence of their behaviour I had to say that I thought they would be cheered rather than upset. He also wanted to know where in Tehran I would be in the least danger and have the lowest visibility. I told him I really didn't have much choice. I needed to be at the Embassy to make my secure calls and to coordinate with the Ambassador, and I had to be at the SCS compound to conduct my business with the Group. I had to carry on with the same routine.

He wanted to know how I could get out if I looked like being trapped. I told him I had already set up a procedure for the Iranian Air Force to airlift me by helicopter from downtown Tehran to Mehrabad Airport. They were ready to pick me up from the Embassy or several other points. I had thought of commuting by helicopter to the SCS compound, but Ambassador Sullivan objected to bringing a helicopter into the Embassy, as it could invite trouble. So we continued to battle with the traffic, changing cars nearly every day to ensure that we wouldn't be bugged, or bombed, or all the other things that can happen when you use the same car. Secretary Brown suggested that I should ask Ambassador Sullivan to reconsider his objection to a helicopter, but it was only a suggestion, and he would leave it to us to decide.

I said that with Khomeini's return, tomorrow would be the most critical day since I arrived in Tehran. The arrangements were still being discussed at the National Security Council meeting. They were meeting late, which was understandable; Mr Bakhtiar needed the very latest evidence on which to make decisions.

I reported on the discussions we had on all the possible contingencies. I said I had great confidence in Mr Bakhtiar but there had been some resignations among his ministers, who had turned out to be weaker than anticipated. The Group would stand firm, even though they had been deeply depressed by the scurrilous media reports, the departure of American advisers, and the reduction of arms sales.

He asked who I thought should continue working with the Group if I left. I strongly recommended Major General Gast, a real professional. He had been at all the meetings, the Iranians held him in high regard and they respected his leadership qualities. I thought he could carry on without skipping a beat.

I was proud to be able to give the Secretary a rundown on the afternoon's display of forces in the streets. It had been more than a division strong, probably a division and a brigade's worth. They conducted themselves as professional military men and looked good. They were well disciplined and there was no violence. I claimed this as a real plus, particularly on the eve of the Ayatollah's return, and suggested that he should put this factor in the equation when assessing the military's capability. I advised that if we could keep the third-party elements out of tomorrow's activities, there was a good chance of avoiding violence.

On the evacuations I reported that, to be best of my knowledge we were complete on the Department of Defence dependents. Between the commercials and the Military Airlift Command, somewhere around 1,000 to 1,400 people had left today. This was having a depressing impact on the Iranian military, but I totally agreed that it had to be done, and as rapidly as possible.

I felt compelled to relay another less than thrilling instalment of the tanker saga. The NIOC was now demanding that we make it a gift from the Iranian military to the people of Iran, and of course we couldn't. Nonetheless, I wanted to keep the tanker anchored offshore in case of emergency. I was sure that if Mr Bakhtiar ordered military action we could get the fuel from the tanker.

Secretary Brown ended by expressing his regrets about the change of signals on my immediate future and asked me to explain it to the Ambassador. The President had reversed his decision after taking into account the picture as seen in Washington. I told him I had no reservations about staying. I didn't tell him that I was pleased it had worked out that way, but it was true. I really didn't want to leave my comrades at this time.

I returned to the residence and went to bed, knowing that tomorrow would be one of the most gruelling days of my life.

3

The Return of the Ayatollah

I was woken about two o'clock in the morning with a request to come to the Chancellory to take an urgent message from the Secretary of Defence. Half-dressed, I rushed down to find that the message merely comfirmed my instructions to stay on. It followed a meeting of all the principals at the White House. I was to tell the Iranian military that it was felt my departure at this time might be misinterpreted, and I'm sure they meant 'misinterpreted by the Iranian opposition'. I should reassure them of Washington's total support for the Bakhtiar government.

I returned to the residence, not knowing whether to go back to bed or sit up and stew for an hour or two. I knew I would have to leave the compound at the crack of dawn to avoid the crowds that would be assembling early. Eventually I went back to bed, rolled and tossed and did a little cat-napping, but was up at 5 am. I showered and shaved and prepared to depart at 6 am for the compound.

Already the crowds were starting to assemble. Especially conspicuous were the fleets of motor cyclists gassing up their machines. I had noticed before that nearly all the demonstrations of any size seemed to be controlled by these flying squads. We were sure that the tapes were distributed in this way. The riders were young, but they seemed to be very well organized. To this day I do not know who devised and operated this brilliant information system, but they seemed to be aligned with the Khomeini faction.

At the compound, security had been dramatically increased. They checked us over carefully as we went in – the only time I was required to show my identification. This time they had two tanks with their main guns trained right through the gates. It was the same story inside the building. In the upper hallways they had set up machineguns facing out toward the gate. Mr Bakhtiar had agreed to put the military on red alert. This had happened before, but they had never gone to this extent to protect the SCS headquarters. The weapons were all manned by young soldiers who were well disciplined and well turned out. As I passed them, they snapped to and saluted.

We had not had time for breakfast, so we had Major Ray Burnette go out and get us some Iranian bread. We had dry bread and coffee for breakfast. About 7 am the helicopters arrived with General Rabii and General Badraie. It appeared that the Group was assembling very early, and sure enough it was only a matter of minutes before we got a summons from General Gharabaghi asking for General Gast – they thought I had left.

When I turned up at General Gharabaghi's office, he expressed a good deal of surprise. What had changed my mind? Why had I not gone? I explained that the President was afraid that the signals might be misread. They seemed sincerely glad that I was still with them.

We were all apprehensive, but I thought my feelings were a bit different from theirs. They no doubt felt that once Khomeini set foot on Iranian soil, then for all practical purposes the Shah was dead. That was not my problem. My problem was to anticipate the reaction of the crowds, of Khomeini himself, and of the military. A germ of doubt had been sown in my mind by the Ambassador and his people about the likely reaction of the military, making it just conceivable that thousands of troops could flip over to the other side.

Judging from his proclamation in Paris, it would not be surprising if Khomeini delivered an ultimatum declaring the Bakhtiar government illegal and installing his own government in the offices. This I knew would lead to pandemonium and bloodshed. With these apprehensions, I had to keep a poker face if I was to have any hopes of being the leader with the strong shoulder to cry on.

At the National Security Council meeting it had been decided, as we had agreed, to have the troops withdrawn from the streets and only to protect the essential elements. The Ayatollah would be received by the military at Mehrabad Airport, escorted to Shahyad Square, and there turned over to his followers. They would be responsible for him until the end of the day, and then the military would pick him up at Behest-e-Zahra cemetery, where he would be making his main address to the public. It was a location that suited his familiar tactic of playing on the key Shi'ite theme of martyrdom.

We started our checklist. The airport was open and ready to receive traffic. Khomeini was en route, and should arrive on time. The military guard at the airport were ready to receive him. They had all the equipment they needed for security. Everything looked in order.

The crowd was now in spate, so we decided to survey the situation with helicopters. By 8.30 there were somewhere between 750,000 and 1,000,000 people in the streets, but they were orderly, and there did not appear to be any trouble.

By now we had received the morning papers, and the *Kayhan* announced: 'Take-off on Schedule'. Just below, in two-inch block letters covering the entire top of the page, was the single word 'Homecoming'. Elsewhere the headlines blared: 'Millions to Greet Khomeini', and in contrast, 'Bakhtiar: "Mine is Only Government" '. The *Tehran Journal* had 'Welcome Home' and 'Millions Converge to Hail Imam Khomeini'. Underneath it said: 'Bakhtiar Reaffirms Stand'.

There was excellent coverage of yesterday's show of force. Some comments were less than complimentary, but there was no doubt we had accomplished what we set out to do. The troops in the pictures looked frighteningly impressive. Reports spoke of at least three people killed and several injured when troops fired into the hostile crowds gathered to watch them. I think this was completely fictitious, as we had heard nothing about it.

The paper said that the Ayatollah's arrival would be live on television and radio. This decision had been debated for several days. The media people had been on strike over some dispute, so one day it was on and the next it was off. I was rather pleased that it would be shown, because we could monitor proceedings better on TV, and it would save us from being blindsighted if anything happened to our helicopters.

The arrival was well planned. The route had been published in the paper, so we knew where he would stop and speak, and more or less when. General Rahimi, the Tehran martial law administrator, had told the opposition the night before that peaceful marches and demonstrations would be permitted, and in fact would not be prohibited at any time during the next three days. He called on them to be on their guard against subversive elements waiting to strike and create terror. He said he was convinced that most Iranians were good at heart and would cause no problems. But there were subversive elements, and to control them it would be necessary to station the military at key points: all the ministries, the Army installations, police stations and federal institutions. Any attacks on them would be dealt with swiftly and severely. Mehrabad Airport would be closed to the public until the military authorities announced on the radio that people could go there. All flights had been cancelled except the Air France flight bringing in the Ayatollah.

With luck, the television and radio coverage might reduce the size of the crowd. Hopefully many would watch the spectacle at home. Already the TV cameras were warming up, mostly testing shots because it wasn't too professionally done. But they helped to stimulate the tempo of the occasion – the hopes on one side and the fears on the other. No one who lived through it could doubt that this was really a peg point in history.

The television crews were all set up at the airport, so we were hopeful of seeing Khomeini's arrival. There were some 1,500 people there, the number granted by the permit. The military clearly had things well in hand, and had planned exactly where he would park and disembark from the aircraft to join his motorcade.

Then we saw the airplane approach. It touched down, taxied in and parked. The door opened. The first people out were the Ayatollah's bodyguards, a rough-looking crowd. We were told he employed thirty or forty highly trained Libyans for the purpose. They looked like they could handle a fair-sized rough-house.

There was quite a delay, and then the Ayatollah materialized at the door. He came down the steps, keeping a slight distance from the group, and was led to his car. Then the military escorted him – some in vehicles, others running beside the car to shield him – out of the gate. We lost television contact at that point, and the rest of the day the coverage was very sporadic. But we got good reports from our airborne elements.

Khomeini gave a short speech on arrival, and it was far from friendly. He said without any ado that the present government was illegal. He would replace it with a government of his selection, a true Islamic government. So we had the first taste of a very bitter medicine. He was still the cantankerous, stubborn man he had always been, but he seemed to project charisma, and he was certainly getting the response.

We then endured many hours of waiting, listening and watching, always fearful that in such a large crowd violence could break out spontaneously. Fortunately, none did. Khomeini proceeded to the cemetery as scheduled, and gave his major speech. This was more lengthy, but along much the same lines, condemning the government, and saying he would replace it within the next two days.

Then things warmed up. As he spoke, the crowds started to press in on him. This caused them to get more compact, and it looked as though he might well be crushed. His people called for a helicopter to whisk him out and take him to his quarters. It was a hazardous situation, so General Rabii dispatched one of his best crews and a helicopter to the cemetery. They had no difficulty in touching down, and there was less trouble than anticipated getting him aboard. But then it was chaotic trying to get the people to back away so that the helicopter could lift off. They had kept the engine running, and people were right under the blades, some standing on the skids and clinging to the helicopter. Finally the crew decided to lift off, which they did with great skill and delicacy. The machine slowly hoisted eight or ten people into the air, allowing them to drop back to the ground.

It headed for Khomeini's prescribed quarters, but was then instructed by Khomeini to proceed to the Tehran hospital. The crew radioed this in immediately, but by the time we had received the information they had almost reached the hospital. This caused panic, because no security had been set up there, and as best we knew there would not even be ground transportation. We had no explanation for the change. We first thought he might be ill after his hectic day. We tried to establish radio contact with the crew by phone, but were not all that successful. General Rabii was almost frantic, because it was his helicopter and his crew, and he felt solely responsible that the mission was correctly completed. Then we got a report that the helicopter had landed at the hospital, a car had pulled up, and the Ayatollah and his aide had got into the car and left. Obviously it had been prearranged. The planning and security must have been very good, because there was absolutely no one else around – only one car and a driver.

This caused near panic in the Group, as we had no idea what might happen next. I suggested that it might be a deception plan, to elude the mob and get some much-needed rest. But that did not seem to sell too well to the Generals. They were sure that something had misfired, and that they had failed in their mission and lost the Ayatollah. Since they hated him, it seemed strange to observe their concern; but they had that military instinct of dedication to mission. We started an investigation to try to discover what old friends he might be staying with, or whether he had a hideaway, but we failed. The fox had got clean away.

The crowds were now starting to disperse, and everything was still orderly. There had been no unforeseen incidents until the sudden change on Khomeini's part. But the Group were in a state of deep depression. They were now sure that the end of the Shah had really come. The uncompromising stand of Khomeini, his invitation to the Army to join him, his declaration that all foreign military advisers must leave, and his announcement of a new government within two days – all this promised hard times for any followers of the Shah.

Because of the massive crowds, we were unable to leave for the Embassy, so we stayed on a while and chewed over some outstanding items. During the day the Iranians had rejected the memorandum of understanding on arms sales which had been drawn up, and they were drafting one of their own. This was disappointing because we had been very close to agreement on a MOU. We did have an alternative, as Washington had softened their approach and said they would accept just an exchange of letters. Now that Washington had backed down, the Iranians had become apprehensive and shifted their own ground. I was anxious to hear what game plan Eric von Marbod had in mind to cope with this deadlock.

I also wanted to make my call to Secretary Brown, so as soon as the streets were negotiable, I moved out. The Group were extremely apprehensive about my leaving before we had found Khomeini, but I had a gut feeling that he had to be all right or we would have heard something. The homeward journey was slow and filled with tense moments. It was a relief to arrive at the Embassy, where I had a session comparing notes with Ambassador Sullivan. Then, as it was now pushing on to midnight, I had to put through my call to Washington. It turned out that the Secretary of Defence was away, so Under-Secretary Duncan took the call, along with the Chairman. I did my best to convey the day's activities, but between the hazards of the phone, my own exhaustion and the magnitude of the melodrama, I felt completely inadequate. I ended by emphasizing that we did not know the whereabouts of Khomeini, but I gave my reasons for thinking that he was intact.

I said we expected tomorrow to be a quiet day. I thought Khomeini would be extremely tired, and so in all possibility would the masses. However, one couldn't tell: if Khomeini suddenly elected to break loose, things could get very lively. I was sure that Mr Bakhtiar was still undaunted, and that the military would stand behind him.

I expressed deep disappointment over the pressure for a memorandum of understanding, and got a little caustic about Washington's vacillations. The delay in getting a relaxed position had caused us serious problems in our negotiations.

I also asked Mr Duncan to press on with the phase-down of contractor personnel. Things could get just as uncomfortable for them as for anyone else, and even though they were moving out quite rapidly, I wasn't clear that Washington had taken a position on the subject.

Telephone communications were getting more difficult. There seemed to be increasing interference. Calls out of country, unless they were going to France, were frequently cut off. We had already discussed getting a team in to safeguard US communications inside Iran and also back to Washington. Mr Duncan now asked whether we still wanted this team. I told him that the Ambassador and I both thought it would be useful, but we felt they should be positioned in Europe and not deployed here just at this moment. If we urgently needed them, we could quickly bring them in from Germany.

While I was talking on the phone I was handed a message saying the Ayatollah had been found. One of his officials had said he was staying in the house of a friend. I read it to Mr Duncan as I received it, and on that ominous note I signed off.

Friday, 2 February 1979

I awoke to what seemed to be a very quiet day. But it was also cloudy and cold, which fitted well with my melancholy frame of mind. Breakfast was becoming increasingly important, because between then and dinner the gastronomic outlook was always uncertain, and we usually had to scrounge for our food as and when we could.

The Ambassador and I discussed the previous day's activities, and I went over my report to Secretary Duncan. Mr Sullivan said he was getting very concerned about the emotion building over my presence in Iran, and the reports he was getting from all sources of acute hostility towards me. He said it went further than chanting and posters and graffiti, for it was now clear that many of the opposition were determined to get me out of the country. With this object, they were threatening other Americans if I did not leave. He said he thought my stay had now become counter-productive. It could even have a detrimental effect on the Iranian military. They might develop a reluctance to take action while I remained because the opposition could accuse them of taking American orders. I had already got full credit for many of the deaths. In all fairness, he thought he should tell me that he was going to ask the State Department for my withdrawal. There was nothing personal about it.

A new practical problem was the difficulty of getting our people out of Tehran to Mehrabad Airport. We were loading buses on the outskirts of the city near the US Commissary, and then taking routes to the airport avoiding populated areas as much as possible. But they were getting a lot of heckling, and one bus was pelted with rocks. Another was stopped and boarded. No harm came to anybody, but it was not a healthy situation. This was the background against which my continued presence had to be judged. The message was: Remove Huyser and your buses will not be molested.

We talked about the extremely hard line taken by Khomeini in his speeches at the airport and the cemetery. Among other clerical pleasantries, it turned out he had said: 'I'll punch the government in the mouth.' He had given a direct challenge to the nation; but he had not yet declared his Islamic Republic, or named a council. Those were the two claims which I would have expected to cause a reaction from Bakhtiar. He came across very hard at the military, offering them a 'piece of advice': he did not want trouble or bloodshed. Enough of Iran's youth had been sacrificed (this is rather ironic when you consider the number of young people he has since sacrificed), while clergy had gone to jail and been tortured. What he really wanted was the independence of the armed forces. He phrased it rhetorically: 'Mr General, don't you want to be independent? Mr Major General, don't you want to be independent? Do you want to be a mere lackey?' He advised the armed forces to 'return to the open arms of the people'. They should not submit to the orders of foreign advisers.

He played this one very hard, though he never mentioned any names, or even a country. Had he done so, our problems would have boiled over at once. All the same, most people knew who he was talking about. He said he was giving this advice to the Army for their own sake. He didn't want the armed forces thwarting the will of the people by spilling their blood in the streets. He thanked those elements of the forces who had 'attached themselves to the people'. He said they had saved the honour of the military as well as that of the nation.

He talked a bit about the Homofars and the Air Force officers in Hamadan, Isfahan and other places. They had done well to realign their national and religious loyalties and join the nation. Clearly Khomeini recognized the Army's link with Bakhtiar as the main obstacle to his success. Hence the promise he made in his speech at the cemetery that 'those of you in the armed forces who have parted company with the regime will be protected in utmost dignity'. The country must have its own armed forces, not a military organization run by foreigners. With this carrot came a very nasty stick. He said that those who refused to break ranks with Bakhtiar were liable to prosecution; and he had already warned that he would take care of such traitors by hanging. Foremost among them, without a doubt, would be the Group.

I left for the compound, and as I had expected the traffic was very much lighter than usual. At the compound, security was undiminished. The military were as smart as ever, and there seemed to be an extra snap to their heels when they 'popped to' to salute me. With the troops still that solid, maybe there was some hope for the days ahead.

While I waited in my office the liaison officer reported that Mr Bakhtiar had summoned the Group for a National Security Council meeting. I hoped he would put the military into action and take control. Time was fast running out.

Things were now getting entirely too tough for our remaining people, and particularly their families, and I reviewed the list to make sure we had all dependents scheduled for departure. I found there were eight who were not scheduled. Seven were Iranians who had married Americans, and the Iranian government were prohibiting their departure at this time. The eighth was a doctor's wife; she was not an Iranian, but she did not want to leave her husband. However, we had reached the point where we were no longer asking people to leave, but telling them. It was a difficult directive to enforce, as our only way of doing so was to cut off all their dependent's rights, which would make it difficult to stay. I found we had roughly 125 people scheduled out today, and tomorrow we could pretty well clean up the last of the 'non-essentials'.

In the message traffic I found that one of the Americans who had left earlier in the week had related his experiences to the press in Athens. He described the bus journey from Tehran to Mehrabad Airport, which took about an hour and a half instead of the normal twenty minutes, as a Wild West wagon-trip through hostile territory, with the Iranian Army riding shotgun. The convoy of buses and cars was escorted by Army jeeps mounted with machineguns and trucks full of armed troops. Along the way there were many anti-American shouts, but on this convoy no one had tried to climb aboard or throw rocks. He was impressed by the way the troops had established a circle of defence with tanks and soldiers at the airport.

I had got the Army's agreement to maximum security for these convoys, and they were supplying specially elite troops. But just in case the system broke down, they were ready to use helicopters. The armed forces proved most willing to help.

It appeared that Bakhtiar was going to keep the Group with him for most of the day. I was anxious to check the morale and status of the armed forces, which I normally got from the Group, so we decided to call the Services' headquarters to see if we could get reports direct from them. Each of them reported that there was no change, which implied no noticeable response to Khomeini's appeals. On the contrary, the troops seemed to have been more alert and if anything more ready for a fight than usual. It was extremely reassuring to know that there had not been a significant change of allegiance on Khomeini's return, and encouraging to hear that they were still holding in there. We also took a reading with the Air Force on what had happened at Khatami Air Base. It appeared that the F-14s were being protected to the maximum degree, and so were all the test equipment, the Phoenix missiles, simulators and spare parts. That too was encouraging.

This took most of the day, and as it was now clear there would be no Group meeting – the first time since 6 January – I went back to the Embassy. There the Ambassador told me that he had very forcefully brought to the State Department's attention the resentment caused by my presence in Iran. His people had again confirmed that the threat level was extremely high, and there was no predicting what form it might take. He also told me that Khomeini was planning to hold a press conference at 8 am the following day. I updated the Ambassador on the status of the armed forces, pointing out that there had been nothing like the predicted outbreak of desertions to the Khomeini camp.

Later in the evening, I reported to Secretary Brown. I explained that we expected the Ayatollah to unveil more of his intentions: he might even declare an Islamic Republic and name the members of his council. His disappearance had been innocent enough: to escape the mob he had gone to a friend's house for the night, and he intended to stay there for the next few days.

Secretary Brown asked about progress on evacuation. I told him that we were right on schedule but that some Americans stood to lose much of the cost of the possessions which they had to leave behind, and the official maximum reimbursement would not cover this. As I had anticipated, he was very sympathetic. On the FMS memorandum I told him that Eric von Marbod had an appointment with the right people tomorrow, but I was not optimistic, as there just was nobody in the mood to do that sort of business.

He wondered if they ought to move helicopters and ships into the eastern Mediterranean as a contingency measure to help with the evacuation. I told him that I appreciated the thought, but really believed the situation was under control. We had our emergency procedures if needed, but up to now we had been fully capable of moving our people by ground to Mehrabad Airport, and there had been no restriction on the number of Military Airlift Command aircraft. In fact we had three C-141s in and out today.

He wanted to know if I believed the press reports which said that if Khomeini announced a council, Bakhtiar would arrest them. My reply was that they would only be arrested if they tried to take over the offices by force. I said we were in a peculiar situation. The physical power lay with Mr Bakhtiar, namely the armed forces; and my reading as of today was that they were still hanging solidly together. On the other hand, Khomeini had the economic leverage, through control of the strikes, and he had a good portion of the masses on his side. Clearly, Bakhtiar also had a large number, most probably the majority, but there was as yet no knowing how big his share was, and they were remaining silent for all practical purposes. We were standing on a large keg of dynamite, but at least Mr Bakhtiar had survived Khomeini's arrival.

With this we brought our conversation to a close and I returned to the residence. I went right to bed. But I had not been long asleep when I was aroused by a message on the intercom asking me to take a secure call from Washington. I got up and returned to the Chancellory. It was the Chairman, General Jones, on the line. He was now really exercised about my continued presence in Iran. Ambassador Sullivan's advice had arrived at the State Department, and they wanted my view on it.

General Jones interrogated me very closely and exhaustively. I told him I could not disagree with the Ambassador's evaluation. He had far wider sources of information than I did. In the last four or five days, my presence had been highlighted more sharply than ever before. *Pravda* and Tass were stirring everybody up with savage accusations of what I was doing, and people believed them. Their theme was that I had taken over the country and was to blame for all the bloodshed.

General Jones then asked whether I thought that the Army would be capable of staging a takeover *if I was no longer there*. I said this was anybody's guess, but I believed they now had the capability to do so, and if ordered by Mr Bakhtiar they would do it. But I added that the Ambassador believed just the opposite. He did not think they had a viable capability, and if a takeover was ordered he believed there would be mass desertions. Further, I wanted us to put more support behind Mr Bakhtiar, while the Ambassador wanted to make an accommodation with Khomeini. Thus, the real question was one for Washington: what are you trying to do? Clearly, anybody who wanted Khomeini in would want me out.

I repeated my apprehensions about General Gharabaghi, and added that Admiral Habiballahi did not seem to think this was the right time for military action. Rabii, Toufanian and Badraie were quite different. If they saw things getting out of control, they would be ready at the drop of a hat to take military action, but they would still need a leader to direct them.

General Jones raised the crucial question of Washington's point of contact with the military if I departed, and I confirmed that the Group, like myself, had great confidence in General Gast. On the other hand, they had grave reservations about Ambassador Sullivan. They mistrusted him. In their mind he was the man responsible for the Shah's departure, and there was no way I could convince them otherwise. But if General Gast had the same access to Washington that I did, I believed that they would seek his counsel, because they knew they could depend on his advocacy.

I did not want to have to make a recommendation about my own fate. I didn't think this was up to me. I told them they must balance the factors themselves, but keep in mind that I was not concerned about my personal security. I was sure I could take care of myself, as I had superb security men, and had already come through a number of difficult situations. General Jones said they hoped to be able to make a decision before another day went by. If they decided I was to go, I would have to leave during daylight hours, as the Iranian airports were all closed after dark, so that anything flying at night would be subject to ground fire. He asked if I could call the White House situation room at 7 am EST, which would be 4 pm in Tehran.

Saturday, 3 February 1979

At breakfast I reported this conversation to Ambassador Sullivan. He then handed me an AP release which said that Khomeini had been out of his house yesterday, which was news to both of us. He had gone to a school-yard and met a small group on a personal basis. It was his first day of rest and prayer back in Iran. He had told the gathering that his goal was to replace the twenty-eight-day-old government now headed by Prime Minister Bakhtiar with an Islamic Republic. They had broken into chants of 'Death to Carter' and 'Death to Huyser'. The article accused me of manipulating the Iranian Army and the Bakhtiar government. I told the Ambassador that I was going to remain neutral on the subject of my own future, as I really thought the decision was above my pay-grade.

We left it at that and I headed for the compound, along streets far more crowded than they had been the previous day. In fact, the traffic was so heavy that we had a hard time getting through. It was very disorganized, and no one would obey either traffic directors or traffic lights. At the compound the security was still extremely good, and the troops were really sharp, including two or three formations marching and training.

In the office, I scanned the local newspapers. One correctly reported: 'Khomeini hands out direct challenge, but doesn't declare a republic or name a council.' Just below, in bolder print was was the memorable phrase: 'I'll punch the government in the mouth.' Illustrating a complete report of the day's proceedings was a dramatic picture of the helicopter at the cemetery trying to retrieve the Ayatollah from a vast sea of people.

This paper considered that the chances were now brighter for a dialogue between Khomeini and Prime Minister Bakhtiar. It said that Bakhtiar had no intention of resigning. The Ayatollah appeared intransigent, but there were signs of a willingness to reactivate the aborted Paris meeting. His intentions should be clearer after his press conference this morning.

Today's meeting turned out to be the Group of Six, and they started by warmly supporting what Mr Bakhtiar had said yesterday about his intentions. He had obviously taken a very strong line. He dismissed the news reports estimating yesterday's crowds at several million, but admitted there were a good number. As he put it, the Ayatollah was just another individual. He wanted it clearly understood that he would do everything to prevent the imposition of a dictatorship, particularly if it was done in the name of a democracy. He said the Army always has the right to march, and he would see that that continued.

He had no plans whatever to seek a meeting with Khomeini. Conditions were not favourable, and he would not be the one to propose a meeting. The supporters of Khomeini could yell insults and shout all they wanted, but it wouldn't mean a thing. He wanted it clearly understood that he welcomed liberty within the law, but when it got beyond the law, and people started throwing Molotov cocktails, prompt and severe action would be taken.

When asked what he would do if Khomeini announced the formation of his own government, Mr Bakhtiar said he would ignore it. If the government side could stand firm, they would be in a better position than they had been before. When the Ayatollah was in exile, there was a mystique about him; now there was no more mystique; he had arrived, and it was up to him to deliver. If he insisted on maintaining the strikes, the people would eventually get fed up, as their losses had already been considerable. They had lost more in the past three months than in the previous twenty-five years. He was ready to take all action necessary, including the use of military force, to defend his government.

I thought I should probe the Group a bit to see just what their own reactions were to the developments on both sides. In reply they all denounced Khomeini as a demagogue and said an Islamic Republic would be a disaster. All, including General Gharabaghi and Admiral Habiballahi, said they must stand solidly behind the Prime Minister. One of them declared that if it came to an Islamic Republic, the armed forces would obviously disintegrate and there would be at least a sixty per cent chance that the country would drift from the Western to the Communist sphere of influence. I personally assessed the odds as higher than that.

Asked what the future would be if our side won, and where the Shah would fit into it, Gharabaghi said he was speaking for the others when he said that Iran could best be served by a Social Democratic government patterned after Sweden, Norway or Denmark, with a King who rode a bicycle.

The Group accepted Bakhtiar's argument that it might be better now to have Khomeini back in Iran. What did worry them was the number of weapons in the country. If Khomeini was unable to make progress any other way, he might call for a religious war. This would also suit the Tudeh party, who would seize the chance to incite the religious elements to violence. We tried to check up on Khomeini's press conference, but were unable to get any definite information. We heard that it was the same old rhetoric, but that he was at least claiming that a peaceful solution was possible.

We reverted to the plans, and once again I urged them to take more positive action. There was now more oil, but food was running short because customs were again holding it up on the border and at the ports. There were about a thousand trucks backed up at the Turkish border, and some sixty ships waiting to be unloaded. I really felt they should get back to the Prime Minister and reopen the issue of customs, and this time they should get the job done properly. Also very soon the other elements must come under control, because there was little question in my mind that Khomeini would move out to take complete charge.

I watched General Gharabaghi carefully during this dialogue. Either he had a very good poker face or else he honestly agreed; and he showed very little expression when they decided it should be discussed with Mr Bakhtiar. The burden was on his back, and progress would only be realized if the military was put into action.

Again we received the status of the forces. The strongest seemed to be the Imperial Guard; the next strongest overall, with almost complete solidarity in all respects, was the Navy. General Rabii had taken a very careful look at his Air Force and he said that if called on to act, he could depend on seventy-five to eighty per cent without question. General Badraie thought the Army was good, particularly the infantry; upwards of seventy to eighty per cent were solid. In the artillery, with their Soviet training, there might be problems. All in all there was far more than enough capability to take whatever internal military actions might be required. This confirmed the assessment I had received from the US officers in the Military Advisory Group.

I laid into General Gharabaghi to get the foreign military sales memorandum signed. I said we had problems with our Congress, and that no commitment was involved, as it was just a memorandum of understanding. We needed to fulfil the obligations of our Defence Department with Congress by having a formalized signature. We appreciated that if the Bakhtiar government fell, the validity of the document might not stand. Previously Gharabaghi had not taken much interest, but this time he more or less took my words as an order. He looked at General Toufanian, and in very curt terms he told him to get on with it. Then they switched into Farsi and had a heavy exchange of words, after which he turned to me and said that action would be taken.

I thought it was time to tell them that my days with them, indeed hours, were now numbered. I must have a helicopter on stand-by somewhere close at hand to get me to Mehrabad Airport. I did not know if I would have to go in the next six, or twenty-four, or sixty hours, but I would certainly be leaving. They quite understood the reason. Some of their own people had expressed reservations about being associated with me. This seemed to derive almost entirely from the danger to their safety. None of them admitted that the threat applied to themselves; it was all in the third person. But the point they were making was obvious. There was no doubt the opposition was winning this crucial round of psychological warfare.

General Rabii agreed to put a helicopter at my disposal. I told him we would use a code: Plan A, I was departing immediately; Plan B, I would not be departing that day. When I called him, I would simply say Plan A or Plan B.

General Toufanian pressed me very hard to have the helicopter positioned near his headquarters; but I was very reluctant to do so because he had continually stressed that when I left, he wanted to go with me. I would very much like to have taken him, but I thought his strength in the Group was urgently needed, because he was the one who could get things done in the days ahead. We considered putting it in the Embassy compound, but I thought that might be too conspicuous. It would be better to have it in the SCS compound, where helicopters were constantly coming and going.

There followed a lengthy discussion in Farsi, after which Gharabaghi told me that they could understand the problem as it affected both Americans and Iranians, but they did not want to say that they agreed I should go. As far as they were concerned, they would have preferred me to stay. I made it very clear to them that the decision was not mine but would be made by our President.

I told them that if I personally had my way I would stay, and for two reasons. One was our lack of progress: we had had the plans ready for days, but none of them had been implemented. When we tried to carry out the customs plan, which could have succeeded, it was cancelled. This was totally unsatisfactory. If they wanted Mr Bakhtiar to survive as Prime Minister, they had to get control of something besides the military installations. They had to achieve economic progress, so that the people would know it came not from Khomeini but from the government. Then I dropped all finesse and said they had to start taking action on their own initiative. I pointed out in clear-text English that the only things which had been done so far were as a result of my constant pressure and prodding. There were some downcast eyes and serious looks, but no one contradicted me.

My second concern, even more compelling, was that the opposition was going to test them very severely in the days ahead. The Bakhtiar government might be pushed to the point of collapse, and if this happened there would need to be rapid, decisive military action. They would have to take control of the country. Then I let them have both barrels. I said I felt that should this occur, I did not think General Gharabaghi had the will or the guts to carry out what would have to be done. This produced absolute silence. I let them just sit there for a while, all looking very serious. I then said that before I left, I needed to know precisely what they planned to do if the government did collapse.

Again there was a long period of silence, and all eyes were fixed on me. I broke the silence. I said I knew this was very difficult for them, and it would be much easier to discuss it. 'But this is hardball, this is big poker, and the stakes are your country.' I thought that this at least would draw a response from General Gharabaghi, and deep inside I was hoping he would explode and tell me I was wrong. But he did not. He just sat there, and his silence simply confirmed in my mind that I must be right. So I stood up and said: 'Well, it appears to me that it is a lost cause, as none of you want to face the realities of life.' They all got up when I did, and this brought a response. General Rabii, who for years had referred to me as his brother, blurted out: 'My brother, if that happens, and if it's necessary to save the country, I will do the necessary things and take charge.'

Under the circumstances, I did not choose to pursue this any further. I had no doubt that General Rabii meant what he said, so I just put my hand out for a handshake which he accepted. I felt that both Generals Toufanian and Badraie would also take whatever action was necessary when the chips were down. There were several others further down the ranks who would back them up, one for sure being General Khosrodad.

I expressed my deep appreciation of their cooperation, coupled with a strong desire that they take a more aggressive view of their duties. I ventured into a philisophical discourse on the importance of maintaining strong ties between our two countries, and how I was fearful of Khomeini's attitude towards the West. I said I would be watching developments closely, and if the situation dictated it, I was certain that my government would send me back immediately.

I had stressed all my points, and it was approaching time for me to make my report to the Secretary of Defence, so I started my farewells. This time it was different. I believe we all had a feeling that it might be our last meeting together. There were no great emotional outbursts, but the handshakes were longer and firmer. There was some embracing and considerable physical contact: a pat on the shoulder, or on the back. To my surprise and relief, after what had been said, there was warmth and sincerity in my final exchange with General Gharabaghi. He still remains an enigma in my mind.

It was with a heavy heart and a strange feeling that I left the Group. I spent the ride to the Embassy in almost complete silence and very deep thought.

At the Embassy I was given a message from the duty officer at the National Military Command Centre in Washington telling me to be ready to start the conference promptly at 7 am EST. I was to call directly to the White House switchboard, and could expect to have at least two additional participants at the other end.

I established the link at the appointed time, and found at the Washington end were General Jones, Secretary Brown, Secretary Vance, Dr Brzezinski and Mr Christopher. They had asked for General Gast to be on the line with me, but this was not possible, as we only had one instrument, so he stood right beside me.

I started my report with an update on the meetings of the military with Mr Bakhtiar. I told them that the Prime Minister had been very strong and definite and intended to stand firm no matter what the Ayatollah Khomeini did or said. He had declared that with the support of the military he would succeed. I said I believed this was true, provided that they now took positive action. The Group had made strong statements about their support for Mr Bakhtiar, and certainly agreed with me that if Iran became an Islamic Republic, it would eventually end up in the Communist camp. Now they had to act. I said we all felt it could be an advantage to have Khomeini back in the country. There was a power struggle within his camp, and disagreement among the opposition groups. These could be cultivated and fostered without precipitating an armed conflict.

Secretary Brown fired off a series of questions. He wanted to know how the Iranian military felt about whether I should leave the country. I replied that I had discussed this at length, and they understood the situation. They were reluctant to take a view, and said it was up to me, by which I was sure they meant 'up to Washington'. They would accept Washington's judgement, without concurring.

Then he asked me directly whether I myself thought I should leave. I told him I still didn't want to make that decision. Personally I had a feeling that I should not leave; but if I were to go, now was as good a time as any to make the transition to General Gast. I knew the Group could work with him. The only advantage I had was my rank, which they respected, and the influence bequeathed to me by the Shah, which was still strong.

Secretary Brown wanted to know how my departure would affect the Group's ability to take military action. I told him this was almost impossible to forecast, but I was certain that General Gast could influence them. If the more forceful ones were to take action – Generals Rabii, Badraie or Toufanian – any or all of the plans could be executed. He wanted to know what impact my departure would have on the Group's readiness to take over the country, if the time came. I said this too was a judgement question, but I thought General Gast could probably do as much as I could to encourage them to do whatever was needed.

Next he wanted to know if the Group still thought that military action was a viable option. I told him they were willing to stand behind Mr Bakhtiar to the fullest extent, and they fully realized that if things got bad, the only way to guarantee protection of the

legal government would be through their intervention. But I
expressed my reservations about General Gharabaghi and Admiral Habiballahi.

Then came a fusillade of questions. How did it really look to
me? What was the overall situation? What was the political/
military balance? What were the odds on Bakhtiar and Khomeini
respectively? I told them I believed Khomeini had been gaining
ground in some ways, and Mr Bakhtiar needed to achieve results
for which the people would give him credit. But this was going to
be difficult. Khomeini had the economy in the palm of his hand,
and could regulate it by controlling the strikes. But Mr Bakhtiar
also had the means to break strikes with the military. The media
seemed to be leaning Khomeini's way, and he was getting more
attention in the press than Bakhtiar. The vocal masses were
certainly for him, though the solid majority might be against.
Many people, including the upper classes, were starting to recognize that Khomeini could put them back in the dark ages. Public
religious observance was not as strong in Iran as it was, say, in
Saudi Arabia. In this respect they were as different as night and
day. The Saudi Arabians practised religion sincerely on a daily
basis. I never observed that in Iran.

I told the Secretary that the best hope lay in exploiting divisions
in the opposition, and making demonstrable progress on controlling the economy. I explained how I had been encouraging them to
take control of customs and to move on to complete control. If Mr
Bakhtiar could get the credit for breaking the log-jam of food
imports, it would have a great impact.

He pulsed me again about the military capability, and I told him
there had been no falling off since Khomeini's return, which was
good news. This had not surprised me, but it must have astonished
Ambassador Sullivan and his people, who had predicted a mass
desertion on Day One.

Secretary Brown again asked me who would be the leader if
military action had to be taken. I said I thought that Gharabaghi,
though smart and capable, just didn't have the stomach for military
action against his fellow-countrymen. Admiral Habiballahi was
very cautious, and seemed to be thinking more along the lines
favoured by Ambassador Sullivan, of amalgamating with
Khomeini now. General Badraie was a soldier all the way, and
he would move into action whenever necessary; with General

Rabii, the ramrod fighter pilot, there were no doubts in my mind. General Toufanian, being the senior, would probably carry most influence and might well take over the leadership of the Group, and in the background there was always General Khosrodad, who was fully capable of implementing the necessary actions.

Secretary Brown wanted to know about the morale of our military team in Iran. I told them that like me they were extremely apprehensive about Khomeini, with his virulent anti-Americanism, but they were all working hard and there was no problem with morale.

I said I had come down very hard on Gharabaghi and Toufanian about the memorandum of understanding, and thought it would now be signed.

With Secretary Vance on the line, I expressed my appreciation for the physical support and cooperation I'd had from Ambassador Sullivan. Mr Vance said that the President and everybody in Washington felt deeply indebted to me; I had operated in very difficult and abnormal circumstances, and in their opinion had done outstanding work.

At this point I was asked to stay on the line and keep it open, as they were going to have a discussion and arrive at a decision as to whether I should stay or leave. I held the line open and waited. It was only a few minutes, but it seemed like an eternity. Back they came, and Secretary Brown said that their decision was that I should leave either today or tomorrow, whichever I preferred. They didn't want me to appear to be fleeing the country, so I should complete whatever additional business I felt necessary with the senior military. Harold Brown said I was to take the C-130 standing by at Mehrabad to Incirlik, Turkey, and then the C-135 to Stuttgart. There I could stop off for a change of clothes, but I was to come straight on to Washington, and the President would expect to see me on Monday morning at first duty hours.

We ended the call, and I informed the Ambassador of the decision. I said I would go ahead and leave tonight, even though it was late, because we had it all geared up and planned that way. My last conversation with the Group had really reached the bottom line, so this was as good a time as any to make the break. I called General Rabii and told him we would implement Plan A. He acknowledged, which meant he would get the helicopter ready for lift-off at the SCS compound. I told my security guard, and General Gast alerted the C-130 crew.

I went over to the residence, packed my bag, and bade farewell to the staff. They had taken very good care of me, and we had developed a solid friendship, so it was a wrench for me to say goodbye and leave them there.

It was drizzling a bit and getting to be dusk as we left for the SCS compound. My security people insisted on sending three men with me in the helicopter for protection until I reached the C-130. One man would stay with me as far as Stuttgart. On arrival at the compound, we found the crew and helicopter were ready to go, so we loaded my luggage and I said farewell to the rest of my security men and to General Gast. This was an extremely difficult parting. We had worked closely together, and had developed that kind of bond which is only created when two people are dependent on each other for survival. I boarded the helicopter and we lifted off into the wet evening air. We rose to 500 feet and set course for Mehrabad.

It was almost dark when we arrived. In the helicopter area I was met by the general in charge of the air base and another Iranian military man. We all went on foot across the dark wet ramp through the parked airplanes to the C-130. On arrival, my bodyguard and I went up the ladder and into the crew compartment. Somebody questioned whether we should leave while it was already dark, because flying had been prohibited after dark in Iran for some time. I said we were going anyway.

I was certain I would not be putting either the crew or the airplane in jeopardy. General Rabii knew my departure plan, and I knew he had control of his Air Force, so the only possibility of being intercepted by fighters was if some opposition group in the Air Force wanted to destroy me. Again, we might get missiles fired at us from disaffected anti-aircraft units. I ran this quickly through my mind, but decided that the chances were remote. By selective routing, the only defences we would need to fly through were right around Mehrabad Airport and I had confidence that there would be proper coordination by the armed forces in the area.

From the look of us, the crew had every right to be suspicious. I was dressed in civilian clothes, and with my bulletproof vest underneath, the upper part of my body was very bulky. My bodyguard had let his hair grow considerably longer than a standard military haircut, and he was unshaven. (They did this so as to blend better into the local environment.) He was also well armed and wore his bulletproof vest. I have often wondered just what the crew did think when they first saw us!

Because of the hazardous nature of their missions, C-130s crews are extremely well disciplined and highly trained in combat tactics. They are accustomed to operating off unprepared airstrips, under unusual lighting conditions, and in hostile areas. This crew, under the command of Major George H. Newton, was one of the best. They didn't waste any time. They started the engines, taxied across the dark airfield and applied full power for take-off. Once airborne they swung the aircraft round to the north-west and set course for the Turkish border.

Tension was high. There was very little chatter on the inter-phone, and crew members were especially alert for anything that might be picked up on the radios. They peered intently into the darkness for signs of trouble. As we crossed the Turkish border the tension snapped, and a spontaneous roar went up from the whole crew. It exactly expressed my own feeling of a great release.

We now came under normal air traffic control for the remainder of the flight to Incirlik Air Base, Turkey. The pilot made a smooth landing and, on instructions from the control tower, parked right beside the C-135 waiting to take me on to Stuttgart. With my bodyguard, I crossed to the C-135. I knew all its crew, so it was an extremely warm reunion; you would have thought I had been away for a year. My officer aide Major Jim Moss was with them, and couldn't do enough for me.

By the time I had eaten and been briefed about events at my headquarters, we were in Stuttgart. In the floodlights I could see a reception party waiting to meet me. When the plane door swung open the first people I saw were my wife, my two daughters, Tracy and Christine, and my son-in-law Mike Murphy. My oldest daughter, Tracy Murphy, broke ranks and ran right up the steps to meet me. The whole reunion was very emotional. My family had been really worried by reports of the huge crowds in Tehran chanting 'Death to Huyser'. I was positive that every day I had been gone, my wife had prayed for my safety and that I be granted divine wisdom. She was a devout Christian, and communicated with the Almighty every day.

It was an enormous relief and absolutely heavenly to be home. But it could not dispel from my mind a deep concern for what might happen in Tehran in the next few hours.

Sunday, 4 February 1979

Before my departure for Washington, I was able to spend a few hours with my family. Especially welcome was a long walk and chat with my younger daughter, Chris. I hadn't seen her in some time, as she had been residing in the US. In the afternoon I called the Embassy in Tehran on the non-secure phone. They told me that things were still stable; but the press left no doubt that Khomeini and Bakhtiar were on a collision course. One of the newspapers asked in two-inch headlines: 'Civil War Looms?' Both men had publicly declared their determination to take full control. Bakhtiar said he would arrest anyone who defied the government, and Khomeini called the government illegal.

General Gast had met the Group of Five, and they were still solid behind Bakhtiar. As to the armed forces generally, it did not seem that Khomeini's arrival was immediately damaging their morale or status. I felt sure that if the leadership stood firm the troops would follow suit. But either of the two adversaries could trigger actions which would abruptly change the whole picture. Predicting the behaviour of Iranians is never easy. Sometimes they seem to have the patience of Job; at other times, much less than Americans have. In the evening I flew to Washington. I spent the whole journey reviewing the notes I had made during the past thirty-one days in preparation for my meeting with the President.

Monday, 5 February 1979

The next morning I checked in with the Chairman of the Joint Chiefs in the Pentagon, and then reported to Dr Brzezinski in the White House. He escorted me to the Oval Office. As we came in, the President rose from his desk and started toward me. I saluted and said: 'General Huyser reporting as ordered, Sir.' The President was very cordial. After an exchange of greetings he excused Dr Brzezinski. He then motioned to the sofa in front of the fireplace and said: 'Let's have a chat.' We spent the next thirty or forty minutes discussing the situation in great detail.

He picked up many of the points from my reports to the Secretary of Defence, and expressed keen interest in all my views on what might happen next. My central theme was that Bakhtiar must take positive action immediately, or he would be in trouble. I told the President that I had impressed this on the Group of Five just before I left. I had also warned them of the strains to which their loyalty would be exposed in the days ahead. I was particularly concerned about General Gharabaghi's ability to pass this test.

The President looked straight at me and said: 'What do you think I should do about Ambassador Sullivan? Should I relieve him and bring him home?' I said No; he was a capable and strong man. 'But,' I added, 'you should give him some instructions.' The President said Sullivan had had the same instructions as I had: why hadn't he followed them? My reply was: 'Mr President, maybe you didn't understand what I said. What I said was, *YOU* should give him his instructions.' I felt certain that the instructions I had received were exactly those prescribed by the President, but I was not so sure about the Ambassador's. I knew for some reason many of his conversations had been with lower-level State Department people, and they may very well have added their own gloss to the President's directives. This was the first notice I had received that there were less than cordial feelings about Ambassador Sullivan.

We completed our tête-à-tête and went into the adjoining room, where several members of his Cabinet were assembled: the Vice-President, the Secretary of Defence, the Secretary of State, Dr Brzezinski, the Chairman of the Joint Chiefs, the Director of the

CIA, and two or three others. I sat to the left of the President. The Secretary of State was on his right.

The discussion centred on the difference of opinion between myself and Ambassador Sullivan. I said I thought this was understandable because we had completely different backgrounds. Mine had been military all the way and his, though he did military duty in World War Two, had been that of a political officer. Further, our contacts in Iran were with two entirely different groups. Mine were confined almost entirely to the military; the only information I had on other groups was through the Ambassador and his people. The Ambassador had been in personal contact with several of the religious leaders, and his people were in constant touch with the opposition, so that he was intimately familiar with their activities and views. I told the President that we had been completely open with each other, but had been unable to see eye to eye on two major issues. One was the reliability of the military. The other was whether the US should support Bakhtiar or Khomeini.

After the discussion I received many compliments from the President, the Vice-President, the Secretary of Defence, the Secretary of State, and others. In spite of this, I could not feel confident that this government was making a united effort to save Iran.

I went back to the Pentagon and had further talks with the Secretary of Defence and the Chairman of the Joint Chiefs. They were due to receive their daily secure-telephone report from General Gast, and invited me to listen in. Gast's report was quite encouraging. The Group of Five seemed to be holding firm. His main anxiety was the totally uncompromising line being taken by both Khomeini and Bakhtiar. The press reports of their speeches indicated an imminent head-on clash. Gast thought this was a duel which, if handled properly, Bakhtiar had a good chance of winning. He had the military behind him, and, though the fight could get extremely bloody, there was no reason why he should not come out on top. It was good to learn that the Group of Five had survived my departure.

After this conversation, I sent a message to Ambassador Sullivan about my report to the President. I told him that I had explained my view that if Khomeini took control and formed an Islamic Republic, the country would drift from right to left. If Khomeini could be accommodated within some type of middle-of-the-road government, this might just work out; but if he took over completely and practised what he had been preaching, the country would disintegrate and eventually fall under Communist influence. I had told the President that this view was not shared by Ambassador Sullivan, who believed that under those circumstances the Khomeini government would drift toward the right. In the same message I also told Sullivan that I had discussed with the President our differences over the reliability of the military, and how they should best be used.

The Chairman's office told me that I would be cleared to leave Washington for Stuttgart the next day, 6 February. They would, however, like me to come back before I left to join them in their briefing from General Gast.

Tuesday, 6 February 1979

I reached the Pentagon about 6.30 am and after breakfast in the Chairman's Mess, reviewed all the message traffic. Secretary Brown had left Washington, so his Deputy, Charles Duncan, joined the Chairman and myself for the talk with General Gast. Secretary Duncan drew Gast's attention to a Jim Hoagland article in that morning's *Washington Post* arising out of my meeting with the President. The article alleged that US officials were extremely pessimistic about the survival of the Bakhtiar government. This was not helpful. One of the points I had made very clear in the Cabinet meeting was that whatever we thought privately we should, as a nation, publicly express full confidence in Bakhtiar. Any other course could have calamitous consequences.

Mr Duncan went over this very thoroughly with General Gast, and told him to pass on to the Group of Five that, no matter what was said in the newspapers, the US government were still firmly behind Bakhtiar and wanted the Iranian military to back him up. At the previous day's Cabinet meeting an 'action' had been agreed for 'amplified instructions to be sent to Ambassador Sullivan', requiring him to give unqualified support to Bakhtiar and not release pessimistic statements about his prospects. This was essential to offset the mistrust which the Group of Five had developed for the Ambassador.

Following the Cabinet meeting the State Department duly dispatched a wire to the Ambassador. General Gast conveyed the message to General Gharabaghi and Admiral Habiballahi and warned them to ignore US press reports to the contrary. Mr Duncan told Gast that this was fine, but he would also like it very strongly emphasized in Tehran that he, General Jones and General Huyser, firmly maintained the same position.

Gast said that Tehran was basically calm. There were more cars on the streets and more streets opening each day. The local press was questioning whether Khomeini could get the economy moving, and this was encouraging to the Group of Five. Gast had been urging them to get Bakhtiar to work with the press and capitalize on the situation. The Group seemed to realize that this was the moment to build up Bakhtiar and foment splits in the opposition, but as usual it was hard to get them to act. General Gast had also been working on them to start breaking the strikes and combating the terrorist groups.

Khomeini had now appointed Bazargan as his 'Prime Minister'. Bakhtiar had said that he did not mind Khomeini forming a shadow government so long as it did not interfere with the real one. Gast had discussed with the Group whether this curious ambiguity could be used to advantage. Could Bazargan contribute by getting the strikers back to work? Was there a chance of some coalition between Bazargan and Bakhtiar?

Then General Gast gave us some startling news. The Bakhtiar government had announced that they were withdrawing from CENTO. We were not sure if the rules of CENTO allowed this, or whether a request had to be submitted one year in advance. But whatever the rules, it was bad news. If it meant neutrality on their part as between the USSR and the US, it would be very difficult to continue to provide Bakhtiar with military support. Certainly Congress would challenge the wisdom of doing so.

General Gast then reported an intriguing conversation he had had with Lieutenant General Bakshejar, J-5 of the Supreme Commander's Staff. I knew Bakshejar well, and had formed a high opinion of his integrity, though he had got crosswise with the Service Chiefs the previous year in trying to introduce some highly necessary reforms. Bakshejar had heard through a mutual friend that Khomeini considered that Bakhtiar was a good man who should be in politics, not in jail. But if he was to continue as Prime Minister he would have to sack all his senior military chiefs — except General Gharabaghi. I was fascinated to hear this because I already had doubts about General Gharabaghi; now to hear that Khomeini would accept him as a military leader gave me profound concern.

Bakshejar had told his friend that it was actually General Huyser who had prevented the coup which General Rabii and General Badraie wanted to carry out. General Gast had been with me for all meetings, so he knew this was absolutely false.

That concluded our conversation with Gast. The three of us stayed on and discussed the implications of what we had heard. I again expressed my apprehensions about Gharabaghi. I also said it was hazardous to let Khomeini think that General Rabii and General Badraie might be the instigators of a coup. But I was pleased to hear that the armed forces were continuing to support Bakhtiar. They had demonstrated this by staging flights of fighter aircraft over Tehran to show the public that they were still very much a force to be reckoned with.

I then departed via Andrews Air Force Base for Stuttgart, where I spent the night with my family.

Wednesday, 7 February 1979

The following morning my headquarters staff gave me a fine reception, as if I had been off to a big battle and come home the victor. They were right about the battle, but I was not so sure about the victory. I had accomplished the specific tasks assigned me by the President, and he had presented me with a magnificent letter of commendation. But what about the future of Iran?

I decided to call General Gast non-secure just to get the latest word. I knew that all the non-secure communications were tapped, so we followed the procedure we had established inside Iran: we did not even mention our own names and were very careful about naming any of our military colleagues. Gast said that things were stable but there had been some significant events: in particular, the leader of the Tudeh party, Mr Nourreddin Kianouri, had publicly endorsed Khomeini. This was a surprise, because the Tudeh had been underground since 1949 and had been declared illegal. Whenever they had attracted criticism they would duck under the skirts of religious groups and fade away. Now they had suddenly gone public.

Another interesting event was that when the new class had graduated from the Officers' College in Tehran, the pledge of loyalty to the Shah had been removed from the oath of office. It was now only necessary to swear loyalty to God, the Holy Koran, Iran's independence, and the national flag. General Gharabaghi had been in attendance, so apparently he had approved this.

The positions of both Bakhtiar and Khomeini were hardening still further. General Gast said that the banner headlines of the *Kayhan* proclaimed: 'Stand-Off'. The armed forces were still in good order and there had been no sign of mass defection. But the question was: who would make the next move, Bakhtiar or Khomeini?

Thus briefed, I decided to call General Al Haig and give him a complete update. He was much exercised about the apparent lack of central direction from Washington. Why weren't the instructions for Ambassador Sullivan the same as those for myself? As this had been the riddle overhanging my whole period in Iran, I naturally had no answer. In colourful language he once again expressed his views on the adminstration's inept handling of the whole situation.

Thursday, 8 February 1979

Later I received a written report from Washington covering the latest discussions with General Gast. It was not reassuring. It seemed that the Group of Five had met for several hours, but without giving him a chance to speak to them, and they had gone directly off to see Bakhtiar. This was unprecedented. Previously, when preparing a visit to the Prime Minister they had always wanted both Gast and me to be present.

Gast said there had been a pro-Bazargan/Khomeini demonstration estimated at up to a million strong. Some 200 lower-ranking troops were said to have taken part, which was not surprising since more than that number were known to have deserted in Tehran. It was a peaceful demonstration but the fervour and chanting had been formidable.

Bakhtiar had said that he was willing to adapt his government to their demands if it were done by legal means and in accordance with the Constitution. He would accept a public vote on who should head the government, and he would do so even sooner than his previous offer of six or eight months. But he insisted that any attempt to install members of the shadow government by force would be severely dealt with.

All in all, the situation was now deteriorating. The economy was sliding back towards complete paralysis. There was little semblance of order; people were just ignoring the law. Elements from the south of the capital were swarming into the northern part, looting and stealing. Bakhtiar was sticking to his word that if there was no work, there would be no pay; and the strikers were now protesting against this policy.

General Gharabaghi had addressed his troops at the Armed Forces College and told them, very clearly, to stay out of politics. This had been reported in the *Kayhan*, and I was pleased that the military could still get attention in that newspaper.

Gast said that the government was planning a demonstration for the following week in support of Bakhtiar. They had come to believe that as the economy disintegrated, a lot of people were looking to Bakhtiar as the saviour of stability, especially in the middle classes. But such people were timid about showing their support, because the opposition forces would take reprisals. A good demonstration could stiffen their resolve. I hoped the government would go ahead, in view of the spectacular success of our earlier pro-Bakhtiar demonstration.

Meanwhile, however, no progress had been made in implementing the plans to take over the power centres of the economy. Without such action, the Bakhtiar government were doomed to failure. I could not understand why they refused even to take control of the customs. This would release food for the masses and simultaneously cut off the flow of arms which at present were going straight into storage in the mosques, where they were accessible to virtually any opponent of the government.

In this situation of political, economic and social collapse the only redeeming feature was the unwavering solidarity of the armed forces. This could yet be the determining factor, if only Mr Bakhtiar had a mind to use it. It should be noted that Khomeini had been in Iran for a week, and the military was still holding together. I contrast this with the statements by the media, and even – in retrospect – by some of our government officials in their books, that I was overly optimistic about the military forces.

Friday, 9 February 1979

The next day's report from General Gast told of further violence and the accumulation of garbage in the streets, which was having an effect on the people. Wherever the environment was disorderly, the people tended to follow suit. Gharabaghi and the Group of Five watched these developments with dismay, but they still showed no signs of taking action.

The evacuation of Americans was continuing, but not fast enough. They could not get on to chartered commercial aircraft, so the only means of transport was that provided by Military Airlift Command. Still, progress was being made, and it looked as if the US military contingent could be brought down to 250 by 1 April, the date agreed with the Iranians.

Bazargan had made a speech proclaiming that Iran was only at the beginning of an Islamic revolution. He predicted that it would spread far beyond the country's borders. He also hinted that he himself might drop out of the running for the new Iranian government. This was important because he was one of the more moderate members of the opposition, and a natural leader in a future coalition. General Gharabaghi was apparently worried about press reports that the US had been dealing with Bazargan. One of our political officers at the Embassy had told the press that the Bazargan/Khomeini axis was rapidly gaining in strength, and the Bakhtiar government was failing. The Group of Five was extremely sensitive to any such statements from US officials. The report suggested to them that our government was about to switch horses. They were now much less sure about the reliability of the US.

However, General Gast's standing with the Group of Five had revived somewhat, as Washington had given him some intelligence data to pass along about Russian movements on the border. They had been pleased to know that the US was closely watching their interests in this quarter.

But the worst was to come. Late in the evening, about 8.30 pm Tehran time, all hell started breaking loose among the military. The TV stations had put out a re-run of Khomeini's arrival in Iran, and this had served to excite the pro-Khomeini elements and inflame emotions on both sides. At the Doshan Tappeh Air Force Base in Eastern Tehran, which was General Rabii's headquarters, some Homofars started to demonstrate on behalf of Khomeini, and fighting broke out between them and the Imperial Guards. It rapidly escalated from fist fights to gunfire, some of which came from outside the base. It was obvious that other elements were working the situation. Eventually, with the aid of reinforcements, the Guards got the situation under control for the night.

Saturday, 10 February 1979

Next morning, however, about 8 am, the fighting resumed. A group believed to be members of the Iranian Imperial Air Force broke into the armoury and took a couple of thousand rifles and a lot of ammunition. This haul was immediately distributed, some of the rifles being tossed over the base fence. Firing continued until late afternoon; but around 4 pm it started to quieten down again. The affray caused the Bakhtiar government to establish new curfew hours for the capital from 4.30 pm to 5 am. It was a very bad business with many killed and wounded. Moreover, it was obvious that the curfew was not going to be obeyed. Meanwhile the incident meant that about seventy Americans had to be evacuated from Doshan Tappeh in CH-47 helicopters.

Later, gunfire broke out in other parts of the city and fires were built in the streets, on a combustible base of vehicle tyres. Many demonstrators claimed that Khomeini was encouraging them, but there was no way of telling whether this was true. Mercifully, to the best of our knowledge, the outbreak was not spreading to other cities. But it spread like wildfire within Tehran.

Bakhtiar had been on television declaring that he was not going to tolerate the disorder, and would use the military to put it down. General Gast had cautioned the military to be very careful about being used in this way. He advised them to consider the principle we had established in the past: that if the masses wanted to kill each other, let them do it; the military should not attempt to control the whole city. They should, however, protect themselves and the vital government elements at any cost.

Throughout the capital the tempo was increasing. Neither the new curfew nor the warnings of Bakhtiar seemed to have any effect.

Sunday, 11 February 1979

By dawn on 11 February, there was almost continuous gunfire all over the city. It was apparent that this was to be the day of reckoning: things must come to a head one way or another. The attack on the Air Force headquarters in Doshan Tappeh flared up again and this time reached such a pitch that General Rabii was obliged to capitulate. Subsequent events suggested that he might have reached some sort of arrangement with Bazargan.

The Chief of the Army, General Badraie, was assassinated outside his own HQ. Some reports said that he had been killed by his own troops, others that the killers had been opposition agents in uniform, but this was far from clear. Nor was it known who had ordered the assassination. To this day, I have been unable to obtain an accurate account of what happened out of the tangle of conflicting stories.

The Supreme Commander's Staff headquarters was attacked with a storm of gunfire. Bullets had shattered the windows in

General Gast's area and he and his staff had evacuated to the command post deep below the headquarters. Before the day was over the Bakhtiar government had collapsed.The military, deprived of their leaders, had fallen apart.

Except for General Gharabaghi, all the military leaders were immediately taken into custody. General Rabii was picked up by armed opposition agents and put in prison. Admiral Habiballahi was seized but soon afterwards released, it has never been clear why. General Toufanian was imprisoned. General Khosrodad, General Naji and many other generals were taken into custody. The demoralized reaction of the troops was inevitable. The military had been over-centralized, but even if it had not, the loss of so many senior officers would have dislocated most armed forces.

General Al Haig had called me in the morning and said he was going to fly down to discuss his retirement plans with me. I alerted my Executive Officer, Colonel Gary Spencer, to open my office and have it prepared for the visit. I picked General Haig up at the airport and we proceeded to my office for the discussions. About thirty minutes later, there was a knock on the door and Colonel Spencer stated that the Deputy Secretary of Defence, Mr Duncan, wanted to speak to me on the secure phone. I suggested to General Haig that he should take the call but he declined, so I suggested a compromise. There was a secure phone on my desk and an extension on Colonel Spencer's desk. I suggested to General Haig that he should listen in on my phone and I would talk on Spencer's extension. This he accepted.

When I started the conversation, I announced that General Haig was on with me. General David Jones, Chairman of the Joint Chiefs, stated that on his end it was himself, Secretary Duncan and Dr Brzezinski. Secretary Duncan then picked up the conversation and asked me if I was up to speed on the situation in Tehran. I told him yes. The next question from Mr Duncan was a heavy one. He asked me if I would be willing to go back to Tehran and conduct a military takeover. I reminded him that I had consistently stated that if the senior leadership of the Iranian military were to leave, then the entire military system in the country would collapse. I considered the present situation with the senior people in custody even more detrimental, so to execute the plans as written while I was there was no longer feasible.

Meantime, a thousand thoughts were running through my mind. Why hadn't I been asked that question while I was in Tehran? The military had been intact and following the orders of their generals. The Imperial Guard would have been strong enough to complete the job. There was a civilian leader, Mr Bakhtiar, to put in charge. Would the United States find a new leader? What would be his role? Then reality set in: I realized he was speaking of accomplishing this task under American rules, which would be to persuade some senior Iranian officer to lead the charge. After all, during the long days when I had been encouraging the Iranian Generals to make a move, the only official in the White House who seemed interested in that option was Brzezinski.

Keeping all these factors in mind, I decided I would test the water; so I decided to pattern my response on the Soviet involvement in Ethiopia. I stated I would consider returning under the following conditions. There would need to be unlimited funds; I would need to handpick ten to twelve US generals; I would have to have about 10,000 of the best US troops, because at this point I had no idea how many Iranian troops I could count on; and finally, I must have undivided national support. No more just having moral support, and I couldn't just be in an advisory capacity.

There was a rather long pause so I answered the question for them. I said I didn't think the people I was talking to were ready for that type of action, nor did I believe the American people would give their support. Therefore, the answer was obvious – it was not feasible.

Dr Brzezinski asked a few questions about military problems in south Iran and then General Jones asked General Haig if he had any comments to which he responded – Nope. The conversation was terminated at that point.

General Rabii, along with three others, was put on trial. In the standard procedure used by the Revolution, the trial started at midnight and ended with execution by firing squad at sunrise. All four were tried, found guilty, and sentenced to death; but before daybreak, Bazargan personally intervened to give General Rabii a stay of execution. He remained in prison until April, when he was tried again, found guilty, sentenced to death, and executed at daybreak. Several reliable sources have reported that Khomeini himself ordered the execution.

General Toufanian managed to escape from prison and after several months made his way out of the country, surfacing in Germany and then crossing to the United States.

Admiral Habiballahi stayed in Iran until midsummer, when he crossed the Turkish border and later reached the United States.

General Gharabaghi remained in Iran and was never arrested. How did he get away with it? There have been many explanations. It has been said that he served on the courts which helped to try and sentence his fellow officers. This has been supported by several solid sources. From his residence in Paris, he himself has denied it, and claims to have been in hiding these many months.

EPILOGUE

Hindsight scores higher than foresight. I am frequently asked whether, if I had the opportunity to handle the job again, I would do it differently. The answer is clear-cut: if I had known then what I know now, then yes; if equipped with the same facts I had available at the time, then probably not. This may sound as though I think that I made all the right moves. I certainly do not want to give that impression.

My claim is that I did accomplish the tasks assigned to me by President Carter and as prescribed by him. Apparently he was of the same opinion, as he gave me a very cordial letter of commendation.

THE WHITE HOUSE
WASHINGTON
February 7, 1979

To General Robert Huyser

I wish to express my personal thanks to you for the great service you performed for your country during your mission to Iran. Your arrival in Tehran in early January came at a moment of great disarray and uncertainty. In a time of violent political upheaval, your commitment, your steadiness, and your perseverance helped the Iranian military leadership to maintain the kind of responsible patriotism that we associate with our own military forces. In doing so, you made a great contribution to the objectives of American policy.

For my own part, your presence in Iran gave me a sense of relief and confidence. During the difficult four weeks of your stay in that country, I was never disappointed by you.

The unique circumstances in which you operated demanded a special combination of wisdom, tact and courage. Your performance under these conditions won the genuine respect and admiration of myself and all of my key advisors. I commend you for a job superbly done.

Sincerely,
Jimmy Carter

General Robert E. Huyser
Deputy Commander-in-Chief
U.S. European Command
APO New York 09128

I ensured that the military leadership remained in the country, and that the military organization held together. As far as I was able, considering their tradition of deep allegiance to the Shah, I swung the military support to the new civilian head of government, Mr Bakhtiar. I encouraged the military to prepare proper plans to enable them to take charge of the country, and those plans were made. Finally, from the military standpoint, I affirmed and demonstrated that the United States would support their logistic needs and stand behind them under all circumstances.

The controversy and questions aroused by my mission to Tehran seem to focus on the exact nature of my assigned task and of the quasi-official extension it acquired. This was, to put it simply, to do all I could to enable the Bakhtiar government, or a civilian government on amicable terms with the West, to take over the running of the country. As I record throughout the book, I was discussing the Iranian situation with the highest levels of my government on a daily basis. They were requesting me to recommend to the country's military leaders methods by which they might communicate to Mr Bakhtiar the value of the one real strength he had at his disposal – his military forces. This developed into recommending to the military leaders that they suggest to Mr Bakhtiar ways of using this power to assert control of the country. From this, some commentators have reached the conclusion that I was either solely or largely responsible for the failure of the

Bakhtiar government. I disagree. I am of the opinion that I maintained intact the means by which the Bakhtiar government might have achieved success, but that my own government failed to provide the catalyst to ensure that Mr Bakhtiar used that capability. Inevitably the result was a disaster, both for Iran and for the West.

The other area where I attracted heavy criticism, which I do not believe was justified, was that of my supposedly over-optimistic assessment of the capability of the Iranian military forces. Ambassador Sullivan maintained this judgement at the time. His position may be partially explained, I think, if what Gary Sick reports in his book *All Fall Down* is true. Sick states that by 3 January 1979, during his negotiations with opposition leaders, the Ambassador had compiled 'a list of more than one hundred senior Iranian military officers who would be expected to leave the country with the Shah'. This should also go some way to explaining why Ambassador Sullivan objected when he heard that I was being sent to Iran, because my task was to keep these same officers in the country if the Shah departed.

Some high-ranking US government officials of the time have claimed in their post-mortems on the Iranian situation that I led our government to false conclusions based on my optimistic reporting of military capability. I disagree that I misrepresented that capability. As I kept observing then, and as I record throughout this book, each time the armed forces were called upon – whether for crowd control, parading in unfriendly streets, air force fly-overs, controlling the Tudeh party demonstration, protecting the Gendarmerie headquarters or military installations, and even safeguarding Khomeini on his return – they responded as a professionally trained military. This was because they were given firm and clear orders to do so.

My estimation of the Iranian military capability was based not only on my daily observations and contacts with the troops but also on evaluations by members of the US Military Advisory Group in their daily contacts at all levels and by our attachés in the Embassy, correlated with the reports of the Iranian senior military leaders. I offset this against what I knew was their major weakness, by Western military standards, namely their dependency on rigid central leadership. I was fully aware of the fact that they had been trained this way, from the lowest to the highest ranks, by the Shah himself. To put this in perspective, it should be noted that for years Western leaders have credited the Soviet Union with a formidable military capability, yet they too have had the same weakness. Their forces have been highly dependent on the top command levels for control and direction. I was asked by the US Secretary of Defence, before I went to Tehran, what I thought would happen to the military if the senior officers left with the Shah. My answer was unqualified. I said that the military structure would collapse.

Yes, the military did collapse, ten days after Khomeini returned to Iran and seven days after I had departed. Why? I believe that the opposition recognized the weakness in the armed services. First General Badraie, Chief of the Army, was assassinated: the Army would have been the main element in restoring control of the key installations and services in the country. Next, there was the overt action at Doshan Tappeh air base, where General Rabii had his Air Force headquarters: the Air Force would have been the next vital element in controlling the country. I believe that the immediate determining factor in their collapse was the lack of central direction from Mr Bakhtiar to the military. After all, the military had been conditioned for years by the Shah to expect and rely upon this type of direction from him. A central question still in my mind today – and as yet unexplained by contemporary historians – is why Mr Bakhtiar never chose to use the only effective lever he had to regain control.

Do I still believe that military intervention in the domestic affairs of the country would have worked? Yes, and for the same reasons that I thought valid then. When the Shah established a military government on 6 November 1978 the reaction was immediate and positive. He just lacked the resolve to take advantage of the situation and maintain control. Would military intervention have resulted in massive bloodshed? Not necessarily, because I still believe that about four-fifths of the population would have backed the constitutional government. This opinion derives from observing the size, location and behaviour of the opposition demonstrations and comparing these with the considerable amount of support we garnered for our own impromptu attempt to have a programmed demonstration. We also found that massed crowds tended to retreat very quickly when there was any use of force, as in the Tudeh demonstration, and in the attack on the Gendarmerie headquarters.

Another false picture painted by several writers is that bad relations between Ambassador Sullivan and myself contributed to the failure of the Tehran mission. This misses the whole point. It happens that our personal relationship was very good. He and his wife were gracious and kind to me during my stay in their residence, and I considered him a personal friend. But we differed fundamentally in our objectives, and in our efforts to achieve them.

Bill Sullivan took a view of Khomeini which has not only been contradicted by subsequent events but which also appears not to have been justified by the information available at the time. Khomeini's pathological hatred of the Shah was never disguised. It landed him in prison three times in the 1960s, and then led to his exile in Turkey and Iraq. It fuelled him to become the unquestioned spiritual leader of the Shi'ite community, which made up ninety-two per cent of the nation. It boiled over after the death of his son, which he blamed on the Shah, in the fall of 1977.

The storm which broke out with the first major uprising in Qom in January 1978 had been predicted by the Shah, but it came earlier than he had expected. No Western government seems to have recognized its significance until the following September, and the British Ambassador, Sir Anthony Parsons, has readily admitted his failure to read the signs. It appears that Bill Sullivan read them, and decided that Khomeini was a 'Gandhi-like' figure whose accession to power coupled with a change in government would be the most suitable course for the US to pursue.

With this in mind, it seems that at the turn of the year he favoured removing the military leaders who were most likely to block Khomeini's plans, and he consistently questioned the capability of Mr Bakhtiar, the man whom Washington wanted to support, in a way which often became public. President Carter's objective was some sort of coalition between Bakhtiar and the military. This was never going to be easy, considering Bakhtiar's apprehensions about the military leadership, and their initial distrust of him. However, it was achieved. But what was the use of my delivering my half of the objective, a coherent military leadership with a workable plan of action, if the Ambassador was making no attempt to deliver his half, a political leadership confident of American support?

The story might have been different if I had had regular access to

Mr Bakhtiar, but all through my time in Iran, we never once met. I have already explained my rationale for thinking this was the Ambassador's job. Ambassador Sullivan has since stated in his book *Mission to Iran* that he met with Bakhtiar on most days. This was news to me, as I knew of only two meetings during my entire stay. I assumed, I think reasonably, that the President's representative, my host in Iran, would notify me of any such meetings and debrief me afterwards. This happened only once, and that was the meeting to discuss General Gharabaghi's resignation.

One of my problems was that I was left in total ignorance of the rift between the Ambassador and the Administration. Perhaps at the time I was sent, on 4 January, the President may still have thought that there was some chance of bringing his Ambassador under control, but there is evidence that I was sent to Iran precisely because the Administration had lost confidence in Sullivan. Yet my briefings gave me no hint either of Sullivan's maverick role or of Carter's response to it.

Another matter that has created considerable debate was my view that, under Khomeini, Iran would drift to the left and eventually end up in the wrong camp. By no means did I think then, nor do I think now, that Iran would go Communist of its own initiative. The two ideologies are much too far apart. In 1979 the Communist (Tudeh) group inside Tehran was growing, but not in significant numbers. Characteristically, its members appeared to be well trained and organized and logistically supported. They constituted an active and disruptive element among the opposition forces, and advocated violence to promote discord and discontent – a long-standing tactic to further their cause.

I believe that under Khomeini the Communists have diminished in number and have been kept under control. What I believed in 1979, and still believe today, is that a Khomeini regime would make Iran more dependent on the Soviet Union for support and technological back-up. This appears to be happening: there are a rising number of Soviet advisers in Iran, and they certainly have grown more dependent on that half of the world for external support. This process typifies a Soviet tactic that has been operated successfully over many years as a long-term method for drawing a nation into their sphere of influence.

Historical events show that Soviet leaders have seldom been satisfied merely with this first step. They continue to work on countries where there is internal discord until the target country is in their domain, or they have established government leaders of their choice. Like the West, the Soviets want to enlist Iran for strategic purposes; but I believe that their end objective is different from the West's, and that Iran is just another piece in their grand design of world domination. With their burning desire for access to warm-water ports and the historical Russian view of the import-ance of Persia, the Soviet Union can be expected to manipulate the situation to their utmost. On this account I continue to believe that Iran under Khomeini's rule could end up in the Soviet camp as the only practical alternative to seeking alignment with the West. The precise degree of linkage remains to be seen, but the loss of Iran as a friend of the West has already had a damaging impact on the stability of the area and on world peace.

Looking back on my mission, I see certain things that, even under the rules established, I could have handled differently or perhaps better, but I am going to be realistic and mention only the one which has become my principal source of regret. (Here I refer to my official capacity; on a personal level I have other obvious grounds for regretting what happened in Iran after the return of Khomeini.) I believe that my trust and faith in the upper strata of our government was a real weakness on my part. My naïveté in assuming that if I carried out the tasks assigned to me with the Iranian military, then the political wing of our government would march smartly along in lock-step, was a gross mistake. I should have asked many hard questions that might have revealed the true positions in Washington and how the other half of the equation was being implemented by the State Department through the Ambassador.

At the highest policy-making level I think there are one or two lessons that badly need to be learned from this story. One is the need to stand by one's friends. This is as important for a country as it is for an individual. In each case it is not only a matter of morality, which in foreign affairs is sometimes spurned by the advocates of *realpolitik*; it is also a matter of expediency. For if a man starts abandoning his friends, he will not long have many friends to abandon. Since the US rejected isolationism in 1941, we have opted for a policy built on alliances and mutual arrangements with friendly powers. These, like friendship in the dictum of Doctor Samuel Johnson, need to be kept in good repair; otherwise the whole network will collapse. If friend X sees friend Y being let down, he will waste no time in hedging his bets. America needs to stand by its friends.

But conducting a foreign policy is easier said than done. Under the American constitution, with its built-in separation of powers, it is particularly difficult. Many have questioned whether the system of checks and balances devised by the Founding Fathers to restrain the Executive is suitable for the formulation of a coherent long-term foreign policy. That may be argued. What must surely be wrong, it seems to me, is to compound the scope for confusion by fragmenting the Executive Branch. There have been any number of instances when our friends have accused us of running three foreign policies at any one time – and they have been saying this for the last half-dozen Presidencies.

Because the Secretary of Defence is habitually at odds with the State Department, it was thought necessary to create a National Security Council, whose head would be Chief Adviser to the President, distilling the options presented from all sides. Is this the best system available? It certainly did not work in my case. The National Security Adviser seemed to be just another voice in a discordant chorus that did not always harmonize with the President.

The consequence was that Washington not only conceived but actually implemented conflicting policies simultaneously. In my case, the proliferation of policies was even more serious, and damaging. Little did I realize until I read his book how Ambassador Sullivan felt about smoothing the way for the Ayatollah Khomeini while his own government was striving to keep him out, some of its members even contemplating a preemptive military coup with varying degrees of zeal.

In raising these political issues I offer no particular remedy, leaving that to specialists in the field. I am only afraid that it could all happen again.

It may be, of course, that the United States has no suitable answer to a fanatic who can command a whole generation not merely to die for his fundamentalist cause, but if need be deliberately to commit suicide for it. The problem dramatized by the Beirut Marine barracks disaster of 1983 offers no easy solution. But I do not believe that a nation as powerful and responsible as ours should admit defeat, and even incur it, by allowing ourselves to fight with one hand tied behind our back. A unified foreign policy may sometimes be wrong; a disjointed foreign policy has to be wrong. It can only confuse our friends and give comfort to our enemies. It means that initiatives, when taken, will tend to be half-baked in conception and half-hearted in execution. In the case of the events in Iran in 1978 and 1979 we are still counting the cost. I guess the bottom line is that a country must get its own act together before it can hope to put another's house in order with any success.

It is a very sad ending to a macabre story. The United States lost a close and sturdy ally which could have provided stability for Western interests in the Persian Gulf. That loss has cost us billions of dollars because of the need to make alternative security arrangements for the years ahead. But perhaps the most poignant loss is that of the Iranians themselves. Their country, on the point of becoming a viable and industrialized nation, has been wrenched back hundreds of years in its values and standards. The people have suffered deeply. Men and women have been executed wholesale. The Gulf War drags uselessly on, bleeding away the human and material resources of both Iraq and Iran, although no one doubts that it would be settled in months if it were not for the sacrificial fervour of the Ayatollah Khomeini. And the carnage is far from over, for it is no longer confined to Iran. Thousands have already been killed to satisfy Khomeini's ambitions in the Muslim world, and we may still not have seen the worst. Khomeini's zeal in fostering and exporting terrorism spells trouble all over the world.

I believe that the principal blame for the fall of the constitutional government in Iran must lie with the Shah. He tried to impose twentieth-century industrialization on top of a medieval concept of rule. It was open to him to make the transition to a style of government more acceptable to his people, and that shift became all the more necessary the more he enabled his subjects to become educated in the West. At the same time, in the last months of his reign he could and should have done more to maintain law and order. I don't know if anyone can answer the question why he lost his will or chose not to keep control. Surely his health must have played a large part; and it has been reported that he was receiving heavy medication. Only his doctor, General Ayadi, could have answered these questions.

By the time Prime Minister Bakhtiar had taken the reins it is questionable whether success was possible, but this then raises the question even more sharply – why didn't he use the one element he did control, the military forces? They were the most powerful element in the country and might well have been the deciding factor.

From the United States' standpoint, the Administration obviously did not understand the Iranian culture, nor the conditions that prevailed in the last few months of the Shah's reign. I believe that Washington should have recognized the seriousness of the situation early in 1978. If it was the real intent to support the existing government, much could have been done to bolster the Shah's lagging confidence and resolve.

I considered my mission as an eleventh-hour effort by the United States to preserve some form of the established Iranian government. When I accepted the task I knew that the chances of successfully maintaining a recognizable version of the existing government were not good. I was apprehensive about the specific tasks of keeping the generals in the country and getting them to support a new civilian leader. General Al Haig was even more pessimistic than I. Then, when I arrived in Tehran and saw the completely paralysed government and chaotic conditions, I grew even more concerned. So the question keeps flashing in my mind: how did the US government rate the chances of success? I took it for granted that the President had access to far more intelligence on the situation that either General Haig or myself. If that assumption appears naïve, I can only say that the opposite assumption would probably be thought both arrogant and dangerous on the part of a senior military officer.

If the President knew how serious and shaky the situation was, then unless he was ready to throw the whole of his weight into resolving it, I believe that the decision for the eleventh-hour stand was wrong. If he did *not* know, then his information system was malfunctioning, which may well have been the case. The previous record of his main sources of intelligence does not support the view that he was getting the information a Chief Executive needs. Two major reports from the CIA in 1977 and 1978 gave no hint of impending revolution – rather the reverse. In the first nine months of 1978, virtually the only warning of rapids ahead came from a single Embassy report made in August, when the Ambassador was on leave.

This lack of advice was particularly harmful because it happened that the US government had several other major issues of foreign affairs on the agenda. There were the 1978 US-Egypt-Israel negotiations, which led to the successful Camp David agreement. These took place against a background of strife on Israel's northern borders, which required international intervention. There was the controversial Salt 2 Treaty, in the last stages of negotiation before signature with the USSR in the summer of 1979. And on top of all that, the Guadeloupe meeting of Western leaders, coinciding with my arrival in Tehran, was dealing with the momentous decision to strengthen Europe's defences with cruise and Pershing missiles.

So could my mission have prevented the final fiasco? As I have already pointed out, most of the criticisms made at the time – based more on a sense of frustration than on any ascertainable facts – were wide of the mark. The commonest – that I was sent to do a hatchet job on the Shah – was simply untrue. I was sent to help stabilize the situation if the Shah should decide that his position was untenable. That was his own decision, and he made it.

Since that time, I have frequently wondered what would have happened if the United States government had laid even a little more emphasis on a successful outcome for its declared policy. A number of small but potentially significant steps were never taken. For instance, the President could have publicly condemned Khomeini for his interference. He could have solicited the support of our allies, and in conjunction with them he could have given material support to the Bakhtiar government. After all, through-out these events the Soviets were publicly castigating the US for my meagre efforts while their propaganda machine argued for reform by revolution. Their story was that I was in control and preventing the revolution from taking its course. It appeared that they were concerned about the outcome, and ready to work hard for what they wanted, while many on our side thought that my mission was irrelevant because the game was all over before I arrived. Those who took this view were begging the vital question: Which game? The Shah was almost certainly beyond saving by then: few in Washington doubted that *that* game was over before even the decision to send me was taken. But the real game – preventing Iran from falling into the hands of some anti-Western regime – was still in my view open. Could it have been won? The question is abstract, but I have offered some concrete facts. In particular, I know that the armed forces turned out to be much sounder than our Ambassador was ever prepared to realize. Instead of collapsing on the day of the Ayatollah's return, the 1st of February, as the Ambassador predicted, the troops remained stable and followed orders for several days. The question I still ask myself, therefore, is *how the story would have ended had Bakhtiar made full use of his armed forces in the vital fortnight – the second half of January – after the Shah left.*

That was the moment when Bakhtiar should have been stiffened in his resistance by the full encouragement of the United States. That was the moment when Khomeini should have been brought up against an Iranian political and military leadership assured of our whole-hearted support. Yet that was the moment when Bakhtiar was being *publicly* undermined by American official voices both in Washington and in Tehran, while Khomeini was riding high with the media.

That, to my mind, was the opportunity missed. For most of the Iranian people, I believe, the removal and humiliation of the Shah could have been change enough. The perceived source of their grievances had been eliminated, and they could have made a fresh start in a climate free of hatred and fear. Khomeini's insistence on a vindictive and puritanical counter-revolution almost certainly placed him in a minority at that time. Plenty of mullahs were urging him to slow down. His own people were ready to practise tactics of friendly persuasion. Certainly the public admired him as a hero, and he had their loyalty as the country's religious leader. But was his assumption of the leadership necessary to fulfil their basic needs? Could not the firm enforcement of better conditions of life, under a constitutional system purged of the alleged corruption, have answered the wishes of the vast majority? For reasons which I have tried to record in these pages, this most promising option was never attempted.

As I bring this tragic story to a close, it prompts me to ask twin questions which are central to the issue of intervention in any nation's internal affairs.

If it is morally right to intervene to protect a staunch ally against invasion, is it any less virtuous to protect a staunch and deserving ally against internal subversion supported and motivated by external elements?

If the latter is the proper course, should not the job be done with all available resources, on a decisive no-punches-pulled basis? I believe that it should. If America wills the end, then it has to will the means.

Index

ABOUT THE AUTHOR

Robert E. Huyser, better known as "Dutch" Huyser, was born on a farm in western Colorado on Flag Day, June 14, 1924. Soon after graduation from high school, he received a draft notice and was inducted into the army as a private on April 15, 1943. In 1944, he joined the Army Air Corp and entered the Aviation Cadet Program, and on September 9, 1944, he received his pilot wings and second lieutenant bars. During World War II, he flew B-24's, B-32's, and B-29's. In 1947, the U.S. Air Force was formed, and he started a long career in the new branch of service.

During the Korean conflict, Huyser was Chief of Combat Operations for the Far East Bomber Command and flew combat in B-29's. Upon his return he made the transition to jet bombers and jet fighter aircraft. He served as an active duty reserve officer until 1957, when he was integrated into the regular Air Force. During the 1950s and '60s, he served at all levels in combat units, culminating in December 1966, when he became the wing commander of a B-52H unit at Kincheloe AFB, Michigan. During this same period, his unit level duty was interrupted by two assignments to 15th Air Force Headquarters and one to Strategic Air Command (SAC) Headquarters as a staff officer.

In 1969, while Chief of Command Control at SAC Headquarters, Huyser was promoted to brigadier general. In 1971, he was promoted to major general and assigned a dual-hatted role: chief of SAC's operations plans and chief of the single integrated operation plan division for the Joint Strategic Target Planning Staff. In the latter job, he developed the strategic nuclear war plans for all U.S. nuclear forces.

In 1972, Huyser moved to the Pentagon as Director of Plans for the Air Force. In 1973, he was appointed to the rank of lieutenant general and filled the position of Deputy Chief of Staff Plans and Operations for the Air Force. In September 1975, President Ford nominated him for his fourth star; when confirmed by Congress, he moved to Stuttgart, Germany, as Commander-in-Chief of the U.S. European Command. In mid-1979, he became Commander-in-Chief of the Military Airlift Command.

On July 1, 1981, General "Dutch" Huyser retired from the U.S. Air Force. Since his retirement, he has worked with youth organizations and has lectured, and is a consultant for the Boeing Company.

General Huyser is the first draftee to have attained the rank of four-star general in the U.S. Air Force—the highest rank possible in peacetime.